COLORADO COLLEGE:
MEMORIES AND REFLECTIONS

COLORADO COLLEGE:
MEMORIES AND REFLECTIONS

collected by
Maxwell F. Taylor

125th Anniversary of Colorado College

COLORADO COLLEGE
1999

Colorado College, Colorado Springs, CO 80903

© 1999 by Colorado College. All rights reserved

Published 1999

Printed in the United States of America

ISBN 0-935052-33-X

TABLE OF CONTENTS

PREFACE

This collection of memoirs is published as part of the celebration of Colorado College's 125th Anniversary, that is, the College's Quasquicentennial Celebration. The memoirs have been written by select faculty and administrators who are bound together by one common trait—a long association with the College. All of the authors in one way or another tell the story of their professional lives at Colorado College, and it is fair to ask, "Do these reflections represent a version of the history of CC?" Some might answer by saying that history is not the same as story; that memoirs, because they are so personal and subjective, distort the reality of the College's history. But let me suggest an alternative way of looking at the selections in this volume. These memoirs, though personal and subjective, represent one way in which we recapture the reality and meaning of our past by providing an opportunity for the readers to interact with these visions of CC's past.

ACKNOWLEDGMENTS

I am grateful to Dean Timothy Fuller of Colorado College for selecting me to edit this special volume of memoirs. He has given much needed guidance and encouragement along the way, not to mention approving the financial support needed to accomplish the end result. Norma Flemming, staff assistant to the Sociology Department, devoted much of her summer to the the tedious task of typing the manuscripts and preparing them for the printer. I have appreciated her patience and commitment in working with me on this project. I also want to thank Dean Fuller's marvelous staff of Marlyn Burch, Rita Zook, and Kathy Conley for their willingness to set aside other tasks to be of assistance with correspondence and particular typing projects along the way. In addition, Sally Hegarty provided valuable technical assistance and much needed advice. Of course, the authors of the memoirs deserve special thanks and praise for their willingness to take time out from busy professional and personal schedules to write in celebration of the College's 125th year. They have indulged my editorial suggestions and my mistakes with good humor and understanding. In turn, I have tried not to tamper too much with their particular styles of writing and expression. Finally, I am especially grateful for the support and understanding of my wife, Jodi.

FOR LEW AND BROSS

INTRODUCTION

Maxwell F. Taylor

History is the past reconstructed interactively by the present through argued evidence in public discourse.

—John Dominic Crossan, *The Birth of Christianity*, p. 20

When Dean Timothy Fuller asked me to serve as editor of a special volume of faculty and staff memoirs to be written as part of the College's 125th anniversary, I accepted with very little hesitation. Years ago, I received my training as an historian at Emory University in the Graduate School of Arts and Sciences.. When I accepted my appointment as an administrator at Colorado College, I did not realize that it would lead to a virtual abandonment of my professional life as an historian. Teaching occasionally, keeping up with the reading in my field of specialization, and following avidly the debate about the meaning and nature of history is not the same as practicing the craft. Editing this volume at least nudges me back toward my professional life. As an undergraduate majoring in history at Vanderbilt University in the late 1950s, I recall vividly my senior seminar entitled "Historiography." Our undergraduate struggles to find our way between so-called subjective and objective schools of history prepared me for the postmodern debate that has emerged in recent years. This volume also frames for me some of the pressing issues about the nature of history.

A survey of various histories of institutions of higher education confirms that our memoir approach is most unusual. More formal, conventional approaches are usually preferred, and, indeed, we are fortunate that Professor Robert Loevy has completed a new history of Colorado College. In this collection of memoirs, published along with Professor Loevy's history as part of the celebration of the College's 125th Anniversary, twenty select faculty and administrators have written about Colorado College. The authors have one trait in common—a long association with the College. Most in one way or another tell the story of their professional lives at this special liberal arts college. Some readers might respond by legitimately questioning whether such personal reflections capture the real history of the College; whether instead a memoir approach unintentionally distorts the reality of history. Although story is not the same as history, I join many other historians in believing that all true history is story. Memoirs represent one way in which we recapture the reality and meaning of our past by providing an opportunity for the readers to interact with these visions of Colorado College.

The collection includes selections from fourteen faculty members and six administrators. Within the faculty representatives are the four most recent Deans of the College. Administrative authors include three former presidents, two vice presidents and a Director of Admissions. Several others chose not to accept the invitation to participate in this project. Sadly, retired President Lloyd E. Worner and retired Vice President Robert Brossman both died before contributing to the collection. By including President Worner's personal essay on the state of the college, prepared for the 1978 accreditation visit by the North Central Association, I have tried to recapture something of his long involvement with Colorado College. Those who recall the close friendship and working relationship of "Lew" and "Bross" will readily recognize Brossman's voice and influence in the essay.

Former presidents Louis T. Benezet and Gresham Riley write about their respective presidencies, highlighting their goals and accomplishments while confronting some of the things that did not work out as well as hoped. Benezet describes a post-World War II college that had slipped somewhat from an earlier status of national distinction, and he outlines the steps taken during his presidency to redefine Colorado College's mission as a liberal arts institution. Riley highlights the importance of his "President Elect" year (1980) as an opportunity to define the issues that framed his presidency over the next eleven years. He concludes with an honest self-appraisal of his strengths and weaknesses as a leader of a college community.

Among the contributors to this volume are the four most recent academic deans, including current Dean of the College/Dean of the Faculty and Professor of Political Science, Timothy Fuller. Professor Emeritus of Physics Richard C. Bradley, who in his personal and professional life epitomizes liberal learning, writes with tongue in cheek about the presidents of Colorado

College. (His 1993 address at a faculty dinner for President Kathryn Mohrman in celebration of her inauguration forms the basis for his memoir.) In his essay, Professor Emeritus of Political Science Glenn E. Brooks shares his views about the late 1960s academic culture that provided the context for the planning process and the politics of change leading to the adoption of the defining feature of Colorado College, the Block Plan. Brooks' personal recollections about the origin of the Block Plan are timely and long overdue. Professor of Political Science David Finley selects from among many possibilities three salient concerns that he sees as of critical importance during his deanship—the diversification of curriculum and faculty, the impact of controversy over apartheid in South Africa on the culture of learning at Colorado College, and the reasons behind the change to the eight-block academic year. Finley's theme of innovation balanced by a commitment to traditional liberal learning is echoed by other contributors to this work. For example, Dean Tim Fuller, in writing about his life and career at Colorado College as an unrehearsed intellectual adventure, gives us insight into the tradition of liberal learning that has endured at the College in spite of times of upheaval and even revolutionary change. He counsels continuing reflection about the implications of ongoing programmatic initiatives. He ends his essay with a impressive tribute to Michael Oakshott, a major influence on Fuller's life as a teacher and scholar.

Five retired members of the faculty have written memoirs for the collection. Professor Emeritus of Psychology Gilbert R. Johns surveys impressively the three "Golden Eras" in the history of the performing arts at the College. His telling of the stories of the long association of the College with internationally famous dancer, Hanya Holm, and the Colorado College Opera Festival are especially poignant. Johns draws on his experience as Dean of the Summer Session (1965–1981) and his personal involvement with the arts as both promoter and critic. Professor Emeritus of English Neale Reinitz reconstructs from the notes in a "spiral notebook" his first year (1953–54) as an instructor of English. Reinitz's reflections are both humorous and historically revealing. Professor Emeritus of Biology Werner G. Heim, without donning the robes of an educational primitivist, observes some of the changes that have occurred at Colorado College and similar institutions during the past twenty-five years. Heim analyzes the reasons for these changes and raises important questions about the dangers of substituting form for substance as we apply models of accountability, efficiency and modern management to the College. Professor Emeritus of Geology William A. Fischer recollects the role of serendipity in his career at Colorado College and remembers appreciatively the evolution of the Geology Department into a champion of liberal learning. Fischer ends his memoir with a moving testimony about the central importance of Geology to the natural sciences and to the public at large. Professor Emeritus of Biology Richard Beidleman chronicles the excitement of the Benezet and Worner years both with respect to changes in the physical plant and the emergence of innovative new academic programs. Beidleman pays tribute to the Ford Independent Study Program, the Selected Student Program, the Summer Session Institutes, the Southwest Studies Program and the Patterns In Nature, the ACM, and the Block Plan for their contributions to his evolution as a scholarly teacher. He concludes with a marvelous statement about the relevance of liberal arts education for the futures of Colorado College students.

Five current members of the faculty are included. Professor of History William R.Hochman, who recently retired after serving eight years as the Dean of the Summer Session, remembers the rich experiences of his forty-three year career at the College. Hochman observes the passing of many of the old practices and traditions and the battles he waged against Division I athletics, Greet organizations, and ROTC. He concludes his memoir with a moving statement about the joy of teaching at a college that has steadfastly maintained its commitment to the liberal arts tradition. Professor of Sociology Eli Boderman tells the story of a wonderful life as a member of the faculty of the College. Boderman's writing about the symposium years is especially valuable to the student of Colorado College's history. He joins other essayists in testifying to the transforming power of teaching under the Block Plan with its many options to move beyond one's field of specialization. Professor of History Susan A. Ashley devotes most of her memoir to an assessment of the culture of teaching and learning at this Block Plan college. Ashley's comparison of two groups of students who graduated twenty years apart is especially valuable for those who struggle with questions about the relevance of liberal learning. Professor of Education Charlotte Mendoza establishes the case for the education curriculum in the mission of the College as a liberal arts institution. Moreover, she underscores the important role this department plays in the community at large with its four MAT programs, its Teacher Placement Program and its summer programs for children. Professor of Music Michael Grace writes from the perspective of someone for whom Colorado College has served as a third parent over the period of a long career that began with his undergraduate days. He reminisces poignantly about his transformation from student to faculty during the turbulent days of the late 1960s and early 1970s culminated by his appointment as Acting President in 1992–93.

Three former administrators are included in the collection of memoirs. Former Vice President for Development Barbara Yalich recalls her close involvement with the College during the last twenty- five years as she wore many hats—Alumni Trustee, Director of Alumni Relations, Director of Development, and finally Vice President. The reader learns of the dynamics behind building strong alumni support and the painstaking challenges of planning and carrying out a major Capital Campaign. Yalich's view of the College confirms the central importance of loyal dedicated supporters of the College's central mission. Director Emeritus of Admissions Richard Wood remembers the circumstances under which he came to Colorado College from the University of Denver's Development staff at the urging of President Louis Benezet. Wood surprises the reader with his pre-Block Plan view of the growth of admissions numbers. Finally, the editor contributes a selection based on his twenty-six years in the administration. He focuses on the development of student life issues—Greek organizations, athletics, and student activism. He concludes with a statement about the administrative philosophy that governed his life as a dean, vice president and director.

Of course, my summarizations do not do justice to the breath and substance of the memoirs that make up this collection. There is much more. I hope those who read this collection will join me in reacting and interacting with delight in and appreciation of the memories of a group of individuals who have given much to Colorado College and in turn have been rewarded immensely through associations that go back, in some cases, more than forty years.

Louis T. Benezet
President 1955–1963

CHAPTER 1

COLORADO COLLEGE, 1955–1963

Louis T. Benezet
President 1955–1963

THE TIME WAS RIGHT TO MOVE

In the early 1950s, life for my family and me at Allegheny College wasn't all coming our way, but we had no reason to complain. For those of middle class and above, postwar America was upbeat. The recession some predicted didn't happen; demand was still catching supply after years of hard goods withheld by government order for military use. The new cars sold fast. I turned in my '41 Ford coupe sans tears for a maroon Chrysler.

David Halberstam's *The Fifties* describes the Eisenhower years as a time of flourishing business and high consumption. Ike's one innovation was the forty-billion dollar national highway system. The number of cars soon rose from 26 to 52 million. Mammoth new home communities like Levittown took over the landscape, while Ray Kroc took over McDonald's to fast-feed the homeowners. Rapid change was everywhere, replacing whole industries. Xerox retired those inky mimeographs for mass copying, and in Meadville, Pa., home of Allegheny College, the zipper industry was born. No more need for a woman to ask her husband's help in buttoning the back of her dress or for him to button his pants. Yet over the years even that revolution slipped away from a town in which an old Meadville family was one whose ancestors had arrived before 1810. After the Erie Railroad was bought by Chesapeake & Ohio, the apparel industry, based hundreds of miles from Meadville, beckoned Talon, Inc. to move closer, and zip it did. Other firms eventually followed. Today the population is just over half what it was in 1955 when we drove away for Colorado.

In what possible way could a fugitive zipper company relate to my move west? Not because postwar Colorado Springs grew from 70,000 to a third of a million. In fact, I prefer smaller cities. For me, Meadville's decline symbolized how people react when a social entity they'd long depended on goes away. To be sure, Allegheny College has changed, as any good school, helping late-adolescents to grow up mentally, changes. Yet down from the hill where Allegheny stands, the city seemed to lose a stability the college had valued. For example, a neoclassic church, the one Unitarian church in the region, was a favorite with faculty families. The church is still there, yet about three years ago a crowd in the public square heard some Midwest radio talk-show host, Gordon Liddy style, blasting out untruths, distortions and clamors for violence. The event was featured in The New York Times, no doubt to show how easily provincial towns can be taken in. No mention was made of a respected liberal arts college with a faculty ready to offer a sharp rebuttal. Reading the story, I couldn't recall anything like it in the Meadville I'd known. One wonders whether 40 years earlier it could have happened. It then occurred to me that the area southeast of Lake Erie over former decades had suffered two downers. First, the great oil vein through Bradford, Titusville, Oil City, Franklin and Butler dried up. Second, the city of Erie never became a major lake port. In the years after the St. Lawrence Seaway was deepened to 27 feet, the large ships, it turned out, sailed right by Erie to Cleveland, Toledo and Detroit. So when Meadville, forty miles south of Erie, saw the Talon zippers leave town, it seemed to some like the dirge of once a loser, always a loser. Again only a symbol, yet one which somehow stuck in my mind. In contrast, 14,110-foot Pikes Peak, towering over the campus, raised my thoughts above banality many times a day.

Summing things up, after seven years of learning, often from my own mistakes, I felt prepared at forty to leave a good college in stable condition for one in financial straits, yet whose faculty was equaled in the West only by Reed, Whitman, Occidental, Pomona and, as of 1955, three other Claremont Colleges. By then Colorado College's straits were more like the Straits of Magellan. More of this in section 2.

You've Got to Know the Territory

In mid-September our family crossed the plains, not in a Conestoga but a yellow station wagon. En route we found how to hitch up the cigar lighter to Barbara's bottle warmer. We arrived at 1210 Wood Avenue to learn my wife and I were expected at a student reception that evening in Bemis Hall. As usual Evaline McNary, who ran the residence halls and dining services, was in charge, having filled up the fridge and recruited Cherry Carter for baby sitter. We scrubbed our faces, put on welcoming smiles and met a roomful of eager if jittery freshmen. From then until we departed eight years later, things never quite slowed down.

For me Meredith Wilson's opening song in *The Music Man* was already a slogan when I saw the Broadway show three years after coming to Colorado. In the Allegheny years, three of our first four summer vacations had been spent in Western high country. By then I thought I knew the territory. However, the first year in Colorado Springs was a lesson in how deeply the people of the Rockies believed the uniqueness of their homeland.

The lesson began early in the fall with mass attendance one evening on Washburn Field, scene of class of 1929 All-American Dutch Clark's glory a quarter-century before. Sponsored by the Junior Chamber of Commerce in cowboy attire, the event was to welcome notable newcomers. This year I was guest of honor. My welcome started in front of a crackling fire, with a brief summary of who I was and what I had done to deserve tribute. The presiding officer then asked, "What shall we do with him?" "Brand him!" the men yelled. I was picked up by the heels and laid face down on the ground with a red-hot branding-iron held above the seat of my pants. At the crucial moment (I'd been tipped off), a board was tactically placed and the iron applied. Then they stood me on my feet and escorted me out with men close behind, shouting, "Keep him decent, boys!" A few years later Russell Tutt told about a senior Air Force general who got the same treatment and turned purple with rage. To my knowledge, the ceremony was dropped 30 years ago. The Air force Academy's coming had perhaps a sobering effect. Equally new is the plague in Colorado Springs of religious fundamentalists whose fierce intent suggests the touch of a branding iron.

The late James Michener's book *Centennial* paints in bold outlines the early times of white settlers in Colorado. Despite the horse operas of my boyhood at the movies, Indian fighting wasn't the source of the wild and free spirit that filled the seats on Saturday afternoon. The economy of cattle-raising rested on having ranches large enough for raising hundreds of Herefords and Black Angus and shipping them east, plus hard winters on open plains that each year called for long cattle drives south. The lonesome cowboy with his wailing songs of gory death was a fact of life—also "First down to Rosie's and then to the card house" when he got to town. More than a century later, the wild-and-free stereotype is earthbound by industry and banking in Denver, fuel and iron in Pueblo and a sprinkling of small plains' cities, the state's farm centers.

While admired in its early days as a resort for wealthy folk as far away as England—some called it Little London—Colorado Springs became known as a haven for health seekers. In 1924 Dr. Gerald Webb's tuberculosis laboratory in Palmer Hall basement helped persuade people that a good liberal arts college had a place in the macho Rockies culture. Still when thirty years later at Rotary Club I took on the task of reselling the college to downtown merchants and professionals, they finessed its accomplished faculty while rooting for the CC Tigers at Broadmoor Ice Palace. As for presidents, Rotarians spoke fondly of Prexy Slocum, who years before had been retired with honors by the board. But most of them fumbled his successors' names except the latest, General Gill. The easy answer is that in three decades Slocum himself had become a memorable institution. A better answer is that following his unique career, Colorado College lived with a series of uneven presidencies which cost it much of the national recognition several remarkably creative professors had earned.

PUTTING THE PICTURE BACK TOGETHER

Nothing is surer to land former presidents in the soup than judging the performance of their predecessors. For one thing, no one will agree on what, when or why things happened. A homegrown example I'll describe later involved my part in the slump of CC hockey after Don Wishart and Bill Hay led the team to the NCAA championship in 1957. Before that happy event it was my part first to focus on the financial slump responsible for an annual operating deficit of up to six figures. Colleagues now gone whom I'll name were involved; their families will I trust forgive me. Any blame centered in delays from actions liberal arts colleges as non-profit enterprise must take to survive. Lacking full information, the trustees lived with an optimism that, when help is needed, someone—perhaps God—will provide. In fact, the Board, led by new chairman Bob McIvaine (class of 1923) called upon a reply used daily in *their* business, "God helps those who help themselves."

The accounts that follow owe much to the late Juan Reid's history of Colorado College as seen by one who from 1928 until 1975 lived through its every moment. I first met Juan as a quick-thinking Dean of Men who regularly beat faculty friends at chess and, knowing every cop in town up to the Chief, could spring a sophomore out of jail within the hour. Of all personnel deans his judgment was the fairest I've known. Blocking for Dutch Clark in the back field was ideal training. Yet as a good historian, he was invaluable to a new head of an unusually complex small institution.

The college I'd left was dubiously blessed by having fifty trustees, most of whom shared their slight knowledge of what went on. To move from that to one with a dozen to fifteen seemed a blessing. In my working years, however, I've learned that few college trustee boards have more than six or seven members prepared to work at the job. Two qualities mark those half-dozen effective trustees: (1) insight into understanding distinctions between the economy of a business and a college; (2) and an ability to help the president select a staff competent to carry out through their various skills the purposes the college is committed to achieve. These two unite in the college's first purpose which, again, is to survive. "So what's different?," you ask; "Every business down to a hot dog stand has to survive." Then comes the distinction trustees can recite (if few have taken it to their inner minds). A business makes profits by producing saleable goods and services at the lowest cost per unit. A selective college survives, nay improves, by 'producing' good students at the highest cost per student the college can afford. A similarity is the luxury goods market. Tiffany's, for example, profits by the same principle of high-cost production of fine goods by top experts. Elite liberal arts colleges—Colorado College is now one—prevail by offering a top faculty, facilities and equipment at the na-

tion's costliest rate per student. In 1955 how many students could have
gone to a school displaying an endowment, tuition and gifts beyond our
dreams? Answer: only those financially able to pick one of the best. It was
left to me to persuade the board that Colorado College was being under-
sold. After making clearer to them the facts of our debts, this was a pretty
nervy thing to do.

Our lean, hungry state hadn't always been so. In Slocum's golden age,
the parade of wealthy patrons started with General Palmer, followed by
Bemis, Van Diest and once even Andrew Carnegie. The president himself
capped the climax with his own cousin, who gave enough in 1914 to build
an entire gymnasium in honor of her father Frederick Cossitt. Yet halcyon
days eventually end. No more buildings except Shove Chapel (1931) were
erected until the first residence hall, Slocum, (1954) was built by a federal
loan from the HHFA. Philanthropy is a tricky business, driven as often by
vanity as by unselfish desire to aid society's best institutions. The institution is accordingly chosen according to the donor's confidence that the
prospective grantee is on solid footing, sure to last for generations to come.
In early years at CC, I pondered what had shaken that confidence. One
reason was simple biology—the 1890s multimillionaires had died off.

There were other reasons. In the years of both world wars, with the
Great Depression between, the school was subject to disruptions by military training units of both Army and Navy-Marines. Meanwhile, the
financial straits of many families throughout the 1930s led to lower enrollments in a western private college circled by public institutions, virtually tuition-free. Faculty salaries were cut and cut again, resulting in a loss
of professors to liberal arts schools academically no better but more
highly endowed. In 1955 when I came, two full professors were paid the
maximum salary, $6,000. The next spring Lew Worner and I announced
salary goals with a top of $10,000 within four years. The faculty replied
with wry smiles and fingers tapping their temples. (Happily, it turned out
we made it in three).

Still, stability in a college, likewise people's confidence in the college,
begins at the top. Earlier I referred to uneven administrations after
President Slocum's resignation, but it's known that circumstances included his personal actions, thereby charges by Dean Parsons and three

professors. Separate from this, the succeeding tenures of Clyde Duniway and Charles Mierow were each in its way visited by disagreements and discontent. My friendship with Charles Meirow permits opinion that the business side of an underfunded college was not his forte. The Depression called for skills his humanist mind hadn't learned. For the college the worst luck then was how two wars eroded the strength of a vibrant leader, Thurston Davies. Of all presidents after Slocum he came closest in dynamic energy to direct college operations, travel to alumni clubs, join multiple boards and committees in town, solicit donors and speak throughout the state on any subject: all with urbanity, charm and apparent ease. As one who ran the circuit 20 years later, I'll testify it can be done only so long. In World War I, Lefty Davies, as his buddies called him, fought with distinction. He was twice wounded. In 1943 the Marine Corps recalled him to duty in its Washington Headquarters. Two years later he returned to organize a capital fund drive and restore the campus after departure of the Navy V–12 unit. Within a few months his health failed, wracked by fatigue and hard drinking. Hospitalized, he was granted leave of absence by the Board. However, after General Gill's appointment as Acting President, Davies submitted his resignation.

Thurston Davies had led the college like a builder on the way to matching the best in liberal education. Had he remained healthy, I think he would have made changes in organization needed to do it. His successor, General William Gill, presided in ways that won respect from students and faculty, including some academics who distrusted the military. We became good friends. More than that, having briefly served in New Guinea, I appreciated what it meant to command the red Arrow Division through the jungles of Burma, so close to the enemy that all rank insignia were removed. One evening at his house, Bill Gill showed me a handsome samurai sword. "Where'd you get this?," I asked. He smiled grimly: "I took it off him." Two of his actions dear to my heart were done when greatly needed. One was to deny by letter the local paper's claim of communism being taught at the college, soon to be followed by a letter to the chairman of HUAC in Washington upholding academic freedom and declining to send information about textbooks and readings in Coburn Library. I'm happy to say that the second action is intact: the honor system, prepared by two former Virginia college students, William H. Gill (V.M.I.) And Lloyd E. Worner (Washington & Lee). Now fifty years old, is it strange to find it a college rarity?

When in 1954 the president decided to retire, inevitably things were left undone that a career Army officer neither reckoned on nor had been prepared to carry out. Some of them, the faculty were impatient to have done. Other items had always been absent—items needed by a liberal arts college to handle problems in postwar capitalist democracy. Here is a short list of the gaps that yawned at me on the first floor of Cutler Hall:

- There was no development officer or even an office. K. Freyschlag, a recent graduate, handled public information, assisted by Tom Pankau.
- There was no vice president of business and finance. The new treasurer was Robberts Simcock, promoted by President Gill after Tom Rawles decided to return to teaching mathematics. There was no business manager.
- There was no vice president or Dean of student affairs. Juan Reid and Sallie Payne Morgan, as respectively Dean of Men and Dean of Women, had their differences now and then, yet were entirely congenial.
- There was no director of student aid. As director of admissions, Dean Ed Mathias had earned his title by managing over the years everything on campus. CC's Pooh-bah added student aid to recruiting and selecting students.
- There was no director of physical plant. A rotund retired Army officer, Colonel Moore, served as superintendent of buildings and grounds. Regarding faculty as corporals, he treated them accordingly—a major sore point.
- The College lacked a first-class library of books with the promise of a new building now twenty-four years overdue. The patron changed her mind and instead gave the money to build the Colorado Springs Fine Arts Center.
- There was an unbalanced athletic program: Division I hockey was reasonably successful, but the football program with a de-

manding schedule against large state colleges and the financial burden of athletic scholarships cost the College dearly.

This list only begins the items waiting each morning at 8:45. My genteel secretary was willing, though elderly, and she didn't type. She had a typist, yet some months later confided to a friend, "The man is killing me!" At noon I jogged home for lunch, amusing the women on sorority row. The time for change was now. My reaction recalled classmate Budd Schulberg's *What Makes Sammy Run?*.. Acting Dean Lloyd Worner met with me nearly every day. (We dropped the 'Acting' at the first board meeting.) By next spring our plan echoed Marshall Foch: "My right is defeated, my left is thrown back; I shall attack with my center." Like his strategy, ours came early in the fight when odds were long against us—attack with the center.

At every college, be it a research university or two-year community college, the institution's center is its faculty. Quality in a teacher, unique to each person, can't be decided by degrees or scholarly output. Still, as Mr. Justice Roberts said of pornography, you know it when you see it. I saw the quality of Frank Krutzke, Doug Mertz, Ken Curran, Glenn Gray, Al Seay, Robert Stabler, Fred Sondermann and a baker's-dozen others, including some later lights: Ric Bradley, Jane Cauvel, Glenn Brooks, Bill Fischer, and Dick Beidleman. Professors like these inspire a president to animate liberal education at its best.

In the winter of 1955–56, Lew Worner and I, backed by Chairman Bob McIlvaine, hunted for animation bright enough to rival Disney, while discussing our academic side with fellow citizens, some of whom lived on Lake Avenue, ending at the Broadmoor and the El Pomar Foundation. The whole town knew CC's WCHA ranking vs. DU's team. Few if any people knew about Colorado College's record in producing Ph.D. scientists, as reported by a Wesleyan University study some years before—13th among nationally known liberal arts colleges. My 'some years before' was the catch–22. Our reputation in recent years had declined with the drop both in salaries and admission standards. The casualties mounted during two ill-favored times: after Slocum's retirement and after Davies' return from the Capitol at the war's end, his health broken by fatigue and alcoholism. When a college is hit at the same time by loss in money, top students and the leader, it identifies with Hamlet's lament, "How all occasions do inform against it." In fact, the problem was a classic dilemma: how to recast the image of success while asking support from the very sources able to make the success real. The first point we soon resolved: much as we loved winning hockey games, for CC to beat even the Edmonton Oilers wouldn't raise a dime towards again being known as the best liberal arts college in an area one third the size of the contiguous 48 states. That being said, our second point was aimed at the center of any college's strength. Quality of liberal education begins and ends with good teaching. Colorado College had always excelled in its faculty. It was time the public be reminded that quality professors expect to be fairly paid.

A private liberal arts college with underpaid professors has two ways to move up fast: develop giving, typically from rich alumni some of whom might never have graduated, or raise its fees. The ways interconnect. Each, however, has problems needing separate solutions. As to the first way, I neither read nor heard from older faculty members that the college had ever had a director of development. From the first with Thomas Haskell in 1873, fund-raising was the president's responsibility. Since he was invariably a minister, it was assumed he could do this through praying to the congregation. Some excelled in this; others argued that praying should be spelled with 'e' plus 'on'. At all events, Haskell had no luck. In fact, after President Tenney's disastrous investment experiment Colorado College had to rely for gifts if not survival on its trustees until W. F. Slocum arrived.

It therefore took me time in early '56 to persuade the Board that we like all schools of our kind must find a top development officer. I had a name to offer: Robert Brossman, Cornell University's director of public information. I'd known Bob as a resourceful Allegheny alumnus in a high post at a renowned institution. Luckily he was on the rebound from rescuing his president who, it seems, plagiarized Harold Taylor in the Inaugural Address. Though he was joining CC at its nadir, Bross agreed to be Vice president of Development. In 1982, after guiding three presidents for a quarter-century, he retired. His legacy was a campus full of new buildings, a faculty twice the size and an endowment nearing $200 million. It was hard for me and many others to hear of his death last fall. To serve as the helmsman for a small college en route to national recognition requires a genuine individual prepared on three fronts: telling the president more than he or she knew about goings-on, giving trustees full facts of the college in plain language, and staying close to the faculty as a friend and colleague, not as a runner for stodgy administrators on the top floor of Old Main. In my thirty years with development people only Ken Beyer at Claremont approached Bross's easy humor and self-critical mind. Bob Brossman left for others a model of development officer to learn from and, I hope, to follow.

The second way to move up fast, raising tuition, led to questions how to raise fees at a school that's already behind its competitors. Mt. Holyoke in the 1970s could serve as an example, though hardly comparable in terms of geography. The Seven Sisters colleges compete at top prices for national standing. Contrast this with the mid–1950s at Colorado College, the quality liberal arts school of the Rocky Mountain region, where $400 for tuition and fees was then thought exorbitant. While that price didn't deter bright upper-middle class kids in our region, in the East and the West Coast it had the reverse effect. Wealthy regions see quality and price as reciprocal: the higher the cost, the better must be the education. In Depression days, Tom Rawles as admissions director traveled the East on a safari for students. The reaction dismayed him: back there such low fees telegraphed a mediocre school, good for skiing and someone looking for easy grades after barely earning their prep school diplomas. Some years before I came, Ed Mathias, who replaced Rawles after Tom became the college's Treasurer, had been directed by President Gill to recruit any admissible student who could pay the tab. The direction was obeyed, but the result was counterproductive.

Here a word in defense of my predecessor is due. In accepting the headship of a liberal arts college, General Gill made no pretense of being either an educator or a financier. Least of all did he expect to raise money for a school in debt to its own piddling endowment or to rebuild student enrollment after hundreds of G.I. veterans graduated. At Fort Carson the first order, keep things under control, was assured by government funds. The commanding general was thus left at peace to oversee troops training for war. Aware of the sharp contrasts in duty assignment, Bill Gill used his V.M.I. background as an officer and a gentleman to learn the new orders of rank in academia. Beyond that he adapted the Army's chain of command to upholding academic freedom and the quasi-democracy of a liberal arts faculty. What he wasn't prepared for, neither was I: the deep inroads from 30 years of in-and-out presidencies on a college's financial integrity after its major donors had died or left town. Ersatz administrators, professors at a loss in matters of business, law and organization, did their best in faith, hope and damned little charity to start paying off the endowment debt.

Gazing back on that scene gives a clue as to why my inauguration was postponed to a year after I came. The year was occupied with the cleanup detail listed above in this section. The two main priorities were development officer, just described, and a senior administrator for business and finance. Filling this post proved to be a longer assignment. Tom Rawles had left as Treasurer and happily returned to teaching math. In his place, to my regret Gill had promoted Robberts Simcock as a reward for long service. Bob Simcock was a small polite man and a good bookkeeper, self-educated but without a college degree or C.P.A. He had, however, grown used to annual audits of Ernst and Ernst from Denver, each year ending with Rawles' dry question, "Well, how much do we borrow from endowment this year?" A series of conferences with Simcock left me resolved to look for someone experienced in college financial management. While serving on the Board of Directors of the American Council on Education, I'd made a friend of its highly regarded financial officer. After one turn-down I tried again. In 1957 Bob Broughton became our Vice President for Business and finance and gave outstanding leadership until his retirement in 1982. In all that time, Colorado College never had an operating deficit.

To keep on retelling how various offices were created or changed would sound like the U.S.S. Reluctant in *Mr. Roberts*, sailing monthly from Tedium to Apathy. With two new vice presidents aboard, our staff was complete except for a properly trained director of physical plant, again non-existent. As building superintendent, Colonel Moore had neither the knowledge nor any concern about campus grounds, which after a four-year drought looked like Alaskan tundra and truly disaffected the townspeople. Meanwhile the Colonel disaffected the faculty so much that offers were made to pay for his replacement—this by professors wretchedly underpaid.

The academic salary problem preempted the call for action. Once more Lew Worner sat for hours with me to prepare a new faculty scale. Since we still lacked a development head, a tuition hike was mandatory. At length we took to the Board of Trustees a schedule whose details I forget except for the top: from the present $6,000 for full professors (only two were getting it) to $7,500. When we then proposed a $50 tuition increase to $450, sober looks greeted the figure but the new Chairman got it through.

In this day of $20,000+ tuitions, the rates of 1956 are as archaic as the predicted 500 Dow average called crazy at a Chamber of Commerce luncheon I attended in 1946. But in 1956, $450 plus fees still put a private college in the Rockies as high as its altitude. Dean Ed Mathias shook his head at prospects of recruiting enough rich students to accept it. It was time for Ed to learn new signals on whom to recruit and whom to deny. Having taught at The Hill School, I knew the convenience of a good college in ski country as a haven for 6th Formers who failed entrance into the so-called Little Three, let alone the Ivy League. For well-heeled prospects our tuition price was a breeze. But for Colorado College to turn down such applications sent a message of intent not to be a dumping ground. This then would open the door to better students from all over, since such messages quickly get around to the best-regarded secondary schools both private and public. True to predictions, the first year of change netted a loss in students; our audit was again in the red. The next year saw a change. Almost by magic the word passed that CC meant what it said. Not long thereafter we were included in the circle of 50 very selective liberal arts colleges. Ed Mathias was content to assume full-time duty in financial aid. After Professor Ross's brief tenure, Dick Wood, a fugitive from University of Denver development, came to stay. In years after, he was known by many as the West's top admissions director.

The state of our physical plant kept deteriorating, as did the faculty's relations with Colonel Moore. When outside engineers pronounced our heating plant moribund—the superintendent said it was OK—I recalled a chat with a friend, financial coordinator of the university system in New

Mexico, who had mentioned a bright young assistant plant director. On the phone to Albuquerque I asked about him. Dr. Russell said I could try, but he thought Richard Kendrick wasn't for hire. We invited him to visit. He came and surveyed the college plant like a surgeon deciding whether the patient would survive an operation. That fall Dick Kendrick, his wife Ruth, also an engineer, and two sons joined the CC community. Dick took over the plant and gave it a father's care. Among other things, to our neighbors' delight, he negotiated with the city a non-potable water irrigation system for the central campus and, behold, the green returned. Since in mysterious ways success breeds success, it must have been kismet when the following year an undesignated bequest of $100,000 from the brother of two alumnae was given to the college. Just in the nick of time the gift materialized as the brand new Williams heating plant. And by then the plant director had been inducted into the oldest faculty poker club at Colorado College.

IMPROVING THE PICTURE: NEW PRIDE, OLD PROBLEMS

In autumn 1958 members of the board of trustees for the most part became believers. Four trustees in particular were behind Bob McIlvaine's spirit of "You ain't seen nothing yet." Banker Chase Stone, Cornell '14, was on the El Pomar Foundation board, recently bolstered by the return from Garden City, Kansas of Russell Tutt, a Princeton graduate in engineering. Familiar with top-grade higher education, the two men delved into money problems at CC in a way not seen for years on its board. In so doing they hoped to inspire other members to do more than move the question. Two who needed no help were Grace Berkley Brannon '27, a keen thinker with classmates on the board she nudged into action, and class of 1897's E. K. Gaylord from Oklahoma City. Gaylord was the state's most powerful influence for progress, founder of its Frontiers of Science, and owner of The Daily Oklahoman as well as many radio stations. He was a true phenomenon who at age 82 had come lately on our board, ready to brighten its eye to the future. From then on until his death at 101 Mr. Gaylord made up in part for the help he might have given had the college not neglected its opportunities. At this writing, his daughter, Edith Gaylord Harper '36, is an active and generous trustee.

With trustees of this caliber, it was easier to believe that indeed we hadn't seen anything yet. This leads me to tell the library story.

Since 1894 when Coburn Library added to Hagerman Hall a new peach-blow sandstone building, Colorado College had prided itself on the finest collection of books in the Rocky Mountain West. By 1931 the ravages of time had brought the need for a new structure, and Alice Bemis Taylor pledged to make it possible. By 1943 she'd changed her will to fund the Colorado Fine Arts Center. At this, Louise Kampf, College Librarian, despaired of a new building. In 1955 when I came, she was still confirmed in misery. In the fall of 1959, an El Pomar Foundation phone call requested our board chairman and me to visit Mr. Charles Tutt. I had an inkling of what could be in the wind, but my chairman didn't believe it. In Mr. Tutt's reception room were his son Russell and Chase Stone. Charlie sat grinning while Chase told of the Foundation's decision to build on our campus the Charles Leaming Tutt Library. Bob McIlvaine was silent for a moment. I glimpsed a tear in his eye. Then he said, "I think this may be the greatest thing that's happened to me." For all his hyperbole I'm glad he said it, because about a year later Bob died of a heart attack. As for our Librarian, on ground-breaking day I said, "Now, Louise, you have your library." She smiled wanly and replied, "Well, it's the closest we've come, anyway."

Still on the theory that success breeds success, Bob Brossman and I planned an approach to the Olin Foundation in Minneapolis. Its president, Charles Horn, who sported several honorary degrees and enjoyed being addressed as Doctor, was said to bark at college presidents, tear apart their proposal and sometimes almost literally throw the president out the door. Using his own methods, Bross learned Dr. Horn was thinking of a Western college for a next Foundation grant, always a building, usually for science and inevitably to be named Olin Hall. My findings disclosed his abilities in Old Testament scholarship, Charles Mierow's field. I also learned that he'd gone to a small Iowa college I knew well, and he liked direct phone calls. The fact that Dr. Horn and I were fraternity brothers, I declined to use. (He discovered it, and later insisted on giving me the grip). In short, I phoned him, withstood the bark and got a next-month appointment. What ensued need not lengthen the account, except for a one-foot stack of CC faculty publications that I carried by hand to Minneapolis to interest a man who I knew did believe in the liberal arts for, as he lectured, "producing intellectuals." Our conversation was lively and pertinent. When the three Olin Foundation officials came to visit us, Russ Tutt reserved the Spencer Penrose suite at the Broadmoor and rolled out the carpet. After two years of reciprocal visits, our combined rewards were two badly needed academic halls. One visit surprised my wife and me, an invitation to informal dinner at Charles and Evelyn Horn's home—so informal in fact that it survived a shaky moment when he spilled soup on his trousers.

Were all these shenanigans a courtly form of mutual hypocrisy—á la Lincoln Bedroom or did one see in Charles Horn a self-conscious oldster with few close friends and a habit of barking louder than other dogs for cover? I came to like Charles, waxed mustache and all. Conceivably he seldom had outside guests. His wife devoted her part to reassuring her older husband, waving covertly each time he spoke at convocations. More to the point, Charles Horn could tell a good from a so-so college. Since he had looked into the kind of graduate a school was producing, he took dead aim at presidents rash enough to claim what they couldn't demonstrate.

Adding three academic buildings, the first in some thirty years, was a major bricks-and-mortar improvement. It was also time for us to remind local people what Colorado College meant to Colorado Springs beyond winning hockey games. The city had grown so fast that its already historic college, now in hard times, slipped from the public's attention as an educational and cultural mainstay. Our citizens needed to hear how many of their civic and professional leaders had won their B.A. degrees from a widely respected school a mile or two from their homes and to share the delights of music, drama and art as well as nationally known speakers open to the public at little or no expense. The first need was met by a Chamber of Commerce luncheon in the City Auditorium. After lunch I described from the platform a mythical civic calamity: the sort of time warp whose effect was to banish overnight Colorado College and its local alumni. Facts were driven home by charts and numbers of all the business, professional, educational, government and humanitarian agencies which awoke to find their leading members gone. Allowing the rather corny ploy, to the surprise of a few skeptics it got a hand and follow-up from the community: this despite my announcement of a capital development campaign soon to begin.

The second reminder, cultural enrichment, was entwined with the Colorado Springs Fine Arts Center, only a block away. In the days before Armstrong and Packard Halls, cordiality with the F.A.C. increased into a cooperative agreement that linked the two institutions in the public's mind. Although their theater lacked a full backstage for major play productions, in my latter four years a trio of professors, Bill McMillen in drama, Don Jenkins in choral music, and Norman Cornick in dance, put on the finest performances of *Brigadoon, The Most Happy Fella* and, especially, *Guys and Dolls* that any of us had seen on a college stage. Never shall I forget the sight of Coach Jerry Carle's beefy linemen down in the sewer, lustily singing "Luck, Be a Lady Tonight." For three decades CC's cultural reputation was buoyed by Hanya Holm's summer dance school, begun in 1941 through the good offices of Carol Truax. The celebrated choreographer of Broadway musicals, climaxed by *My Fair Lady,* was fairly matched by Max Lanner's diplomacy in bringing national artists to play in the string quartet, often joined by Max on the piano. Such virtuosi did as much for us in the nation as in the city, especially in relations between Aspen's summer program and our own. For instance, violist Paul Doktor went over to visit his old colleague William Primrose, then America's premier violist. All in all, Colorado College in those years regained its place of former years as a center for the humanities, and I hope will continue. In view of Jim Dobson's Focus on the Family haranguing the town, my hope becomes a prayer.

THE QUESTION OF BIG TIME HOCKEY IN AN ELITE SMALL COLLEGE

Since the 1890s when baseball was the top college sport, Colorado College has fielded teams in intercollegiate competition. As a small institution in the Rockies against the state schools CC held its own, with boys coached in city high schools while state college players were often from small towns and villages. From early in the century until the 1940s, football was king at our college. Perhaps because of better coaching and headier players, on a good day CC was able to beat the best university teams in the region. The years of Dutch Clark are still savored as Colorado College's golden age of football. After World War II, university football became professionalized as egged on by the thousands of student and alumni spectators. Well before then the major universities in our region had withdrawn from the Rocky Mountain Conference, leaving CC to regroup with none but state schools. By 1955 the group comprised Montana State and Idaho State Universities, Adams State and Western State Colleges, and Colorado School of Mines. Although Mines remained our annual rival, the less academic state institutions were clobbering us. With negligible gate receipts a change had to come. In '58 CC left the Conference, ironically as a co-champion.

As often happens, the move had a precedent in Thurston Davies' attempt, after seven universities withdrew in 1936 to arrange a liberal arts college conference with Whitman, Occidental, Washburn and Grinnell. For reasons mainly involving distance, the effort failed as did another I briefly tried soon after I came. Yet the far flung spaces of the West are not the biggest obstacle against matching like with like in liberal arts college football. In '58 Athletic Director Jerry Carle agreed to leave the RMC provided the college would pay travel costs to our kind of school. The pact followed my showing him the net costs of 40 football scholarships (tuition + fees) in a conference of low-cost schools with lower admission standards, Colorado Mines excepted. As for football, a real downer came with the Air force Academy in 1956 about 12 miles north of our campus. The frustration of watching plebes and 3rd class cadets beat our seniors prepared the college for today's no-charge games with unsubsidized players who compete for the joy of winning. Few loyal fans would pay to see us lose, facing such odds. What's more, the periodic downtown CC Booster Clubs, called on to raise money for football scholarships plus store jobs, faded into history after the advent of NCAA Division I hockey, to which the discussion now turns.

Colorado College's hockey team, born in 1938 after the Broadmoor Hotel delivered an ice rink from the weary loins of its old riding academy, had by the time I assumed office become a national power. Two years later in 1957 at the Ice Palace, Don Wishart, Bill Hay, Bob McCusker and their fellow tigers devoured the University of Michigan, 13–6, for the NCAA title. (A few years later, after expansion of seating capacity, the name was changed to the Broadmoor World Arena.) A college holiday was declared, celebrated by a mighty beer putsch in the Garden of the Gods. The picture on page 1 of *The Free Press* showing distraught men and women students gazing at a wrecked car recalls the event to mind. What happened to CC's hockey fortunes in the next five years is a story agreed upon by few in my time. Enough to say, the Benezet tenure survived, but barely, a long interim between winning seasons. Like Thoreau I took my beat from a different drummer. Let me explain my belief in changes I felt were needed since things eventually went that way.

The heart of my feelings about college amateur athletics is their influence toward enjoyment of life for the sake of living. Alexander Calder's mobiles and stabiles were objects that refused to be classified according to values or emotions. A big, blunt man, when asked what his creations meant he'd say, "Look at them. They're not a philosophy; they're what you see, objects you like to watch and feel good about." I feel the same way about college sports—good to try and good to win at but mostly good in themselves. Sports build body condition and are fun to play. Every day of his life Calder made a new object, either floating or still. Granted it brought lots of money, he gave away to old and young folk most of the objects he made and got a kick out of watching the enjoyment it gave them.

Applying this to Colorado College hockey, both the school and the town took the sport so seriously they spoke of it as if in church. The team became widely known in 1939 after a star player returned to the college with four other Canadians and CC won two games with the University of Michigan. After that our hockey was a sport for those north of the border. When I came sixteen years later, Bucky Reinking, a local lad, was one of two American players. He was an alternate on the 3rd line. The other, Jeff Simus from Minnesota, was goaltender and a good one.

To set things straight, I loved watching hockey and learned to ice skate at age nine in New Hampshire. Canadians I like and admire. At Harvard summer school John McDonald, a McGill law student, was my roommate, and I'd gone to high school with dozens of French-Canadians.

In western Canada the high schools' 13ᵗʰ year bolsters preparation for college. Few of our players had trouble making grades. True, the El Pomar Foundation in its scholarship program for CC students included athletic scholarships for hockey. Yet, during my tenure I recall that virtually all hockey players would have qualified for need-based aid. My objection to having an all-Canadian team was its discouraging American high school players from competing with Canadians who came from one to three years of Junior-A hockey during or after high school. Junior-A was virtually a semi-professional league of farm-clubs for the NHL. So close was the tie that if a Junior-A player signed a contract for even a NHL try-out, he was barred from playing amateur hockey in the U.S. By that *faux pas*, we lost one recruit, Orrie Kinasewich, who then spent his CC years on the golf team. Ironically his brother Gene four years later sparked Harvard's hockey team who beat us on Broadmoor ice.

The Junior-A player issue moved me to propose that the WCHA restrict Canadians to Junior-B's, good players but not semi-professional. I carried the idea to Ann Arbor, Michigan, where President Harlan Hatcher who spoke at my inauguration and his wife were hosts. Harlan was gracious as ever, but next morning it was plain he liked hockey as it was and saw no pressing reason to exclude the Junior-A's. In Minneapolis for an alumni evening I saw our team lose to Minnesota and had to hear the fans call Jack Smith on our front line "Pop" because of the grey in his hair. Coach John Mariucci, who for years had seen his teams beaten by ex-Junior-A's at North Dakota and Michigan, was obviously delighted with my idea. Back home Tony Frasca, former CC great from Boston and successor-coach to Canadian Tom Bedecki, was willing to forego Junior-A's, given recruiting funds to cover north and northeastern U.S. I met with the team to explain my reasons for the action. They were good sports about it though they were shaking their heads. Next year we enrolled a 1ˢᵗ-class Junior B, along with two from Quebec and some top Americans. After three losing years the team found its will to win. In 1962–63, my last year, with Don Stouffer and Art Berglund at the fore CC defeated DU in spite of its Junior-A's. That night at 11:30 our doorbell rang. It was Bill Dixon the captain presenting a hockey stick, signed by all players, to give to our 11 year old daughter Julie. It seems she'd written a fight song which

Coach Frasca read to the team before they went out for the 3rd period. Thirty-six years later Julie can show it to her 11 year old Zoë, who's getting good at basketball.

In years following, what happened to the Junior-A hockey issue has escaped my knowledge. Apparently teams like the Edmunton Oilers were upgraded to the NHL. *(Editor's note: The NCAA eventually banned the recruiting of Canadian Junior A hockey players.)* In any event, the 1997–98 Colorado College hockey roster shows 23 of 32 players to be Americans. In ending a saga of my lone attempt to level the playing ice, I thank the late Thayer and Russell Tutt for their patience and faith that the effort would right itself after a while.

DEVELOPING A SUPERIOR FACULTY FOR LIBERAL EDUCATION

Speaking of ironies, one I've lived with nearly all my life is the need to attach a word to *liberal* when talking with trustees or wealthy alumni. *Liberal Arts* is safe on first; *liberal education* purses their lips but gets by. Calling a professor *liberal* or *liberal-minded* is antsy business and best avoided, while to call him or her *a liberal* is out of the ball park. Once I was in a play (*Milestones* by Arnold Bennett and Edward Knoblock, Walter H. Baker Co., Boston, 1912) whose leading character, a British shipbuilder about to be knighted warns his daughter against a suitor, blurting out, "He little guesses I know he's a Socialist!" At this point the father's spinster sister says to no one especially, "Why are men always so frightened by names?"

To the best of my memory the Colorado College board, while it had quite conservative trustees starting with E. K. Gaylord of Oklahoma City, never raised the question at meetings, though our faculty covered a normal range of political beliefs, averaging what F.D.R. liked to call a little left of center. Along with Mr. Gaylord the trustees were all for progress to be the best liberal arts college in the Rocky Mountain West and one of the few dozen considered the best in America. The path to distinction is led by men and women on the faculty with a broad grasp of knowledge outside as well as in their specialty. During eight years in office it was my great pleasure to watch the faculty's breadth of intellect stretch to students in every field.

In Colorado Springs recruiting creative minds for teaching and research has an unearned increment, climate, the main cause of its founding. My surprise that such competent people were teaching for meager pay was answered as my wife and I visited faculty families on the edge of town with flourishing gardens and ingenious hobbies amid America's most glorious views. Granted that when time came to decide on salaries Dean Worner and I were reminded you can't eat a scenery, the autumn picnics at Bob Stabler's and Woodson Tyree's farms on the mesa enlarged the picture of a faculty that had come to stay. Far from taking advantage of nature's beauty, we were all the more determined to sell the college back to its constituents at values its hectic but unique academic history had earned. If nature's beauty is irrelevant to raising funds for faculty salaries, it *was* relevant to remind the faculty that effective teaching is the best way to impress philanthropic sources as to the quality of a college. Those sources include affluent alumni, also local business people preoccupied with last night's hockey score. Today's hot market for "America's Best Colleges" has led to endless schemes to convince a fickle public that College X rates so many points better than College Y. Intricate charts and scales to prove this appear in magazines competing for circulation like dogs growling over a bone. Has anyone invented a way to prove which college faculties best move students to learn how to understand people who are different from themselves? Some great teachers I've known would settle for the ability to help students learn to understand themselves.

During 29 years at or among (i.e. Claremont) ten selective colleges, faculty bonding was the variable that for me best distinguished one school from another. By bonding I don't mean the hail-fellow-well-met of a social fraternity that's more like an Odd Fellows Club. On the contrary, college professors shy away from back-slapping, finding more pleasure in argument. At two colleges, conflicts reached a point where one professor no longer spoke to another in the same department, a situation which at the time for signing up courses required note-passing carried by interceding students. I could name some places where faculty members have been united in common defense against *the administration*, an abstraction for the president. At others, if colleges went under fire such as after World War II when the Dies and Veldes un-American activities committees were snooping on certain campuses, most of the college faculties stood firmly together. The others joined in condemning a few that turned stoolpigeon on suspected colleagues, who then ably defended themselves. These goings-on in a time of postwar hangover leave ample room for belief that faculty bonding is an integral part of effective learning. In a select liberal arts college, faculty bonding helps ensure the learning will last. Among the ten I've had the luck to serve, Colorado College's faculty bonded the most closely, yet in ways distinctly their own. My story ends with some of the ways that kept me aboard until I felt sure the next captain would stay the course—enough of a metaphor for an aging ex-Naval reserve lieutenant.

First, faculty appointees will usually stay if all the department shares in recruiting them, not the chairman only. It isn't a truism. Just before my arrival the history chair by himself appointed four new members, in effect a whole department, and then informed acting Dean Worner of the *fait accompli*. Needless to report, that department never quite came together in spite of surface good humor. Within five years two left us. Lew Worner, himself a top historian, for once in our years together confessed that he found the presumption personally too close to handle. Naturally I asked the chair to come talk it over. The agreed solution was his special appointment as Professor of Southwestern Studies with funds for travel plus a department search for a new chairman, reporting their findings for the Dean's approval. I might add, Harvey Carter said he never liked being chairman.

This regrettable faculty glitch is cited because nothing else like it happened at the college while I was in office. In contrast, here are three examples which to me display the character of *scholar-teacher*—a redundancy if ever there was one—that made up the fibre of Colorado College's faculty in the days when its rejuvenation was in the making:

- Bob Stabler, called Doc I think because of his wide expertise in bird's diseases, especially pigeons, came in 1946 as biology chairman. A robust extrovert who could have been a professional athlete, he served as coach of both swimming and lacrosse, the latter because of Johns Hopkins' championship teams, where he lettered and earned his Science Doctorate. Bob was a competitor from toe to crown and didn't care who

knew it. I found it out on the tennis court. In 1958 the department recruited Dick Beidleman as Associate Professor of
Zoology, a sparkling teacher and scientist who published in half
a dozen fields. As a man intent on winning, Doc Stabler
had cause to spot a rival who'd test his mettle. Able academics
are prone to run for the wire like race horses. In small colleges,
news of a faculty tiff soon gets around. Still in the five years before I left, the two were not close buddies, yet nothing but team
loyalty in the biology building ever came my way—another
example of the oft-told Sherlock Holmes tale in which there
was no murderer. Holmes solved it by observing that the dog
didn't bark.("Silver Blaze" in *The Complete Sherlock Holmes*,
Doubleday, Doran & Co., Garden City, N.Y., 1930.)

• Fred Sondermann, archetypical teacher, had fled as a boy with
his family from Nazi Germany. A small but dynamic man,
from 1953 when he joined the political science department he
never stopped running. Unlike Budd Schulber's Sammy Glick,
he ran for the sake of others, not himself. His writings gave
way to a succession of committees which in turn were given up
when he was elected member of the City Council. Fred was
also president of the Reform Congregation. At his invitation,
one Friday evening I tried a brief sermon on Jacob's struggle
with the angel. All this time students lined up to take his
courses since his knowledge, relieved by a saucy wit, was well
known on campus. One day I had a phone call from John
Bonforte, an engineer-businessman, asking about a professor
who had predicted future relations between the U. S. and
China. (It was well before Nixon himself opened the door, later
his one claim to a diplomatic feat.) Mr. Bonforte, President of
the Rose Society, a club noted more for local gossip than growing roses, named Fred Sondermann as having made the infamous claim about a Communist power. I asked John to lunch,
where we discussed a book on Epictetus he'd written with help
from our philosophy chair, Glenn Gray. At length John agreed to
have lunch with Fred. Two days later Mr. Bonforte phoned,

saying, "Your man is O.K." When I told Glenn he said that after a lot of help Bonforte had sweated out the book.

- At each college I have known there's at least one professor who is looked on by colleagues as the faculty sage. At CC we had two: Kenneth Curran, Economics and Frank Krutzke, English. Ken replaced Lew Worner as Dean after I left. Frank remained the senior professor who said little at faculty meeting but closely watched the actions. In one contested issue the question was moved, to be voted by secret ballot. In the interim he was asked, "Frank, how will it go?" In measured tones he said, "It will pass by a small margin." And so it did. Professor Krutzke's serenity was bought at no small price. By circumstances beyond my understanding, his doctorate at the University of Pennsylvania never went through. In 1937, he joined the CC faculty as instructor. From the lowest rung, eighteen years later he was full professor and one of two professor who met my plane at Denver for the first visit. The other was Kenneth Curran. Throughout my stay Frank Krutzke was a quiet source of wisdom. A special contribution was his kindness to one student, Dick McCabe, the son of Thomas McCabe of Swarthmore, trustee of that college and president of Scott Paper Company. Dick had been meat in the sandwich between two aggressive brothers, a shy, lanky boy looking for friendship. Frank and his wife, who'd had a problem with their own son, opened their home to Dick. Neither he nor his dad ever forgot it. When we honored Tom McCabe with an LL.D. at commencement I saw by a tear in his eye that our college had formed a bond which Harvard and perhaps Swarthmore itself couldn't have made. Perhaps no more deserved honorary doctorate has been awarded than the one CC granted to Frank Krutzke upon his retirement.

THE MOVING FINGER WRITES ONCE MORE

On June 29, 1962, my birthday, Colorado College announced a $2.2 million grant from the Ford Foundation, subject to its raising $5.5 million in the next three years. This was one in a series of awards to liberal arts colleges judged to have arrived at, or to be on their way to, high academic quality. Since the year before we'd missed the grant and immediately tried again, the Ford officers took another look and presumably saw what they hadn't seen before. Pragmatically not cynically, more likely our opening of two major buildings, Tutt Library and Olin Hall of Science, had evoked the hoary law of *to whom who hath, it shall be given.* In either event, earlier that year I had been visited by two trustees from the Claremont Colleges concerning the presidency of their coordinating institution. A meeting in New Mexico with a second delegation soon followed. In view of the Ford grant my course was clearly to decline or at best to postpone any acceptance of a firm offer. Claremont asked for the latter and I returned to our campaign.

Looking two ways at once the next months were not easy. I flew to Los Angeles and ran the gauntlet of interviews with trustees and presidents of four undergraduate schools; Pitzer College hadn't yet opened. The Board of Fellows then sent me a firm offer to be President of Claremont Graduate School and University Center, the central institution's latest name. (In 1997, it became Claremont Graduate University). I agreed to take office in July, 1963 on condition the announcement be delayed till next spring. The Board held by its word. I refocused on Colorado College, including a trip that fall for the first visit to David Packard in Palo Alto. The request, a gymnasium to be named for Sperry Packard '02, his father, wasn't accepted. Yet in view of what followed in later years the trip was more than amply justified.

That last year for me saw two actions that were unconventional if not hazardous for presidents on the eve of leaving. The first was a climb up Crestone Needle with Glenn Brooks, led by Bob Ormes, a mountaineering guide whose full-time appointment in English came long after it should have. The second was fraught with more hazards, an action contrary to all advice for a departing college head. The number 1 rule is to take no part in selecting his or her successor. Instead, I wrote individual detailed letters to each trustee on why Lloyd E. Worner should become Colorado College's next president. The reasons were only partly based on his record of leading every college organization from fraternity president to head of student government, the youngest professor on key faculty committees, and Dean of the College. To my best knowledge Lew Worner enjoyed the confidence of every member of the college community, including even faculty known for a penchant to think otherwise, borrowing the immortal words of Carl Becker. That same confidence spread throughout the Colorado Springs community and among the deans of Middle States Association colleges.

The replies were heartening, mainly because I didn't get any. What I did get was one or two phone calls asking whether Lew Worner could go out and raise money like other, less-academic, presidents. I had evidence prepared for that one as the ensuing eighteen years have abundantly shown. At the board's next meeting it was voted without dissent, and at the next faculty meeting a standing ovation greeted President-elect Lloyd Worner.

Success in finding the ideal next leader in my favorite college job is a tough act to follow. Hence this memoir ends while it's ahead. In closing, I can only repeat that good leadership rests upon quality performance by the leader's executive team. In having Bob Broughton, Bob Brossman and Lew Worner, I was blessed by the finest team of vice-presidents I ever hoped to have. To college presidents of the future, the most obvious word is the one least often achieved, *"Go and do thou likewise."*

Lloyd E. Worner
President 1963–1981

CHAPTER 2

A PRESIDENT'S VIEW OF COLORADO COLLEGE
ON THE OCCASION OF THE
1978 ACCREDITATION VISIT
Lloyd E. Worner
President 1963–1981

INTRODUCTION

For this ten-year accreditation review of Colorado College by the North Central Association of Colleges and Secondary Schools, I should like to depart from the traditional "institutional self-study" and to venture instead a more personal and partisan statement concerning a College which I have known as student, teacher, dean and president over a period of almost four decades.

I do so for three reasons. First, and most important, because the review team will have access to the preliminary findings of a comprehensive and independently monitored evaluation of the college and its block plan, which will show us for what we are in much more objective terms than any self-study could hope to do. Second, because this will be my last opportunity to be associated with an accreditation review visit before my retirement. And, third, because as a historian who still attempts to practice his craft, I believe in the value of the illuminating essay which attempts a measured judgment.

1968 REVISITED

The last visit to this campus by an accreditation team from the North Central Association occurred ten years ago this Spring. It is instructive and generally encouraging to reread the report of that review. In sum, the review team found the enterprise sound, especially with respect to its commitment to the liberal arts tradition, but it pointed to several areas where improvement appeared indicated.

The review report observed:

> The commitment of the college to the aims of an undergraduate liberal-arts teaching institution is explicit and widely accepted, a condition that seems to be both the cause and effect of significant faculty participation in the formulation of institutional policies. This sense of involvement, together with a sense of freedom which each faculty member enjoys, probably accounts in large measure for the strong feeling of faculty loyalty to the college. The standing committees are numerous (perhaps there are more than is necessary) and active in conducting faculty business.

That statement was a fair appraisal ten years ago. I believe it can stand scrutiny today—even, alas, with respect to the abundance of our faculty committees.

The 1968 Report was also on the mark, I believe, in observing that "the first concern of the College is for good teaching, an emphasis which has not denigrated scholarly work, which is also encouraged, and a fair amount of research and publication has been going on." I like to think that our priorities are still firmly ranked in that order.

Comparative numbers deserve mention. In 1968, the full-time faculty of 114 taught a student body of 1600, compared to a full-time faculty of 136 and a student body of 1900 today. Mean salary for all faculty ranks was $10,668 vs. $17,250 today. Median class size was 17 students compared to 14. Tuition was $1700 vs. the present $3600. And the endowment fund was about $10 million vs. the present $23 million. Clearly, we have made gains, but we take no satisfaction from the fact that our tuition charge—while below that of most comparable institutions—has had to rise so sharply in order to keep pace with escalating costs.

The Report had this to say about curricular ferment:

> Although the approach of the faculty to curriculum change has been evolutionary rather than revolutionary, the curriculum has been receiving a good deal of study, and the faculty has been open to change, in-

cluding a willingness to cut off curricular outgrowths and consolidate them around the liberal arts.

It went on to summarize three experiments of the time under which students were not required to follow the usual mandates of the curriculum. An *Adviser Plan* freed a group of fifty freshmen from certain regulations, including distribution requirements in general education, and permitted them to work out individual arrangements of study in close consultation with their advisers. A *Selected Student Program* was an enrichment program for well-qualified freshmen and sophomores, with special courses and careful analysis of the students' work substituted for normal letter grades. The *Ford Independent Study Program* enabled a group of twenty-five students to go through the four-year period using combinations of course work and independent study which seemed appropriate to them and to their advisers, all without required courses, credit hours or formal grades.

These experiments have disappeared from the scene and although in retrospect they may appear to have been part of a trend toward abandonment of long-respected tenets of a liberal arts experience, they did provide important background for us as we moved toward the revitalization of our overall program through the adoption of the block plan.

The Report has positive things to say about our then-new venture into the Master of Arts in Teaching, our library facilities and program, and what it described as a generally healthy state of student well-being and involvement in the educational process. It observed a need, however, "for greater diversity in the student body," remarked upon the absence of a modern gymnasium-field house, noted plans for expanding fund-raising and called, in conclusion, for "a systematic evaluation of (the) educational program, particularly its innovations and experiments . . . "

As I reread the 1968 Report, I am reassured that we have moved forward. An excellent evaluation program is advancing toward culmination; our fund-raising programs are making progress; we have made gains in attracting different kinds of students to our campus; and, thanks to another in a long series of benefactions by El Polar Foundation of Colorado Springs, we have a splendid new gymnasium-field house. Throughout, we have strengthened our allegiance to traditional liberal arts education, which it is becoming increasingly evident was never more sorely needed in our Republic than it is today.

THE CONDITION OF THE COLLEGE

By the usual norms, Colorado College is a favored institution: The books are in balance, enrollment is stable, and the educational program is sound. Just why is it that this College is in generally healthy condition at a time of trauma for so many institutions of higher learning? We are asked the question often, and we are not entirely satisfied that we know the answer. I am convinced, however, that our positive estate derives from factors such as these:

Singleness of Purpose. Plain and simple, we are a college of liberal arts for undergraduates. Despite our modest excursion into the Master of Arts in Teaching, we are not a graduate school in any sense of the term. Nor are we a research institution, although it is still true, as it was in 1968, that "a fair amount of research and publication has been going on." The block plan has not changed our fundamental commitment to the liberal arts experience as it has come down through the centuries. We reject contemporary pressures toward vocationalism, and we are confident that we shall be proved right as current conditions of the employment market improve.

Institution-wide Involvement. The block plan originated in our Faculty Committee on Academic Programs. Our program of Summer Matriculation for freshmen was proposed by a member of our administrative staff, who had seen it mentioned at another institution. Our Campus Design Committee brings members of the faculty and staff together with students in common concern for the aesthetic environment of our campus. What these and other examples like them have to say is that this is an institution where the campus community contributes to the learning experience and to its improvement. Our committees may indeed be numerous, but they have a great deal to do with the fact that ideas find ready hearing here.

Concern for Students. Students are our central concern. Thus, our library hours are as extended as any that I know for a college of our type, and our Boettcher Health Center is a model for this kind of campus. We know our co-curricular program can be improved and that our Career/ Placement Center has only begun to explore its potentials, and we shall continue to strengthen them in order to provide a positive campus environment to enhance and support our educational offerings. Luckily, we have the good fortune to enjoy a budget condition which enables us to entertain student thoughts affecting their educational experience, and we shall continue to do so.

Faculty as the Core. The 1968 Report remarked on the expensive process which the College uses when appointing new faculty members. For each opening, we invite as many as three or four candidates to come to the campus for several day visits, and put them through a rigorous regimen of interviews, informal sessions open to faculty and staff as a whole, and actual teaching trials. We make mistakes in appointments nonetheless, but I am experienced enough with the luck of other institutions across the country to believe that ours is as fail-safe a procedure for faculty appointments as any.

We believe in making teaching conditions attractive and have made strong gains in both compensation and fringe benefits. I shall have some things to say later about the heavy burden which we place on the faculty under the block plan; it is an indicator of faculty morale here that we have generally positive feelings toward a curricular format which is as arduous as the block plan is for the teacher. The fact that 46.1 percent of our educational and general budget goes for instruction is an item in which we take pride.

Conservative Management. Colorado College rejects the blandishments of a "total-return" concept for its endowment funds, holding to the old-fashioned notion that the use of capital gains to support the operating budget is not a wise policy for the long term. We maintain fiscal reserves, we build buildings only when we have the money, and we have been successful in resisting the allure of government and foundation grants which commit an institution to continue expensive enterprises after the grant money has run out. (Distance can sometimes be a problem here, but I have often taken comfort at our remoteness from the grant-making centers of New York City and Washington.)

Regional Commitment. Colorado College draws its student body from the nation as a whole, but believes that it must first be firmly rooted in its own region. Thus, we insist that at least a third of our students come from Colorado. As a result, Colorado College is fortunate to enjoy a solid relationship with its home constituency. The fact that we have been able in recent years to attract more scholars than any other institution under the state's most prestigious scholarship program (the Boettcher Foundation scholarships) has been a vindication of this commitment to our region, as well as a source of a group of very able freshen each year.

Change of Pace. The block plan is arduous for both faculty and students. We attempt to compensate by providing a wide-ranging program of so-called "Leisure Time" experiences under the leadership of student-faculty committees, and we have made it a central feature of our program to maintain a broad diversity of intramural, recreational and intercollegiate sports activities for both men and women. We have not perfected our Leisure Program—far from it—but we shall keep working at it out of concern to enhance our classroom offerings while providing healthy change of pace to our intensive-learning format.

The Honor System. The 1978 Report made only briefest mention of the Honor System which has been a part of our academic program since 1948, yet the Honor System is one of our great strengths. Our system is essentially student-controlled, and I can think of few instances in which student judgments in honor cases have not been sensitive and sound. I would place our Honor System among the foundation stones upon which Colorado College is built.

The Block Plan. Simply, the block plan is a rearrangement of the academic calendar. We divide the academic year into nine blocks of three and a half weeks each. A normal "load" for the student is a single course at a time, although there are certain options which modify this slightly. For a faculty member, too, the norm is one course per block. The result is a liberation of faculty and students from the multiple-course restraints, the encouragement of extended field-trips and independent-study assignments, and the opportunity to bring to the campus as one-block teachers, individuals who would not be able to get away from their responsibilities for a conventional semester-long course.

The single most salient quality of the block plan is its intensity; and while a great majority of our students and faculty members are strong adherents to this way of learning and teaching, there are signs here and there that we must find ways of relaxing the pressure somewhat. For faculty, especially, the block plan can prove all-absorbing; under block-plan conditions, for example, it is difficult to pursue scholarly endeavors or to find a little time away. Happily, a generous grant from the Andrew W. Mellon Foundation is enabling us to look at some of the problems which our plan presents for faculty and to make at least a beginning toward their solution. We are pleased also that a gift from The Gates Foundation of Colorado has permitted us to provide a handsome common room to which members of the faculty may adjourn for interdisciplinary give and take, or simple relaxation.

I shall leave it to the Evaluation Report to go into detail about the block plan and its effects on learning. Let me remark, however, upon the dramatic drop in academic suspensions and warnings which the block plan has produced. In 1969–70, for example, we suspended 58 students for academic reasons; a year later, under the block plan, that number dropped to 14. The trend continues and it is obvious that the intimacy of a block-plan class (average class size: 14 students) does not allow a student to get into difficulty without having both student and faculty member recognize the fact early enough to be able to do something about it.

The block plan makes certain problems for management, but so far we seem to have been able to cope with them. Library use is extraordinarily high, for example, and it has taken brilliant ingenuities on the part of our Registrar's Office to cope with the some 30,000 "drop-add" transactions which result from our nine-block schedule and limitations on class size. We have insisted from the first that each class under the block plan should have its own "course room" to use for as many hours a day as it wishes. We were forced to use some improbable spaces at the outset, but the provision of our fine new Packard Hall of Music and Art, with the consequent remodeling of former music spaces in Armstrong Hall, has given virtually all classes most congenial places in which to hold formal sessions or simply to allow students to work on their own.

We are fortunate in having as director of our evaluation of the block plan, Dr. Paul Heist of the University of California at Berkeley. I know of no one in higher education who is better qualified to oversee this project for us. We look forward to the formal report next year.

SOME QUESTIONS

Colorado College did not entirely escape the extremes of the Sixties which led to the abandonment of long-established, central academic requirements. We share the general desire of liberal education to rebuild the center, and we are committed to make sure that a student who leaves Colorado College with its degree can properly be said to have received at least a balanced introduction to the broad sweep of liberal learning. Our faculty committees are grappling with the problem, and we look forward to early proposals.

Admissions. Our "applicant pool," for several years an almost unmanageably large one, has shrunk to much more modest proportions. We are working to stabilize application numbers at the 2,000 level for freshmen, and we are favored by the fact that Colorado is projected to escape some of the strongest impact of the forthcoming downturn of eligible-age population, but we know that this will not be an easy assignment in an area so heavily dominated by low-tuition, open-access public institutions.

We have made encouraging progress in recruiting minority students, notably those from Hispanic backgrounds, but we are far from complacent and especially must do more to attract Black students. The recruiting efforts of our MECHA students in attracting other Spanish-surnamed students is a successful model which we hope to replicate with the Black group.

Funding. Although our endowment fund at $23 million is the largest at any institution in Colorado, we cannot relax. A $50-million endowment is a first-stage goal to provide firm underpinning for the kind of program which we offer, but endowment is not a cause which excites the average foundation or corporation. Our endowment progress will come largely through sophisticated estate-planned giving in the form of bequests and trusts, and this at best is a relatively slow process. This is something to which we intend to devote priority attention over the years ahead.

Our Annual Fund is beginning to reach respectable levels and is projected for a ten percent increase each year. To supplement this, we intend to seek budget-supporting restricted gifts for a variety of needs. We shall continue to give special attention to our President's Council activity, which seeks donors at the level of $1,000 or more a year.

Colorado College has not had a traditional capital campaign in recent years, yet has managed to rally $46,788,107 in private gifts and grants since 1955. We must begin to lay the groundwork for a comprehensive capital campaign to take place in the early 1980s if we are to be sure of holding the ground that we have won.

Bricks and Mortar. It is a happy situation to have a modern, well-maintained physical plant which has been essentially completed through the gift of Mr. and Mrs. David Packard of our fine building for music and art. Our needs are relatively modest—expansion of our science classroom, addition of playing fields, and remodelings such as in our student union and our original gymnasium, Cossitt Hall. I am confident that we can find the means with which to accomplish these ends without intruding upon the sources to which we must turn for operational support.

Regional Position. The way of an independent college is not an especially easy one in our part of the United States. There are only sixteen accredited private four-year colleges and universities in the eight states of the Rockies put together, and it is a constant battle to hold independent education high in an area which turns so readily to the tax dollar for its institutions of higher learning. (The general budget of the State of Colorado this year, for example, allots 23 percent of its monies to public post-secondary education.) Yet our offering is distinctive and single-minded, and I have no doubt that consistent attention to making our case in our region will enable us to stand against the numerical odds which are ranged against us.

A WORD OF CONCLUSION

I have been fortunate to have been able to devote most of my professional life to Colorado College. It is impossible in a short statement such as this to remark upon the many things which have built the institution which the review team will examine. Let me make inadequate acknowledgment to the hardest working faculty, staff and board of Trustees that I know. I regret only that I shall not be in office in 1988 to greet another North Central Association review group at what I am confident will be a still more vigorous and adventuresome Colorado College.

Gresham Riley
President 1981–1992

CHAPTER 3

Ten Plus One: A Memoir

Gresham Riley
President 1981–1992

Lest we forget, the 1980s was the decade in which:

Ronald Reagan was elected twice and George Bush once to the presidency.

The Chernobyl nuclear power plant "melted", Mount St. Helens erupted, and Exxon's *Valdez* spilt its oil into Alaska's Prince William Sound.

Mikhail Gorbachev succeeded Konstantin Chernenko as leader of the USSR.

Sandra Day O'Connor became the first woman appointed to the Supreme Court, but Robert Bork failed to make it.

The United States imposed partial sanctions on South Africa because of its apartheid policies.

Great Britain defeated Argentina in a dispute over the Falkland Islands, and the United States notched a victory in Grenada.

Messrs. Reagan and Gorbachev signed the INF Treaty.

Anwar el-Sadat and John Lennon were assassinated; similar attempts on the lives of Ronald Reagan and Pope John Paul II failed.

The rulers of China crushed student demonstrations in Tiananmen Square.

Jim and Tammy Faye Bakker fell from grace.

And on the 19ᵗʰ of October 1987 the market on Wall Street
lost 22% of its value, the biggest hit in history.

Meanwhile, high school students (the very ones soon to be en-
rolling in our colleges and universities) were identifying,
through annual polls, their heroes and models: Burt
Reynolds (2); Alan Alda; Sylvester Stallone; Michael
Jackson; Eddie Murphy(2); Bill Cosby; Tom Cruise; and
Michael Jordan.

I remind myself of all the above to insure a sense of perspective on
what was happening at Colorado College at the same points in time.

My first official day in office was July 1, 1981; but in fact my presidency began in the summer of 1980, a few weeks after an early June telephone call from Russell Tutt, Chairperson of the College's Board of
Trustees, and Lew Worner, the College's President, announcing my selection, by the Board, as Lew's successor.

During the academic year 1980–81 I carried the title of president-
elect of Colorado College while completing my term of office as the Dean
of Faculty of Arts and Sciences at the University of Richmond (Virginia).
On June 23, 1980, however, Mr. Tutt, Pam, and I traveled to San
Francisco for a courtesy call on David Packard; Pam and I returned to
Colorado Springs for the first of what would be four, one-week visits to
the College over the course of the next nine months; and the work began.
On these four visits I met with faculty and student leaders; faculty committees; the senior administrators who would later become members of
my Executive Staff; all other key administrators; and most members of
the Board of Trustees who lived in either Colorado Springs or Denver.

In large part these visits afforded me an opportunity to increase my
knowledge about the College in general and about its needs and aspirations in particular. I was in the fortunate position of being able to listen
and to ask questions without having the responsibility to make decisions
about what was currently taking place on campus.

Few people know, and no written records reflect, the importance of
these "president-elect visits" for decisions about longer-range issues.

Rather than try to capture the essence of an eleven-year tenure in a brief memoir, the historical record might be best served if I focus on those months that preceded my first day in office and explain why they were so important for what was to follow. Five issues can serve to illustrate the substantive nature of the discussions held and decisions made during this formative period.

General Education Requirements. In meetings with Glenn Brooks, Dean of the College, I learned that the faculty, both at the departmental level and through its various committees, had discussed the need to make changes in general education requirements for a period of at least five years and that those discussions had reached a stalemate. Consideration had been given both to a set of interdisciplinary courses that all students would be required to take and to more flexible options for meeting general education requirements that would allow for choice. In spite of much hard work and careful thought, no set of recommendations for change could gain faculty approval.

Although I was disappointed that so much time and effort had not produced a consensus, I was not surprised. I remembered Woodrow Wilson's comment while he was still President of Princeton: "It is easier to move a graveyard than to get a college faculty to change the curriculum."

It was encouraging, however, that the Colorado College faculty had been grappling with the complex issues of what should constitute general education requirements, especially at a time when Ernest Boyer (as knowledgeable an observer of higher education as one could find) declared this to be "the disaster zone of American undergraduate education."

As a reminder to the reader, general education requirements (in the post-WWII period) constituted an important third component of an undergraduate's program of study—the other two being the student's major discipline and second, a body of elective courses. The idea was (and continues to be) that the major requires study in depth; electives provide breadth; and general education requirements create the sense of an academic community through "common" educational experiences. Put the three together and the result is a "liberally educated graduate."

There is ample evidence that this formula did not work precisely as intended, but long before coming to Colorado College I came to view general education requirements as the most important value statements an institution of higher education can make. These requirements proclaim: "Certain forms of knowledge are most worth having; and certain forms of ignorance cannot be tolerated." It is for this reason that college faculties should have taken (and must continue to take) seriously the course of study required of all students.

Against this historical background, Dean Brooks and I decided in the fall of 1980 to appoint an Adjunct Professor of English, James Yaffe, to lead an effort to breathe fresh life into the general education reform movement. The plan was for Professor Yaffe to meet with each academic department during 1980–81; to review past discussions of reform; to identify areas of consensus (if any); and to be prepared to move the debate to appropriate faculty committees in the fall of 1981.

Without belaboring details, this agenda was essentially followed with the result that Professor Yaffe's findings and recommendations were delivered on time to the faculty's Academic Program Committee, chaired by Professor Susan Ashley of the History Department. Professor Ashley and her Committee skillfully and cleverly created a formal proposal from the information provided them; conducted extensive hearings on the proposal; and brought an integrated package of reform to the faculty in the fall of 1982.

In my judgement the Academic Program Committee's proposal was a carefully crafted integrated unit, the parts of which reinforced each other. Consequently, when the Committee's report came before the faculty for debate and action, I ruled, as chairperson of the faculty meeting, that whereas the various components of the proposal could be debated separately, the final vote had to be on the entire document. There was of course opposition to my ruling, but a strong majority of the faculty supported it. The outcome was approval, at long last, of a substantially restructured general education program.

Paramount among the areas of study from which students were required to choose were science courses with a laboratory component; western history and culture; the history and culture of minority groups within American society; and courses focused on nonwestern societies.

It should be noted that almost half a decade before it became politically correct, Colorado College acknowledged through its curriculum the cultural and intellectual contributions of women, people of color, and countries other than the United States and those in Western Europe.

A Campaign For Colorado College. During the interview process when I was a candidate for the presidency, the Board of Trustees made clear that the primary expectation of the new president would be to organize and to complete successfully a fund-raising campaign on behalf of the college. Although the College had been successful in raising money in the past, efforts had tended to be specific-purpose drives, rather than a comprehensive, constituency-wide, multi-purpose campaign. The Board believed (and I strongly agreed) that securing the College's future required a bold, new effort.

Among the senior administrators with whom I met during these early visits was Robert Brossman, Vice President and General Secretary of the College. Bob had served in this position for a total of 25 years, with a break along the way for work at another institution. Although his title would not suggest it, Bob was in fact the College's chief development officer—the person who would have to play a key role in a campaign for Colorado College.

Because of his age and knowing that a campaign would be two—three years in the planning and at least five years of actual fund-raising, Bob was thoughtful and kind enough to inform me that he intended to retire at the end of December 1981, six months into my presidency.

With this advance information, I was able to initiate immediately two efforts that would prove to be instrumental to the eventual success of the Colorado College Campaign. The first was to arrange for Gerald Quigg, Vice President for Development at the University of Richmond, to come to Colorado College in the early summer of 1981 as a consultant to advise me on what changes (if any) would need to be made to have a successful campaign. Jerry had been a colleague at the University of

Richmond and had the reputation of being one of the premier fund-raisers among college/university development officers.

The major weaknesses revealed in Jerry's report were: no development staff engaged in the tasks of prospect identification and research; the lack of an estate planning program; and too few people, and a development budget too small, to conduct a major campaign. These deficiencies were addressed and other recommendations were implemented during the planning phase of the campaign, thus laying the groundwork for fund-raising efforts throughout the 1980s.

The second action taken was to begin immediately the search for Bob Brossman's successor. I appreciated the lead-time because, as a seasoned administrator, I knew the difficulty of finding a good, senior development director. Past experience had convinced me that there were more charlatans per one hundred in the fund-raising field than any other area of college administration. Because we could take our time and be careful and with the help of a hardworking, on-campus search committee, we were able to bring Richard Chamberlain from UCLA as the new Vice President for Development and College Relations, effective September 1992.

Dick was uniquely prepared to take on this assignment because of his prior experience in planning a major campaign (UCLA) and in active participation in a successful fund-raising effort (Brown University). His experience proved invaluable, enabling him to serve as a mentor to both the Board of Trustees and me about the task we were soon to undertake.

Many academics consider fund-raising to be a necessary evil at best. I disagree. Along with the reform of general education requirements, raising a grand total of $51.2 M in the 1984–89 campaign ranks among the significant accomplishments during my tenure. It should be noted, however, that this campaign was not primarily about money; it was about people, programs, and new physical facilities in which dedicated educators could make real their bold dreams.

Campus Master Plan. As I listened to faculty and administrators talk about their hopes and frustrations during this early series of visits, it became increasingly clear that a campaign would have to include money for "bricks and mortar" projects, for new facilities.

Olin Science Hall, built in 1962 prior to the implementation of the Block Plan in 1970, was too small for a student body of 1, 900 and, more importantly, was ill-suited for the small-class, research oriented approach to teaching the physical and biological sciences that emerged after 1970. Rastall Center was not only an eyesore; it failed to accommodate the student-life and leisure programs that were important ingredients of the Block Plan. Armstrong Hall, which began as a home for the humanities and the dramatic arts, evolved into a combination academic/administrative facility with the result that it became a building in which a person had extreme difficulty in getting there from here. The total campus was generally agreed to be too small for the resident student body and a teaching faculty of some 140; on-campus parking was a problem and two major traffic arteries (Cascade and Nevada Avenues) that intersected the campus complicated student safety.

Quickly, it became obvious that priorities regarding physical facilities and campus design had to be set; otherwise, these projects would totally consume a campaign. I concluded that a campus master plan was required, something that did not exist and had never been developed.

So, during my year as president-elect I began to make inquiries about master planners for college campuses, and the search continued into my first year in office. Presidential colleagues at Brown University, Grinnell College, and other institutions directed me to Richard Dober, of Dober and Associates, Inc., in Belmont, Massachusetts, and the more questions I asked the more Dick Dober's name surfaced.

The result was that in 1982 Dober and Associates were commissioned to study the physical needs of the College and submit a comprehensive campus plan, a document that subsequently became known as The Dober Plan.

Dick Dober proved to be a genius disguised as a leprechaun. And as with the mischievous elves of Irish folklore when caught, he revealed the hiding place of treasure. I say this because The Dober Plan served as our blueprint for making decisions about capital projects in the campaign and, equally important, provided a much-needed sense of direction for enlarging the campus.

The Dober Plan was the genesis of what are now the Barnes Science Center and the Worner Campus Center. It was also the stimulus for the

College's quiet but persistent acquisition of properties in what I dubbed the Dober Zone, the area bound by Cache La Poudre on the south, Uintah on the north, Nevada Avenue on the west, and Weber Street on the east. Russell Tutt, then chairperson of the Board, and El Pomar Foundation enabled me to begin acquiring these properties with a $750,000 grant, and by the end of my presidency the College owned most of this 12.5 acre Zone. I, of course, did not have the opportunity to plan how the College would use this space, but by expanding to the east we secured much-needed breathing room for the campus.

As a footnote, I am pleased to learn, from a recent issue of The Colorado College Bulletin, that the Colorado Historical Society has made a $89,953 grant to the College for restoration, rehabilitation, and landscaping projects within the Dober Zone.

The Computer Revolution. In the summer of 1980 a massive Burroughs 6805 dinosaur, named "Mnemosyne" as the result of a campus competition (not to be confused with the earlier Hewlett-Packard computer known as "Smedley"), serviced the administrative computer needs of the campus and what little was being done on the academic side. Discussions with John Pearce, the then Director of Computing Services, were replete with stories about how "the system" was being held together by "baling wire, chewing gum, and rubber bands." Indeed, in late 1981 or early 1982 we were informed that replacement parts were no longer available.

These discussions led quickly to my asking the Computer Policy Board, chaired at that time by Professor Bill Hochman and later by Professor Robert Lee, to undertake a study of campus computer needs and to make recommendations for reform. Over a period of years, the adopted reforms became a revolution.

The College moved from a totally centralized computer operation featuring the Burroughs behemoth to a radically decentralized program of desktop computers. A critically important, early decision was made in this transition, and that was to equip all offices with the same Texas Instruments personal computers. Because we were short on computer personnel, the assumption was that if everyone had the same computer, colleagues would teach each other. And that is what happened.

Other moments in the revolution were: the College subsidized the purchase of home computers by faculty; Tutt Library (with the inspired leadership of John Sheridan) became fully automated; administrative and academic computing became separate divisions; and computers became fully integrated in the teaching and research mission of the College. I am proud of the fact that when I left office the Boettcher Academic computer Center in Barnes Science Center and the Keck Computer Laboratory for the Humanities in Armstrong Hall were powerful signs that technology had been transformed into the servant of liberal arts and sciences education.

Alumni Affairs. While still a candidate for the presidency, I visited the campus in the late spring of 1980 for a round of interviews. In one plenary session I remember that Barbara Yalich, at the time Director of Alumni Affairs, asked rather pointedly,"How much additional money are you prepared to spend on the Alumni Office?" Not knowing how much was being spent at the time (a detail I had failed to research in preparation for my visit), I had to deflect the question by talking at some length about the importance of alumni and an office that supports their efforts. The point was not lost on me, however, that this was a topic to which I would return should I be appointed president.

During the course of my visits, Barbara Yalich, Bob Brossman, and I had several opportunities to talk about the alumni program in considerable depth. A number of points became clear: in general, alumni viewed the College positively but were not organized in a way to allow their feelings to be transformed into action; as a consequence, alumni did not perceive themselves as important stakeholders in the institution; the lack of organization was reflected in the fact that no formal alumni chapters existed in major cities coast-to-coast; the alumni Office was understaffed and underfunded to provide administrative support for a national alumni network; and since they did not perceive of themselves as stakeholders, alumni did not support (in large numbers) the College through the annual giving program. As I recall, only about 25% of alumni made financial contributions to the College on an annual basis in 1981. Clearly, if there were to be a major, successful fund-raising campaign, the alumni would have to be brought into the fold as active participants.

As with the other examples cited above, 1980–81 was a year in which the groundwork was laid for major changes that would come shortly and swiftly. Most importantly, based on my conversations with Barbara and Bob, I decided that a stronger commitment had to be made to create an active, vital, national alumni association. As a start, shortly after I took office Barbara scheduled Pam and me for visits to every large city in the country where there were alumni who had demonstrated an interest in working on behalf of the College. It would not be until a final tour to alumni chapters after I announced my resignation in 1992 that we would log as many frequent flyer miles as we did in 1981–82.

Later developments would prove how successful these visits were, but the critical ingredient to our success were the people we met in that first year—John Chalik, Jeanne Hopper, and Bob and Joyce Selig in the San Francisco Bay area; Garry Knight, Dianna DeGette, Ed and Stephanie Benton, and Sue Arnold Mitchell in Denver; Bob Williams, and Joel and Jessie Solomon in Chicago; Dan and Beth Cooper in St. Louis; Cal Simmons in the Twin Cities; Angie Konugres Coupounas and Don Manzelli in Boston; Carky and Mary Rubins, Hank and Betty Otto, and Sally Jameson Bender in New York City; and Joan Dobrowolski Urbaniak and Sam Coleman in Los Angeles. Without the labor of love of these, and other graduates, the Colorado College Alumni Association as it exists today would never have come into being.

We didn't just travel, however; structural and organizational changes were made. Beginning in 1984, the College, at its expense, brought annually alumni leaders from around the country to the campus for a long weekend of seminars and workshops. These sessions were intended to keep graduates current with what was happening at the College; to provide an insight into early stages of planning for the future; and to create a common base of knowledge that could be used as alumni served in the role of ambassadors in their local communities. Important by-products of these "homecoming weekends" were an invigorated Alumni Admission Representative Program and a newly created Association of Minority Alumni who aided the College in many ways to recruit and to respond to the needs of students of color.

In response to the lack of a formal organizational structure, we quickly assisted more than 20 cities to establish alumni chapters with officers, charters, and a commitment to schedule educational, cultural, and social programs throughout each year. These chapters in turn gave new life to the National Alumni Council, the elected body who served as an advisory/planning group for Barbara Yalich and her staff. In short order, a number of creative ideas came from the rejuvenated Council that were immediately implemented. Representation from the National Alumni Association on the College's Board of Trustees was expanded; alumni recognition awards were established in the names of former presidents, Louis Benezet and Lew Worner (Gresham Riley, I am proud to say, has been added to the list); and a special category of honorary degrees for alumni in mid-career was created, to be given each year at Opening Convocation.

The original objective was to transform passive alumni into active participants in the College's life. We succeeded beyond my hopes and expectations as evidenced by the clamorous responses I received in 1987 when the faculty (with my support) initiated a discussion of altering the Block Plan by moving from a nine-block academic year to one of eight-blocks. The 1984–89 Colorado College Campaign was hugely successful in part because 85% of the alumni made restricted or unrestricted gifts, and in 1993 a College record was set when approximately 65% of alumni contributed to the Annual Giving Program, up from a mere 25% in 1981.

Others will have to assess the official period of my presidency, 1981–1992. As I look back on my association with the College, however, the year during which I had no formal responsibilities looms large in terms of everything that followed. I feel good about that year; I feel good about what followed.

Be this as it may, these reflections would be less than honest if I did not mention briefly two areas in which I failed to provide effective leadership.

During my presidency the faculty never developed what I considered to be an appropriate sense of pride in the College; they never manifested the conviction that they were part of a truly great institution. There were of course individual exceptions; my sense of personal failure relates to the faculty collectively.

Virtually every day that I walked into my office I had the sense of being involved in something special, working with an uncommonly talented faculty, administration, and staff to elevate an already strong college to a new plateau of accomplishment. I think that many of my administrative colleagues shared this mind set, but I never sensed that it was so with the faculty.

Every institution, great or marginal, has its problems, and Colorado College was no exception. The difference is that at institutions where a shared awareness of strengths is part of the culture, problems are matters to be solved; they don't define the way in which people think about themselves and their colleagues.

Early in my presidency and thereafter, I heard from many faculty that all standing between the College and greatness were sororities/fraternities, Division I athletics, and the Business major. As long as these three features of college life survived, these faculty seemed unable to keep foremost in their minds what truly defined Colorado College for me: the quality of teaching; the strength of the faculty; a dedicated Board of Trustees; the commitment of students to learning; the flexibility of the Block Plan; a curriculum that possessed integrity; the successful integration of teaching, learning, and scholarship; successful alumni; a sound physical plant; no indebtedness; and a growing endowment. I believed that these characteristics defined a profile of strength, characteristics capable of shaping an institutional ethos.

This profile, however, did not constitute the accepted, natural, day-to-day way of thinking about the College. Rather, specific "problem" areas (if not the three I mentioned above, then some topical substitute) seemed to come to mind. Furthermore, these problems were not viewed within the context of an institution of strength for which one felt pride; instead, they defined both foreground and background.

Another example. In 1988 the College stood for reaccreditation by the North Central Association of Colleges and Schools. Professor Robert Loevy of the Political Science Department wrote the self-study report that served as the basis for an on-site visit by a team of faculty and administrators from other colleges and universities. Confident (as he should have been) that the College would retain its accredited status, Professor Loevy wrote a rather low key, matter-of-fact narrative of what had transpired in the ten years since the last North Central visit, including recent accomplishments made possible by the Colorado College Campaign. Keep in mind that this was 1988—four years into a five-year fund-raising effort that would exceed $50 M, one year after the opening of a new student center, and about the time of the dedication of a new science center.

One would think that anyone who read the report (and it was conveniently available in departmental offices and the Library) would reinforce Professor Loevy's account of a ten-year record of growth and success. Not so! In the exit interview the chairperson of the visiting committee informed me that there was a serious problem of low faculty morale and inadequate administration/faculty communication because of negative personnel decision that had been made in the Drama and Dance Department and supported by the administration.

Clearly, there is room for different opinions about the case of Joanne Klein. My point is that a localized issue, a very specific problem, defined for a moment in time the institution and its preceding ten-year history. The visiting committee left with the impression that strong disagreement about a single personnel decision reflected faculty attitudes about the College.

Common wisdom says that faculty members are trained to be skeptical and critical, that faculty will allow no good deed to go unpunished. While I believe the former, I don't believe the latter. I also believe that faculty are uniquely trained to handle evidence—what is and what is not relevant support for a given belief; how much weight to place on various data; etc. So, at some level the faculty had to be aware of the good work they were doing; they had to be aware of the positive things that were happening at the College. Nevertheless, awareness never got transformed into a collective sense of public institutional pride. As I look back, part of my role as president should have been that of an alchemist to make sure this transformation took place. It didn't, and I have to take responsibility for the failure.

Since leaving office I have reflected on this failure, trying to understand why the transformation did not occur. At the heart of my conclusion is a set of personal strengths and weaknesses combined with a clearer perception of my leadership style.

At the risk of lapsing into psychobabble or dubious typologies of leadership, I think it is fair to say that I am (and have been) more interested in solving problems than in the processes by which they are solved. Consequently, I often underestimate the impact of emotion and affect on decision making. Being results oriented, I tend to emphasize analysis, understanding, strategic planning and persistent execution of a strategy, assuming that once a task has been successfully completed or a problem solved people will naturally feel good about the accomplishment.

As President, I was energized and excited by the numerous projects that challenged the College community, whether the planning of a fundraising campaign, recruiting new faculty, creating an alumni network, changing the curriculum, or seeking the proper role for research in an undergraduate college. Taking a cue from "if you build it, they will come," I assumed that "if we complete the tasks (solve the problems), we collectively will take pride in the institution where these things happen."

In short, I think that by temperament and style I am (and was) more task oriented than people oriented, with the result that important factors such as team building and personal stroking are (were) either neglected or de-emphasized. I am told that I fall neatly into a well-defined category in personality inventories such as the Myers-Briggs Type Indicator.

Early in my presidency I gave an Opening Convocation address in which I argued that we should think of a college more as a "community" than as a "family." While I continue to believe that my analysis was fundamentally sound, the notion of "family" does embody the personal dimension of human relationships to a degree that "community" does not.

In retrospect, I know that I paid insufficient attention to the ways in which a college is like a family; I slighted the nurturing role of a leader. A result of that failure, in my judgment, was the absence of a pervasive culture of pride in an institution whose strengths were in large measure the products of the faculty's work as teachers and scholars.

The second instance of failure in leadership, I believe, was in one area of my working relationship with the Board of Trustees, and its explanation is essentially the same as the one just given.

The Board was never comfortable with the amount of controversy that occurred during my tenure, and I was unable to bring it to an understanding that a sign of a healthy, mature institution (especially, a college or university) is open discussion about differences in what people believe and value. I rather suspect that the Board thought I was not in "proper control" of the campus because I not only tolerated controversy, but also in some instances encouraged it.

I have already alluded to the long-standing differences of opinion about the appropriateness of sororities/fraternities and Division I athletics on a campus such as Colorado College. This debate was very much in the open for the eleven years that I was president. There were also disagreements about personnel decisions, beginning in my first year when I refused to renew the contracts of two, popular young faculty members who had not met agreed upon conditions for contract renewal. And I have mentioned the emotionally charged case in the Drama and Dance Department. In addition, controversy swirled around the decision to drop the Business major, and the debate became even more intense about two subsequent issues—retaining in the endowment portfolio stocks of companies that conducted business in South Africa and moving from a nine-block calendar year to one of eight-blocks.

What some viewed as an untidy state of affairs, possibly an unruly campus, I saw as a mature educational institution that had the self-confidence to bring the same critical intelligence to bear on campus politics as was encouraged on the part of students in the classroom. My philosophical training made me comfortable with disagreement and with the arguments that accompany differing points of view. Furthermore, in supporting a broad application of First Amendment rights on college campuses I went beyond defending the "Socratic method" as a path to knowledge and self-understanding. In an opinion piece for *The Christian Science Monitor*, for example, I wrote that: "colleges and universities exist, among other reasons, to give offense by confronting their students with new ideas and by challenging their beliefs and systems of values, no matter how cherished." Freedom from conflict may be a virtue, but it is reminiscent of the celibacy of the castrated.

I understand and appreciate the fact that much is expected of Board of Trustee members. Not only are they asked to volunteer their time and expertise; this is done with the expectation that they will also pay for the privilege. Board members have a right to expect that the administrators who report to them insist upon a civil society on campus and are good stewards of the college's resources. For those who do not live, work, and move about daily on a college campus, however, it can be unsettling to be part of what might seem to be unending debates, not to mention having coins tossed at your feet in anger as happened in the midst of the divestment protests.

A college or university is a special culture that must be understood and protected if our nation is to remain strong. As a full-time faculty member I was told often that I was an inspiring teacher. Even after going into academic administration, I continued to see myself primarily as an educator. In my role as educator/president at Colorado College, however, I failed to bring the Board to an appropriate comfort level about that special culture which fosters, indeed is nourished by, debate, disagreement, and controversy.

I cannot end these reflections with *mea culpa*, even though an honest confession is supposedly good for the soul. I cannot end in this way because "failure" was not what we were about during my tenure. Upon the announcement of my appointment to the presidency, David Riesman, a friend and mentor, wrote: "Now, Colorado College has the opportunity to see whether that always difficult match between individual and institution—in which so much depends on others and over which the president has so much less control than is generally thought—will work out as I hope very much it does: to the maintenance of Colorado College's distinctiveness and distinction, and to the satisfaction of the Rileys in the colleagueships they may find in the College's spectacular setting."

In my judgment, we exceeded David's hopes. The match between individual and institution made possible not only the maintenance of the College's distinctiveness and distinction together, we enhanced both. On the personal side, Pam and I found far more than satisfactory colleagueships; we found warmth, friendships, and affection that will never be surpassed.

Richard C. Bradley
Professor Emeritus of Physics and
Former Dean of the College

CHAPTER 4

PRESIDENTIAL PREDICAMENTS AT COLORADO COLLEGE (AN HISTORICAL OVERVIEW)

Richard C. Bradley

Professor Emeritus of Physics and
Former Dean of the College

(Professor of Physics and former Dean of the College and Dean of the Faculty, Richard C. Bradley gave this address at the reception and dinner with faculty on the occasion of Kathryn Mohrman's inauguration as the Eleventh President of Colorado College, September 11, 1993.)

President Mohrman, Dorry and I are delighted to be here with you this evening to help celebrate this happy occasion and to join with everyone else in welcoming you and Bill into our community. As I look around at the sea of faces before me, I am reminded all over again what a splendid handsome faculty we have at this college. I know you will enjoy working with them and getting to know them, just as I know they are all looking forward to working with you and getting to know you.

An inauguration is a cosmic event in the life of a college, a time for celebration (which we did for an hour and a half before dinner), and a time for sober reflection (as if that were even possible after the celebration). I think I'm supposed to be the designated sober reflector this evening.

In that capacity, I would like to take a few moments to review where we came from and how we got here—where by "we" I mean the College. Then I would like to focus on a few of the activities and antics of your predecessors. And finally, in case all of this leaves you feeling a little bit nervous about your new job, I will close with a sure-fire recipe for your success, kindly provided by another eminent college president (who shall be nameless).

So, how did we get here? Well, as with many evolutionary success stories, the probability that we would all be here this evening celebrating your inauguration would have been deemed slightly less than the cube root of a gnat's eyebrow, as viewed in, say, 1865. There were lots of other colleges struggling to be born out there on frontier primordial soupland that weren't making it, and even our own college, once started, went through some pretty anxious times.

By 1865 people knew that there was gold in these hills, and some of the eastern emigrants who previously would have kept right on going toward California or Oregon, or possibly Salt Lake, now began settling here. And it seemed clear to a handful of thoughtful folk that the settlements here would benefit from having some schools and libraries and churches, and not just saloons and houses of ill-repute. But Colorado College was *not* the automatic outcome of those lofty notions.

Six years before CC was born, in 1868 that is, the Reverend Edward Payson Tenney, a fireball of a man who then resided in Central City and who later would preside over Colorado College, proposed to the Colorado Congregational Conference that a college be established on the divide south of Denver, to be called the Rocky Mountain Institute. But the time was not yet ripe. The necessary double helix was incomplete and disappeared. In the same year Fountain College was incorporated in Colorado City, just west of here, but never got beyond the paper stage. For lack of nourishment, it too expired. And within the next decade, so also did Longmont College in Longmont and the College of the Southwest in Del Norte.

Nor did Colorado College even have first claim on the patch of prairie on which we now celebrate your inauguration. In 1872—over a year before our institution was even a gleam in anyone's eye—a group of Jesuit Fathers looked this site over for an institution they had in mind, and passed it up.

The magic combination of circumstances that brought Colorado College into being in 1874, more than 500 miles from any other, and gave it the potential to endure, consisted of: (1) a dedicated promoter in the person of the Reverend Thomas Haskell, who very much wanted to establish a college in loving memory of his daughter, a recent victim of consumption; (2) the sponsorship of the Congregational Conference and (later) of the American College and Educational Society, both of which helped raise money for our institution; (3) a generous grant of land from the Colorado Springs Company; and (4) strong personal support from General William Jackson Palmer, the man who founded Colorado Springs in the first place and who wanted it to be a city of culture and parks, not just your usual railroad town.

And besides all this, the college was needed—or at least so some people claimed. George Marden, an early fund raiser for the College, put the case this way: "East of the Mississippi," he said, "there is one saloon for every 175 voters, whereas west of the Mississippi there is one saloon for every 43 voters." Edward Tenney, when he became president, told his eastern friends that Colorado College was more needed in the Rocky Mountain west than Harvard College had been needed in Massachusetts in 1636. "At that time," he said, "there were not 30 houses in all of Boston." But now in Colorado Springs alone there were several hundred.

Actually, Harvard College and Colorado College were founded for very similar reasons. The people who governed the early Massachusetts Colony had been well educated at places like Oxford and Cambridge, and realized that their own children were growing up more interested in hunting and fishing than in Latin and Greek, and decided to do something about it. And so it was out here—except that in addition to the hunting and fishing there was also the prospecting for gold.

But as luck would have it, 1874 was a tough year to start up a college. Economic conditions were bad. Back east a panic was sweeping the country, and out here a plague of grasshoppers was doing the same thing, devouring all the crops. Yet, despite these handicaps, Haskell, working with his brother-in-law Jonathan Edwards, managed to found not only the College but also the Congregational Church in Colorado Springs.

The College opened in May of 1874 (Block 9??) With a couple of faculty and a handful of students—actually 16 as compared to Harvard's initial 4, though most of the 16 were doing preparatory rather than college level work. Admissions standards were not particularly high then. "Where did Cicero live?," one candidate was reportedly asked. No answer. "I'll give you a hint," the examiner said. "He was a great orator." "Oh," was the reply, "in that case he must have lived down in Boston."

Haskell had to give up after only a few months. He couldn't raise the money to pay his two faculty members, and that made it hard to hold them. You can appreciate that.

The trustees replaced Haskell by the Reverend James Dougherty from Kansas, and gave him the title of "President." So, officially, he counts as the first president, although in fairness to Haskell I really think Dougherty should be considered the second. Dougherty told the trustees when he arrived: "I'm here to stay." But in fact he did well to survive nine months. His daily schedule was worse than trying to teach Anthropology 101 under the Block Plan and do research (I've been listening to Mike Nowak). Besides running the college, he taught every day from 8:30 AM to 1 PM, and gave one or two sermons on Sunday in the church Haskell had built. He also wrote and published the first *Catalog*, hoping to convince potential eastern donors that there really was a college out here on the Rocky Mountain Plateau. It was a well padded document in which hopes for the future and current realities were conveniently blended together. For example, "Music" was listed as one of the subjects of instruction, and yet no music was taught here for at least another 20 years.

His pastoral work was supposed to provide Dougherty his salary, but a problem arose: the local church, which paid Dougherty, depended for *its* income on the Home Missionary Society, and when the Society learned that the minister of the church was also teaching at the college, it refused to provide the money to pay him. So Dougherty abandoned the pulpit and hit the road to raise the money himself. But back east he found the same situation Haskell had found: tight money and failing banks. After serving nine months as the President of The Colorado College, he had received for himself a total of only $200—which wasn't a lot even in those days.

He wrote the trustees, saying he could not continue this way much longer (you can see he was a real complainer!), and the trustees replied that they could not promise him continued support (whatever that meant), and would not *urge* him to continue unless he had "faith and courage and a reasonable hope of success." Dougherty resigned at once, adding: "I am unable to assume the entire financial responsibility for the college." Later he commented: ". . . with continued hard times, with a wife and three children to support, I did not have the faith, courage, patience, or the foolishness to continue the good work."

That was surely the lowest point in the history of our institution, and the college actually closed its doors for one term to regroup.

The amazing thing is that the trustees *did* succeed in finding another person with the faith *and foolishness* to carry on—the same Reverend Edward Payson Tenney who had tried to establish the Rocky Mountain Institute in 1868. Tenney must have felt his mission in life was establishing and nourishing new colleges. Before coming to Central City he had worked hard to establish the College of California—whatever that was. The trustees told Tenney he could preside over Colorado College provided he put them (the trustees) under no financial obligation, and *if* he would assume sole responsibility for providing instruction and meeting all the expenses of the college. And Tenney accepted!

He proved to be the person for the occasion. He, too, ran the college single handedly: he was the president, dean, business manager, admissions director, development officer, and librarian—all rolled into one. He was also a prolific writer, and his book *The New West*, which was widely read in the east, really put Colorado, Colorado Springs, and especially Colorado College on the map and in the minds of potential donors. The College and Educational Society pledged support, and money from that quarter and elsewhere began pouring in. During his eight years in office he did many significant things: he recruited several good faculty—some of whom came for their health, and they stayed. He built the first permanent building (Cutler Hall), graduated the first class, staged the first inauguration (after being in office six years, I would add, not the mere 90 days that is the current practice), and established several feeder academies (prep schools) throughout the southwest to ensure a supply of students. (There were no public high schools around yet.) He was literally all over the place. Tenney might indeed have become a great president, but he speculated in land in what is now the North End—all with the best of intentions and on behalf of the college—and he simply overextended himself. When two or three eastern creditors got nervous and tried to withdraw their money, a kind of panic developed, and down came his house of cards. A paltry $20,000 would probably have saved the enterprise, but he didn't have it. If Tenney had pulled it off—and who would say nowadays in Colorado Springs that speculating in land isn't a very ordinary way to raise a lot of money?—if he had pulled it off, Colorado College would have had a fantastic endowment for its day. As it turned out, both he and the College were financially embarrassed, and he had to resign. Once again the infant institution was laid low with the croup.

This time, however, there was no question of survival. Tenney had given the college the strength to endure, and it went along quite well for a couple of years with no president at all. (Make of that what you will.) Strong local support helped pull the college out of its financial difficulty. I was delighted to read an editorial in the *Gazette Telegraph*, written about that time, urging the townsfolk to dig deep into their pockets on behalf of the struggling institution. "The College needs us," it read, "but more importantly we need the College." When did you last read an editorial like that in our local paper?

And now, of course, came the great Age of Slocum, King William and his Table Round (I'm mixing metaphors but who cares?), the Golden Age of Colorado College—or as we would say nowadays, the first Golden Age. William Frederick Slocum must have done his homework well concerning trustees and presidents, because he refused to accept any appointment unless the trustees guaranteed him a salary for at least two years. There was also a tacit agreement that he would not have to raise money, which I'll bet none of our present trustees made with Kathryn Mohrman. And this time they, the trustees, accepted the terms!

So you see we have made great progress in a decade and a half. The first president wasn't even called a president and he wasn't given any salary. The next two had the title but no salary. And now comes Slocum with both the title and a salary.

Slocum came and he stayed—29 years, longer by far than any other president, and in spite of the tacit agreement, he raised a lot of money and built a lot of buildings, including Palmer Hall, perhaps the best classroom building in the world. He also assembled a truly outstanding faculty and a cosmopolitan student body.

Slocum did some things you don't hear much about, and were certainly not spelled out in his contract. For instance, one spring at the height of a big Chinook windstorm, he noticed that the corrugated metal roof on the college engine house was about to be carried away by the wind, so he climbed up on the roof and sat there, just to hold it down, until the wind abated. Given his considerable size, he may have been the best person around for the job.

CC got two for the price of one when it hired Slocum, for Mary Slocum was a most active participant. She helped establish the Women's Educational Society which raised the money to build the first women's residence halls. When asked if all this education bit wouldn't cause some women to want to rise above their station, she snapped: "You bet! We *want* them to want to rise above their station." According to our local historian, Marshall Sprague, if the early buildings on campus don't seem to match too well, architecturally, it is at least partly because William and Mary had very different tastes in architecture.

It was indeed a great age—with the Harvard faculty exchanges, the creation of one of the first Phi Beta Kappa chapters west of the Mississippi, and all the rest. It's fun to read some of the scholarly papers written by the faculty of the time, as they appeared in the publication Colorado College Studies. (I am indebted to Tim Fuller for putting me on to this.) The articles range from the broad to the specialized, but like many scholarly articles of that era, most of them are remarkably accessible. One I didn't finish reading was called "Pulsations in the Aortic Arches of the Earthworm." One I read only enough of to decide whether the subject belonged to zoology or literature was entitled "A Passage in the Frogs." And one that I just know Horst Richardson and Armin Wishard assign to all their beginning German students is a 20-page paper entitled "On the Use of the Conditional in German." Florian Cajori's name appears again and again.

I mentioned Palmer Hall a moment ago. It was completed in 1904, and shortly thereafter a student wrote a poem about it, a poem that appeared in the College yearbook the following spring. I would like to read you a few lines from that poem, They clearly show that the energy conservation program was already in full swing way back then. They also show that not everybody would agree that Palmer Hall is the world's best classroom building.

The Song of Palmer
by
Julia Ingersoll

It begins:

> You shall hear a tale of Palmer
> Of that great and wondrous building…

Then on opening day:

> On the morrow, o'er the campus,
> Came they slowly, came they quickly,
> Taking each his own pet foot path,
> Straight across the grass to Palmer.
> Then ensued long days of suffering,
> Days of icy chill and horror,
> Then the youths with upturned collars,
> Then the maidens blue and shiv'ring,
> Sought to find aesthetic pleasure
> As they sat congealing slowly.
> They to get the warm side inside,
> Turned their coats the wrong side outside,
> Turned the inside skin-side outside,
> And to keep the cold side outside,
> Turned the outside fur-side inside.
> Thus they wandered, slowly learning
> How to reach their recitation

Ere the recitation ended,
How to thread the mazy hallways,
Intricacies labyrinthine
Of the great, the grand new wigwam."
(And so forth)

Well, as you know, William's Round Table eventually collapsed, with the faculty clamoring for a bigger role in determining the policies that affected their lives. The popular phrase "The faculty *is* the college" may not have been invented yet, but if it had it most certainly would have been invoked, for Slocum's style was autocratic. A charge of improper conduct sent him on his way (Van Shaw would say he failed to keep his office door open), and his academic dean of 13 years was dispatched shortly after. According to Marshall Sprague, 50 of the 60 faculty that Slocum had hired, retired or resigned within the next very few years.

The trustees brought in Clyde Duniway to replace Slocum, but though his academic credentials were impeccable, he wasn't the person for the times; at least he wasn't the person to calm troubled water, and he, too, was gone in a few years amid cries of "Do away with Duniway!"

Then came an insider, a faculty man and great scholar, Owen Cramer's illustrious predecessor, Charles Mierow. And incidentally, if you faculty sometimes get the feeling your time is being swallowed up by too much committee work, you probably have Mierow to thank, for it was he who brought the faculty into the decision-making process through a committee structure very like our own.

Mierow presided over the college very successfully all during the latter 1920's but was sent to the mat by the Great Depression of the 1930's. Enrollments dropped, residence halls closed, and various sources of income dried up. Eventually Mierow had to do something that no faculty member in his right mind would ever wish on any president: *He cut faculty salaries 20% across the board!*

He was replaced by Thurston Davies, once again the right person for the times, a man who could look the Great Depression in the eye and go out and hustle up support. But of course he got caught by World War II and all the upheavals that that brought, and in the process of trying to patch things back together after the war, his health broke down and he, too, had to resign. (None of this can sound very encouraging to you, Kathryn, but be of good cheer, the worst is yet to come.)

By now the college no longer enjoyed robust health. Shear survival loomed once again as an issue. The college was spending its small endowment capital just to pay its housekeeping bills. There are those still alive who can remember the year a faculty member, having received a $50 increase in his salary for the year, charged into the president's office, tore up his check, stomped on it, and shouted: "Obviously the college needs this money more than I do!" and stalked out.

When it came to replacing Davies, the trustees tried a different tack: they hired a military man, General William Gill, recently retired from the Army and a proven organization man. The trustees also used a novel approach in offering him the job: one of them leaked the news of their decision to the press, and a Denver Post reporter called Gill and asked him for his comments. Gill, who knew neither that he was being considered for the job, nor even that there was a job, nor even in the fact that there existed a Colorado College, is reported to have said: "Young man, you must be either crazy or drunk." Later, when trustee chairman Judge William Jackson was showing him the premises, they were nearly run down by a woman speeding by on her bicycle. "Who the hell is that crazy woman?" he asked. "Oh" said the Judge, "that's my sister Helen." (I just know you got off to a better start than this, Kathryn.)

Gill did some good things for the college, one being that he staunchly defended academic freedom at a time when Senator Joe McCarthy was skinning generals alive on national television, and when the House Un-American Activities Committee was more than a little interested in what was being taught at Colorado College. But after a few years in office, Gill recognized that the money still wasn't coming in at the rate needed for survival, and he too resigned.

And now came the great Benezet-Worner era, some would say "the second coming" (to further confound the metaphor watchers). When Louis and Lew took over the administration of the College in 1955, both men were less than 40 and well embarked on careers of putting down-and-out colleges back on their feet, one of them working his magic on sev-

eral different institutions without spending very long at any, the other focusing his entire life on just one. Enrollments swelled as did the endowment, the curriculum was overhauled, and new buildings sprang up across
the campus. Optimism prevailed for the first time in years.

But like Dougherty, Slocum, and every other college president who
ever lived, both men faced situations that had never been spelled out in
their contracts. Benezet says that absolutely the worst moment in his entire life occurred here one October afternoon when a Colorado College
student, hopelessly entangled in an affair with a faculty member, drank a
beaker of potassium cyanide, more or less before his very eyes, and expired. As for his greatest triumph, he says it was surviving being stranded
high up on Crestone Peak in the middle of the night in the company of
new faculty member Glenn Brooks and their intrepid leader—Mountain
man Bob Ormes.

As for Worner, the story about him I like best concerns an irate citizenry (including I believe the Mayor of Colorado Springs) who called
Lew on the carpet before TV cameras, asking for an explanation of some
of the so-called outrages that had occurred during the "Symposium on
Violence" at the College in 1969. Worner was neither defensive nor offensive. Instead, he just shrugged and said in his broad Missourah drawl:
"Well, I guess the College will just have to take its lumps on that one." No
excuses. No self-righteousness. Just Lew Worner. It may not have satisfied
everyone, but it sure stopped the conversation cold.

And this, of course, brings us down to your immediate predecessor,
Gresham Riley, who among other things taught his entire staff to ski, and
who—with great energy and vision—carried on the traditions of the
Benezet/Worner era in bringing to our college many new and wonderful
programs and facilities. Forty years hence, when I am giving this same talk
at another cosmic college event, I promise to include in it a selection of
tidbits from both the Riley and the Mohrman presidencies.

And now I would like to proceed to my final topic: "How to be a
Great College President." This prescription comes from an obviously very
successful college president, who is nameless only because I do not know
his or her name. I first learned these words of wisdom from a friend who
had gotten them from *The New Yorker* magazine. I think I should also point

out that a somewhat similar recipe was provided by W. S. Gilbert and Sir Arthur Sullivan more than 100 years ago. Anyway, the current version might be called "I am the Very Model of a Modern College President" and it goes something like this:

The College President

I am the very model of a modern college president.
I'm always on the job, though nearly always a non-
resident.
I tour about the country to assemblies gastronomical
And make all kinds of speeches from sublime to broadly
comical.
I keep the trustees calm and the alumni all benevolent,
Restrain all signs of riot and publicity malevolent;
I know the market value of each wage-slave
professorial,
And how much less he'll take for honorarium tutorial.
I'm on to all the intrigues and the rivalries divisional,
And on the budget how I wield my fountain pen
excisional!
So though I pile up mileage being generally non-
resident
I am the very model of a modern college president.
I mix with all the business kings—the Lions and the
Rotary;
Of heiresses and oil-tycoons I am a hopeful votary;
I'm fond of giving dinners in a layout that is squiffycal,
And talking on the radio in accents quite pontifical.
I use the phrase "distinguished guest" at every
opportunity;
I welcome all alumni to my parlor every June at tea,
And though I like to see the neutral's lonely-hearts-that-
burn at ease
I always have a kindly word to say about fraternities.

I've shaken every human hand that's manicured and
    squeezable;
I pass the hat among the rich, the buck whenever
    feasible!
So though I pile up mileage being generally non-
    resident,
I am the very model of a modern college president.

Glenn E. Brooks
Professor Emeritus of Political Science
and Former Dean of the College

CHAPTER 5

THE ORIGINS OF
THE COLORADO COLLEGE PLAN
A MEMOIR

Glenn E. Brooks
Professor Emeritus of Political Science
and Former Dean of the College

On the evening of October 27, 1969, a group of Colorado College faculty members, administrators, and students came over to my house to talk about something that had happened two hours earlier. The faculty, by a vote of 72 to 55, had approved a proposal to end the conventional semester system and to replace it with a program in which faculty members would teach and students would take one course at a time, and in which extra curricular and residential activities would be integrated with the academic life of the student. That evening, we asked questions about this major change in the College.

How did the Colorado College Plan come to be? What prompted a faculty to vote for a program that, by several measures, increased their teaching obligations by fifty percent, and required substantial changes in their teaching methods? What motivated dozens of students to work as volunteers in the development of the plan at a time when many of their peers in other colleges were busy occupying their administration buildings (the campus president of Students for a Democratic Society was one of the most active workers)? And what persuaded the trustees and administrators of the College to support a scheme that was rife with uncertainty at a time when the College was already educationally and financially sound?

71

The questions persist to this day. This essay is the effort of one active participant to offer some personal answers.

Over the years since the introduction of the Plan in September, 1970, certain theories have arisen to explain the change. One view is that the faculty was caught up in the mood of change that pervaded higher education in the late Sixties and early Seventies, and simply was ready for something new. In this version, a different program would have been adopted if the Colorado College Plan had not appeared. (Indeed as I will mention later, a second, highly plausible plan was waiting in the wings at the time of the faculty vote.) Another explanation focuses on academic politics. It is that the President, Dean, and Faculty Assistant to the President designed a new program and pushed it through the faculty, using strong-arm tactics to pressure reluctant faculty members to support the plan. Finally, there is the view that the adoption of the new program represented a rational educational judgment consistent with the objectives and strengths of the College.

The best answer, in my opinion, involves the complex interplay of the spirit of the times, the particular structure, strategy, and yes, politics that were employed in the process, and the role of a sizeable number of key faculty members, administrators, and students whose part in the development of the Plan has not been fully recognized. And if rational judgment is marked by the choice of appropriate means to achieve a well-understood objective, then the decision was, on the whole, a rational act.

A full answer also requires attention to the particular sequence of events. *(The reader might also want to see Dr. Maxwell F. Taylor, The Block Plan: A History of the Early Development of the Colorado College Plan, unpublished manuscript, 1978.)*This essay begins with a commentary on the academic culture of the late Sixties, proceeds to an analysis of the way in which the planning process began, examines the process from the perspective of a participant, and offers some closing interpretations of how everything added up to a Plan that became a defining feature of Colorado College.

THE SPIRIT OF THE TIMES

Anyone who was around in the late Sixties recalls the strange combination of excitement and apprehension that gripped U.S. colleges and universities and American society in general. The Vietnam war increasingly polarized American public opinion. Institutions of higher education were hotbeds of sit-ins, marches, and demonstrations. Colorado College had its share of anti-war marches and civil rights protests. Military Intelligence plainclothesmen from nearby Fort Carson were conspicuously present at College events, possibly also in classes posing as students.

Student protest groups, especially different varieties of a Black Power Movement, led to the disruption of classes and the occupation of administration buildings at Cornell University and several other universities. Students for a Democratic Society demanded greater freedom for students and attacked the foundations of an elitist, capitalist university system. The Free Speech Movement made its strident entrance at Berkeley and introduced four-letter words into the public campus vocabulary.

Hippies, flower people, rock music, and drugs appeared all over the country. Charles Reich wrote *The Greening of America*, confidently proclaiming that the United States was undergoing a profound and irreversible culture change. Shortly thereafter, Herman Kahn, author of the infamous *On Thermonuclear War*, wrote an article called "The Squaring of America," in which he correctly argued that the Age of Aquarius was a passing fad and would be replaced by a return to conventional life and values. But in 1967 through the early Seventies, international and domestic events appeared to signal a profound shift in the life of the nation.

In higher education, the most vocal advocates of change called for greater independence for students, a more "relevant" curriculum, a loosening of requirements, collegiality among students and professors, an end to the political neutrality of educational institutions, and "participatory democracy." No one was quite sure what these terms really meant. Their philosophical and educational assumptions were, at best, vague, and at their worst, foolish. But they had a compelling tone, causing colleges and universities to begin searching urgently for suitable responses.

Throughout higher education, there was a vague feeling that there was a national crisis and that, one way or another, things were going to change. But who would be the instruments of that change? Radicals thought the entire system should be thrown out and replaced with genuinely revolutionary education. Conservative educators and trustees believed that the best course of action was to continue straight ahead with traditional academic objectives and values. Reformers, especially in faculties, thought that adjustments could be made within the existing structure of higher education to accommodate new demands.

The reformers were the dominant force. Experimentation became the order of the day. Special programs appeared in colleges and universities. Among these were independent studies, tutorial groups, more off campus courses, the elimination of departments in favor of cross-disciplinary programs, the reduction or elimination of requirements, and greater student participation in faculty and administrative committees. New courses addressed to contemporary political issues and social action proliferated on most campuses. So-called four-one-four schools such as Florida Presbyterian placed emphasis on intensive, full-time courses during their month-long "winter term," a precursor of the Colorado College block program.

While most innovations affected only one part of an institution or one period in the academic calendar, other colleges and universities made comprehensive changes. Conventional grading systems—the old A,B,C,D,F grades—often gave way to Pass-Fail grading or other variants. Brown University introduced its Adviser Program, in which students had no formal course requirements but rather worked out their programs with faculty advisers throughout their four years of undergraduate work.

New institutions also flowered in this period. Evergreen State University was established as a new campus with an interdisciplinary, non-departmental curriculum. The State University of New York at Old Westbury and Hampshire College attracted national attention as experimental institutions.

Most reformers in this period honestly believed that the new freedom from old requirements and expectations would not affect academic standards, that students would work even harder with positive, self-directed motivation, and that faculty members would find new inspiration in the rejuvenated academic community. In retrospect, this was a naive and incorrect assumption.

The late Sixties and early Seventies also marked the beginning of grade inflation, the loss of coherence in disciplinary courses and requirements, and, in some institutions, a reduction in admission requirements.

Popular topical courses often replaced traditional subjects. On the grounds that students should be able to express themselves in their own style, some faculty members allowed students to write garbled and senseless personal essays instead of disciplined analyses of a subject. Feeling and opinion became the equals of careful factual reasoning.

Not all institutions suffered from this confusion of reform and the breakdown of academic tradition. St. Johns with its Great Books program and a number of Catholic schools stayed tenaciously with their traditional curriculum, yielding here and there to student demands for more involvement in academic decisions or for more relevant courses.

This was the context in which Colorado College began a reexamination of its academic and non-academic programs.

The Inner World of the College

In 1968, Colorado College stood somewhere in the middle of the spectrum of educational change. The institution was academically and financially sound. The curriculum consisted of traditional liberal arts and science programs. The Board of Trustees confined itself largely to its fiduciary responsibilities. The Chairman of the Board, Russell Tutt, ran the Board with a firm and sometimes arbitrary hand, brooking little dissent in meetings. He had a close relationship with President Lloyd Worner, and trusted him to manage the affairs of the college.

President Worner was a graduate of the College, a former professor of history and Dean of the College before assuming the presidency in 1963. Probably no person in the history of the college had shown greater devotion to the institution. His fierce devotion to the liberal arts, his sense of history, and his cautious approach to any major decision would, on the surface, identify him as an educational conservative. At the same time, however, he was receptive to innovations that preserved the character of the College, and did not hesitate to support ideas that, in his view were educationally sound.

The Dean of the College who replaced Lloyd Worner in 1963 was Dr. Kenneth Curran, a respected member of the Economics faculty. He was a traditionalist, a fair arbiter of disputes, and a clear-headed decision-maker, but hardly an innovator. Serving under him was a bright young Associate Dean, George Drake, a former Rhodes Scholar and historian, who stepped in as Acting Dean in the fall of 1968 while Curran was away, and assumed the Deanship in the summer of 1969 when Dean Curran retired.

The faculty of the College had grown considerably in the previous decade, starting especially with the arrival of President Louis T. Benezet in 1955. The senior faculty was competent and reasonably receptive to change. Under Presidents Benezet and Worner, they were joined by a number of young faculty members who believed that Colorado College could be at the forefront of high quality colleges. The faculty as a whole was overwhelmingly white and male, with wives who stayed at home and brought dishes to faculty parties. Although the faculty differed on particulars of academic policy and practice, they were almost without exception committed to the liberal arts and sciences. This consensus on the fundamental purpose of the institution was a critical element in the events that unfolded in 1968 and 1969.

Students at the College were an able and energetic group. They worked fairly hard and got along with the faculty, administration, and trustees. While some were interested in radical causes, their antagonism was not directed toward the college. On the contrary, they joined hands with the faculty in the pursuit in improvements in the institution.

Three factors set the stage for the initiation of a reexamination of the institution beginning in 1968. First, the 1960s had already been a period of innovation in the academic program of the College. The faculty had modified degree requirements and credit-hour designations of courses. The College introduced a Selected Student Program in 1964. A pilot "Adviser Plan" was introduced in 1967. This plan exempted students from regular degree requirements, allowing them to work out tailor-made programs under the guidance of selected faculty advisers.

The pace of innovation picked up in the academic year 1967–68. The number of semester hours required for graduation was reduced from 128 to 120. Course distribution requirements among the three academic divisions were loosened. A freshman seminar program was designed and made ready for introduction in the curriculum.

Not all proposals were approved. In March, 1967, the faculty soundly rejected a plan to have students take only four courses per semester and to assign equal credits to all courses. Although the defeat of this proposal was a setback for the administration and the faculty Academic Program Committee, it can be viewed with hindsight as a rehearsal for the more ambitious proposal of the Colorado College Plan in 1969. In general, the faculty was receptive to change.

Second, the College had undergone an accreditation review by the North Central Association. The college earned praise in virtually every phase of its operation. One criticism, fully justified, was that the College was not engaged in effective long range planning. President Worner was personally concerned about the review team's criticism, and held long discussions with faculty members and administrators about how to improve planning.

The third and decisive factor came from the Committee on Committees, the central faculty executive committee of the College. Professor Fred Sondermann of the Political Science Department was a far-sighted member of the committee and a steady source of fresh ideas. He recognized that the College centennial was only six years away, in 1974, and began to think about what the College should be doing to prepare for the centennial year. He was also aware of the North Central Association's comment about the lack of planning at the College.

In April, 1968 Professor Sondermann submitted a memorandum to the Committee on Committees outlining a scheme for the establishment of a "Committee for 1974." In Sondermann's plan, this body would represent all major College constituencies. The Committee for 1974 would ". . . address themselves to the task of figuring out what kind of a College we wish to be, what kind of a College it will be possible for us to be, and how these two projections can be brought into meaningful and productive relationship." Sondermann posed questions that the committee should consider: the nature and size of the student body and faculty, the direction of curricular change, college finances, the campus physical environment, and the relations of the College with the community and other educational institutions.

The Committee on Committees endorsed the Sondermann proposal. Committee Chairman William Hochman placed it on the agenda of the faculty meeting of May 13, 1968. In the debate that ensued, the faculty did not endorse the Sondermann proposal, but instead asked the Dean of the College to discuss plans for the 1974 centennial with department chairs.

The Dean and a new Committee on Committees chaired by Professor Bernard Arnest pursued the issue in the summer of 1968, and through informal discussions came to the conclusion that a faculty member should be appointed to orchestrate a far-ranging self-study of the College. The method of that investigation was not spelled out by the Committee. They agreed that I should be asked to undertake the assignment.

During the academic year 1967–68, I taught at the University of East Africa-Nairobi under the sponsorship of the Rockefeller Foundation. Like so many of my colleagues, I had been distressed by the events in my own country and felt a need to get perspective by spending a year away from the United States. Although I was out of touch with the College, my year in Africa convinced me that, for better or worse, I was an American whose work should be done principally in my own country, not in some far away land, and that Colorado College, as an institution moving up in the ranks of elite colleges, was a place where I could teach well-to-do future leaders without feelings of liberal guilt. Therefore I returned home in August, 1968 with a new sense of excitement about the College.

As well as I can recall, President Worner, Acting Dean Drake, and Professors Arnest and Sondermann asked me in mid-August to accept the assignment. Within a day or two I began to discuss possible approaches with faculty colleagues and administrators. On September 20, 1968, I submitted a report to President Worner proposing ways to organize the planning operation. He agreed, and the process began.

THE STRUCTURE OF CHANGE

The revised planning scheme was a clarification of the broad ideas that had been worked out in the committee on Committees.

The purpose of the project, I suggested, was "to work out a master plan for Colorado College during the next two years which will give us a running start into the centennial decade of the 1970s and beyond." This differed from the original idea proposed by Professor Sondermann, who did not envision a "master plan," but rather a general self-study. The revised approach included:

A. a statement of general objectives for the college for the rest of this century.

B. a set of specific operational goals for the college—that is, goals which can be translated into policies, programs, and budgets—for the 1970s.

C. a detailed program package for the first half of the 1970s, in which we spell out the actual costs of our programs, the kind of people we will need, and the changes that are to be made.

D. a procedure for continuing review and modification of the plan so that it becomes a working document rather than a one-shot statement.

The procedure assumed that "faculty, students, administration, and trustees will be intimately involved in the study from the beginning, and that a great amount of the work will be done by existing groups, committees, and individuals . . . By 1974, then, we will not simply state what we intend to be; we will show what we have become."

The process would include practically all areas of college life. The President would be the chief planner. The Committee on Committees would serve initially as the principal coordinating body, but other committees and groups would become involved as planning moved ahead. As Faculty Assistant to the President, I was to be responsible for the design of the general format of the plan, the assembly of information, liaisons with individuals and groups involved in planning, the drafting of materials. In addition, President Worner gave me authority "to serve as an independent voice and advocate within the bounds of fair play." The understanding that I could be an advocate turned out to be an asset in the early stages of planning and a mixed blessing if not a liability in the later and more controversial phase.

Three points deserve notice about the agreed-upon procedures. The first is that they differed from the original proposal made by Professor Sondermann primarily in that they included the idea of developing a master plan for the College. There was no controversy over this change. The second is that the procedure was designed to have a plan in full operation by the centennial year 1974. The third is that no one involved in the design of the procedures had the slightest idea, in late September, 1968, what direction the plan would take.

At a regular meeting of the faculty on September 30, I reported on the proposed procedures. No vote was taken; the faculty gave its tacit approval. President Worner then called a special faculty meeting for October 14 to begin an open discussion of general College priorities.

On October 3, effective supervision of the planning process passed from the Committee on Committees to the Academic Program Committee, a faculty body with responsibility for the development and analysis of general academic policy and practice. The Academic Program Committee did not oversee detailed curricular matters such as the approval of new courses. That task was handled by yet another group, the Committee on Instruction. Instead, the Academic Program Committee was free to set its own agenda and to address broad policy matters.

The Committee on Committees had given special attention to the membership of the Academic Program Committee when it was appointed in May, 1968. The committee was a particularly thoughtful group of faculty members, students, and the President and Dean. The chair of the committee was professor Don Shearn of the Psychology Department, who would play a central role in spawning the basic idea of the Colorado College Plan and in guiding the committee through the intense and complex activities during the academic year 1967–68.

Other members were Professor Owen Cramer, a classicist who was a steady source of fresh ideas, Biology Professor Werner Heim, whose talent for analyzing programs and data was unexcelled, Professor Lester Michel, a quiet, thoughtful chemist, Art Professor James Trissel, author of a plan to allow professors to teach one "X" course each semester, that is, a course which could be designed and taught freely according to the interests of each teacher, Professor Ray Werner of Economics, a clear-headed academic conservative who became a strong and fair-minded leader of the opposition to the Block Plan, and Political Science Professor Timothy Fuller, whose academic and political sensibility made him another major figure in the evolution of the plan. I attended meetings of the committee by virtue of my planning assignment, but Don Shearn made it clear that "while the Committee should be working closely with Mr.

Brooks, it should also remain somewhat aloof in order to carry on its traditional function of developing new ideas for the academic program."

In early 1968, the role of student members on faculty committees was not well established. The student association, the CCCA, appointed student members erratically and sometimes forgot to appoint them at all. Three students, Charles Mullen, Sharon Dregne and Tyler Makepeace, attended several meetings that year and took an active part in the discussions.

The October 3 meeting of the Academic Program Committee reviewed planning procedures and agreed to an ambitious calendar of departmental meetings and separate meetings of students. The Committee assembled teams of students, faculty members, and administrators from all corners of the campus to participate in the discussions. Before the meetings began, I sent a questionnaire to departments, asking them to comment on a variety of departmental and college matters: What do you believe the objectives of the College are? What do you see as the potentially revolutionary changes in your discipline? Should your department have a major? What would be the effects if you did not? What do you need to do a better job?

At about this same time, I prepared a list of other groups and committees who would be involved in the campus-wide planning effort. Practically no one was excluded. We talked about the college operating as a "Committee of the Whole," and in fact as well as theory this is what happened.

THE GENESIS OF THE IDEA

The structure was in place. The process had begun. Yet in early October, no one had a definite plan. The October 14 faculty meeting on College priorities was a wide ranging discussion of ideas and aspirations, but no consistent theme emerged. Even so, the spirit of change was present in the meeting. Just after the meeting, I wrote down these impressions:

> We can reasonably expect to get a working agreement in the faculty on means of education, but not on substantive ends, either expressed as specific subjects to be taught or, in Carl's (Carl Roberts, Professor of Psychology) unfortunate phrase, the terminal behaviors of our students.

This became an important assumption in the development of a strategy for change—to get agreement on means but not on substantive ends.

The departmental meetings began on October 16, two days after the special faculty discussion of priorities. In these meetings the department faculties advanced many different ideas, some of which could be seen in retrospect as fragmentary elements of the plan that evolved. In September and October, Professor Heim had proposed to the Academic Program Committee an idea for a "leading questions" approach to learning, built on new degree requirements, class size limits, the option of some very large classes, and an interdisciplinary course structure. In the Classics Department review, Owen Cramer suggested that "an intensive version of Heim's plan" warranted further study.

Geology, on October 17, sought ways "to loosen the chains" of the semester system and wanted to strengthen off campus studies. Similarly, Anthropology expressed frustration about scheduling problems wanting to find ways to do more off campus courses. Religion was interested in a scheme that would allow professors on leave to take a group of students with them. Biology called for "team trips" and more courses that resembled the summer interdisciplinary institutes at the college. Dick Taber, in Chemistry, thought the College should consider abandoning the conventional calendar and find ways to do more intensive work. But where, he asked, would the time come from? And the staff? He thought there had to be a reexamination of how we used our time.

The Education Department, on November 11, was concerned about the problem of scheduling "blocks of time" for student teaching. Psychology focused on the questions of faculty time and environmental design, noting that the College Summer Session had a better ambience than the conventional semester. German and Russian also commented on malapportioned time, and thought students were spread too thin under the current system.

While the departmental reviews were going on, students from the Academic Program Committee and other volunteers were meeting with student majors. Small squads of students and faculty went into the residence halls to talk informally to students about academic, social, and residential life.

A rough pattern ran through most of the discussions. Virtually everyone agreed that:

- Colorado College was a sound institution with a capacity for further improvement;
- The college should stay with its historic commitment to the liberal arts and sciences;
- We trusted each other and there were no fundamental differences among students, faculty, administration, and trustees.
- We wanted to create greater opportunities for freedom for students and faculty alike, more student responsibility for learning, more independent study, more off campus work, smaller class size, better integration in the curriculum, and more effective contacts between students and professors. People felt pulled in different directions but weren't sure what to do about it; and
- Better use of student and faculty time was essential.

Yet in the formal sessions with departments, no one had put forth the core idea of having one course at a time. That came in a conversation one afternoon in late October or very early November at Murphy's Bar. Don Shearn, Tim Fuller, and I were taking stock of the departmental reviews, trying to distill some of the central issues. At one point, Don Shearn said, in effect, "Just give me fifteen students and let me work with them." For the three of us, there was a click, a sense that Shearn might have gotten to the heart of the matter. We continued to talk about this remarkably simple idea, and realized that it had the possibility of addressing many of the concerns that we had heard from faculty and students. We also realized that it was fraught with complications.

Several faculty members, especially those in the Academic Program Committee, began to focus on Don Shearn's idea, although other general reforms continued to have currency in faculty discussions. Werner Heim's "leading questions" idea, James Trissel's "X course" plan, and more conventional notions of a 4–1–4 calendar or the scheduling of packages of related courses. Students were proposing major changes in the grading system and the introduction of student-taught courses.

Since other ideas for reform were present at the time, it would be incorrect to say that the idea of the Block Plan was the only, or even the dominant scheme in the middle of the fall semester, 1968. Scientists speak of the "signal to noise ratio" in communications. In retrospect, the Block Plan could be regarded as the signal, and the rest noise. That is only because the Block Plan was accepted and the others were left by the wayside.

Nevertheless, the one-course-at-a-time idea—and it was very rough hewn in early November, 1968—started to gain momentum. The Academic Program Committee touched lightly on the proposal at its meeting on November 7. Conversations about the idea spread around campus, especially among faculty members interested in substantial changes in the academic program. There was no unanimity about what the problems were; instead individuals were thinking about how one-course-at-a-time would address their own concerns.

Professor Doug Freed, a colleague and good friend of Don Shearn in the Psychology Department, believed that the central issue for the academic program was class size, and indeed his view was shared by many faculty members. He was aware of the irony that a small college with a purported student/faculty ratio of 13 to 1 (counting coaches and several administrators) had an average class size of 23 and many classes that were in the 35 to 40 range. Freed homed in on the crucial arithmetic fact of the conventional semester system, and in so doing advanced Shearn's idea to a new stage. In a memo to me on November 12, he wrote:

I am so convinced that far away the main complaint of faculty members at Colorado College at present concerns class size ... Many of the suggestions in the faculty questionnaires solved his problem by adding three or four art historians, two or three biologists, or by doubling the size of the music or anthropology departments. It does not seem to me that any of these are reasonable expectations. It seems, on the other hand, that what is required is some ingenuity in trying to find ways of making better use of the faculty members for the student-faculty ratio that we already have.

Freed's suggestions clarified important features of the emerging plan. He understood that the reason classes were so much bigger than the student-faculty ratio was mainly that the students took more courses—usually four, sometimes five—while faculty members taught only three. He continued:

> If the number of courses taken by the student at one time could be re-
> duced to correspond to the number taught by the faculty, this would, by
> itself, reduce class size by a factor of somewhere between 1/3 and 1/4.

Freed added other suggestions for achieving the goal of smaller classes; teaching a few very large classes to make small classes the norm; use more credit-by-examination and self-teaching methods; increasing faculty hours in the classroom, possibly by sub-dividing large classes into two sections; providing more technical assistance for professors in the sciences; and incorporating lectures, concerts, and plays "as integral parts of the student's load." His conclusion was:

> Above all we must get out of the pattern of courses of 35 to 45 students
> being lectured at on factual information better available elsewhere—
> this is probably not only the most common pattern for courses on the
> Colorado College campus, but also the least possible effective use of
> faculty time.

Shearn's seminal thought of having one course at a time was now supplemented by Freed's proposal to create smaller class size without costly faculty additions. A major question remained: how could more intensive courses and smaller classes be worked into an academic calendar?

Professor Will Gateley of the Mathematics Department heard about Shearn's idea and sent two memos to the Academic Program Committee. On November 14 he outlined a calendar of eight blocks during the academic year, with one course at a time. Five days later he revised his thoughts, offering instead a calendar of two blocks at a time. In both memos, he tried to find ways to give the faculty more freedom for field courses and greater control over their schedules in class. Gateley's memos were the first step in addressing the technical complexities of a block system.

By mid-November, my own thinking had become focused on one course at a time, and my interest was reinforced from an unlikely quarter.

I was reading Peter Drucker's *The Effective Executive* at the suggestion of Mrs. Elaine Freed, who had agreed to help me part-time in the planning work (in the fall semester, 1968, I was still teaching a full complement of courses). Drucker cited evidence from the corporate world that the best work gets done when executives build on the strengths of their firm, concentrate on one task at a time, and maintain clear priorities. Elaine freed and I carried on a lively discussion of Drucker's analysis and wondered how his ideas could be applied in an academic setting.

In late November and early December, as the faculty and student conversations continued in offices, classrooms, and residence halls, I pulled together the main ideas that had been advanced in order to report to the President and Acting Dean Drake.

We met in the President's office on a Friday in mid-December. I had prepared a twenty page outline, built on a general theme of "Unified Learning." I argued that the college community had no reason to change its central purpose of liberal education, that is, to educate students to be free and to make responsible choices. Quoting the College motto, *Scientia et Disciplina*, I noted that the College provided knowledge *(scientia)* and discipline of thought *(disciplina)*, engendered commitment, provided leisure for students to develop perspective, and sought to enhance community.

The diagnosis I offered was that our means were not well aligned with our ends. Although we had major strengths in our academic and non-academic programs, we could do better. Then I cited the problems of the management of time, fragmentation of effort by students and faculty alike, and large classes. Realistically, I said (influenced by Freed's idea that it was not necessary to enlarge the faculty dramatically), we should keep the faculty and student body at about the same size, and find ways to do better with the resources we had.

The prescription was "Unified Learning: a restoration of the classical triangle between a teacher, a subject, and a small group of students, working in one place without major distractions for a period of time sufficient for genuine learning to take place." Drawing upon the proposals of Shearn, Doug Freed, Gateley, and others, I sketched out the basic scheme of a new academic and non-academic plan and offered my own view of how the plan could address our problems. I also identified the practical difficulties and points of resistance to a switch to a system of "Unified Learning."

President Worner and Dean Drake listened attentively. They asked a number of questions about specific programs that would be affected by the proposal, for example, pre-medical studies, teacher certification, and athletics. At the end of the day, however, the President authorized me to concentrate on the emerging plan and to review it extensively with faculty, students, and administrators. The President's authorization marked the end of the formative stage in the development of the Colorado College Plan.

THE POLITICS AND STRATEGY OF APPROVAL

The sequence of events in the academic year 1968–69 shows that the process did not move from a general theory of education to a specific plan of action. On the contrary, we began with a broad understanding of what some of the issues were, locked on to an appealingly simple idea—one course at a time—then embellished it with the specific mechanics of blocks, and only later, in late November and December, 1968, began to devise a philosophy for the enterprise that would be educationally and politically appealing to the faculty and students. The truth of the matter is that we did not go in search of educational theory to support the plan until after the main ideas were formed. When we did search, we found little on either side of the question.

In this phase, events were more important than philosophy. In early January, 1969, the College held its annual week-long symposium, an occasion on which faculty and students attended lectures, films, and plays without the conflicting demands of classes. The topic for 1969 was "Violence." A series of speakers from right, left and center drew large audiences, including many participants from the city. The topic alone was enough to induce some anxiety in the larger community. The most controversial event, however, was a play, *Dionysis '69* done completely in the nude by Richard Scheckner's Performance Group from New York. Church groups and civic clubs in the region attacked the College with resolutions, phone calls, and letters to the editor of the local papers. The College was under siege from the local community.

The assault from the community drew the College together. Students, faculty, administrators, and trustees joined forces in a defense of freedom of expression. The President and Chairman of the Board of Trustees were resolute in support of the organizers of the symposium, even though they probably had a strong personal distaste for the nude performance. Students and faculty rallied under the campus flagpole to voice their appreciation to the administration and trustees for their unflinching stand. The controversy created a remarkable sense of unity at the College, and indirectly, in my opinion, added to the atmosphere of good will that pervaded the campus during the months leading up to the faculty vote on the plan.

On January 29, 1969, I presented to the faculty a broad outline of what was then being called "The Master Plan." ("Unified Learning" had dropped out of the working vocabulary.) I stressed the ways in which the proposal was not a departure from the traditional mission of the College, but rather was designed to permit us to do a better job. I said that the idea had "evolved from a review of the academic program, and from numerous memos, meetings, and conversations with faculty." I used catch-words that had currency with the faculty to make the point—an honest point—that the ideas had arisen genuinely from the College and were not copies of some other institution. The themes of *Scientia et Disciplina*, commitment, community, professional development, and control of time were becoming more pronounced.

More important than the formal report to the faculty, however, were ongoing discussions with small groups of faculty members and students, in which I tried out the ideas, got new suggestions, and gauged reactions. These meetings included virtually all faculty members, but were not departmental sessions. It was important to get faculty and students to think about College issues rather than narrow departmental concerns. I was often joined by colleagues from the Academic Program Committee or others, but the process was highly informal. From these sessions, we gathered a better picture of practical problems and possible solutions. Faculty members advanced ideas of "half-courses" which could be taken two at a time in subjects requiring more time for reflection. We faced up to the questions of finding enough classrooms to accommodate all courses simultaneously, the conversion of credit hours to some new system, and one overriding issue: could courses of varying length and format be offered at the same time? It was clear that we had to produce solid answers to such questions.

The early months of 1969 were also a time of sorting out faculty support and opposition to the proposal. The faculty members in the Department of Economics and Business were beginning to show signs of strong resistance to the Plan. Political Science was generally in favor. Other faculty members tended to take pro or con positions without regard to their departmental identity.

What was still lacking for many faculty members and students was a sense that the proposal was not just another theoretical idea that would find its way into the college archives. What made a great difference, in the Spring of 1969, was an exercise, operated through my office and supported by the President and Dean Kenneth Curran, who had returned for one semester before retiring in the summer of 1969, to have each department prepare a hypothetical schedule of block courses. In turn, students would try to work out a course plan using the schedule.

For the first time, departments were obliged to change their semester courses into blocks, if only as an experiment. Some resisted the idea. Professor Albert Seay, Chair of the Music Department, saw the move as a not-very-subtle way of implicating the faculty in the process. He was, of course, correct. After much cajoling however, he prepared a schedule.

The Planning Office put the hypothetical courses onto big boards in a room in the basement of Armstrong Hall. Student volunteers in the office dragooned students into the basement, inviting them to try to plan out a year's schedule. To the delight of the Planning Office and supporters of the new plan, the students were able to work their way through the year without major difficulties. Although the courses were randomly scheduled, the exercise demonstrated an important feature of student course selection: under any calendar, students choose from among the courses that are available in a given time slot. Only when their requirements or strong preferences are at stake are they troubled. Otherwise, they pick from the menu without complaint. If this were not the case, no calendar of courses would be successful.

The course mock-up did more than anything else to convince passive faculty members that the plan had gathered momentum and could, for better or worse, be adopted. The Spring of 1969 was principally a time of discovering questions that deserved answers, drawing lines of support and opposition, and thinking ahead to a timetable for faculty action. Here again, the unchallenged assumption was that the faculty would make any decision on a proposal, even though it included changes in the residential and extra-curricular life of the College. Student, administrative, and trustee views were significant but not controlling.

An implicit strategy for the approval of the plan was now falling into place:

- Keep the traditional purpose of the College;
- Keep the content of the liberal arts and sciences curriculum but change the mode of instruction to intensive courses;
- Let faculty members support (or oppose) the plan for their own good reasons instead of trying to force agreement on the exact goals to be achieved;
- Emphasize the new opportunity that faculty members would have to organize their courses according to the needs of the subject and their teaching styles, freed from the restrictions of the fifty minute class period;
- Show how the plan was specifically addressed to concerns expressed in the departmental reviews in the fall of 1968;
- Involve students as supporters of the change;
- Take into account the legitimate worries of faculty members and try, where possible, to resolve them;
- Keep the proposal at the forefront of attention in the entire campus community through memos, meetings, and articles in the student newspaper.

As the Spring semester came to a close, the Academic Program Committee, the Committee on Committees, the President, and the Planning Office were in accord. The summer would be devoted to detailed homework on technical aspects of the proposal. We would bring a formal plan before the faculty in the fall of 1969 if it seemed to be ready.

The summer of 1969 was politically quiet. With strong assistance from Mrs. Judy Finley, who had replaced Elaine Freed in the Planning Office, and several student assistants, I prepared three reports on the feasibility of the proposal. The first dealt with scheduling, enrollment procedures, and classroom spaces. With his sharp eyes an good imagination, student David Struthers found dormitory lounges and foyers that could be used for classes along with conventional classrooms. In the process, we developed a better idea of the "courseroom" as an environment for learning that could be shaped to the style of the course.

The second report contained a more comprehensive description of the plan, a restatement of the educational rationale, and a detailed commentary on how faculty members could go about teaching courses without the restriction of hourly schedules. It recommended a revised calendar for the academic year, consisting of eleven three-week blocks (later revised to nine three and a half week blocks), and offered responses, admittedly conjectural, to objections that faculty members had raised about the intensity of blocks, "soaking-in" time for math and language courses (we offered the option of extended half courses), and pedagogical literature that supported the plan (in fact, there was no convincing evidence either way; the College was going out on an educational limb).

The third report dealt with non-academic aspects of the plan, including campus design, the leisure side of student life, residence halls, and administration. Northing was yet solidified, but the foundations were now more elaborate, and the College was ready for the final, highly political phase leading to approval of the plan.

ACTION AND DECISION

At the beginning of each academic year, the faculty of the college holds a fall conference. The Committee on Committees decided in the spring of 1969 that the proposal for the new plan should be the topic, and asked me to make a presentation. By this time I was an unqualified advocate of the plan. My comments to the conference were based upon the summer reports to the faculty and were heavily laced with references to the new freedom the plan would provide for the faculty and the educational benefits we would give to our students.

The faculty discussion was noteworthy in that most faculty members did not attack or defend the main idea. Instead, they concentrated on specific adjustments in the plan that I had submitted in the summer reports. For example, one significant suggestion by Professor Van Shaw was to include strict upper limit of 25 students on courses except for courses which had formal faculty approval to have unlimited enrollment. It is doubtful that the conference changed many minds. Faculty members left the conference with their biases intact. Everyone knew, however, that the faculty was moving toward a decision.

Shortly after the conference, on September 16, I gave an address to the opening convocation in the College chapel. It contained little that was new, but was a strong restatement of the benefits of the new plan, so much so that several faculty colleagues resented the language and the impression that I was trying to mobilize students to put pressure on the faculty. I had referred, for example, to the "Procrustean bed" of the fifty-minute class schedules, and said that students were "whipsawed" by multiple demands. History Professor Louis Geiger protested that I was "a member of the faculty openly inviting students to revolt." Afterward, I realized that I let my penchant for vivid images outrun my better judgment, and I regarded my talk as a setback.

The first regular faculty meeting of the fall semester was on September 22. In part, the agenda included further debate over the details of the plan. Once again, I made an error of judgment. Clouded by fatigue and anxious to get an accurate account of the discussion, I brought a tape recorder to the meeting, and was openly sitting with the recorder in my hand when Professor Jack Rhodes, an opponent of the plan, rose in indignation to point out that I was recording the discussion. The tension was palpable. I apologized and was instructed to erase the tape.

It may be that the events at the fall conference, the convocation, and the September 22 faculty meeting released some of the pressure that was mounting and helped cooler heads to prevail. The faculty agreed to have a vote at its meeting on October 27, but the conditions of that vote were not yet spelled out. Two actions had a crucial effect on the outcome.

Shortly after the faculty meeting, Dean Drake and I met to talk about the state of affairs. We decided that it would be prudent and fair to gather the principal opponents of the plan to see if they could agree on a single alternative proposal that could be put before the faculty if the block plan was rejected. The Dean called two meetings in the Board Room of Armstrong Hall, inviting virtually all faculty members who had advanced different plans. The result was prompt agreement on a single alternative, supported by Professors Jane Cauvel, Glenn Gray, Douglas Fox, Douglas

Mertz, and Frank Krutzke. The plan provided for twelve week semesters in which students would take three courses and professors would teach three. In the middle of the year, the College would offer intensive, full-time six week courses.

My job then was to work with the proponents of the alternative to bring the plan up to a level of legislative detail that would make it genuinely comparable to the main proposal. Since many of the questions posed by the main proposal also applied to the alternative plan, we had little difficulty in working out the details. On October 8, I sent a memo to the faculty outlining the alternative proposal and reminding them that there would be a discussion of the main proposal on October 13 and a vote on October 27.

The greater significance of developing the alternative proposal was that the opposition had a fair chance to put forward their ideas in a systematic way, and to present a plan that was educationally sound. This not only generated good will among opponents of the block plan, but gave the faculty the assurance that a real choice had been placed before them.

The new faculty Academic Program Committee provided the second crucial element in the weeks leading up to the faculty vote. In a series of intensive meetings in early October, the committee, now chaired by Physics Professor Charles Bordner, made last minute changes in the plan, put the main proposal into legislative form, and laid out a precise procedure for debate and voting on October 27. The faculty would have an open discussion for forty-five minutes. There would be no amendments until the conclusion of the general discussion. Then amendments could be offered, preferably in writing. The first vote would be on amendments, then a secret ballot on the proposal as a whole. If the proposal failed, the faculty would schedule a discussion and vote on the Cauvel-Gray-Fox-Mertz-Krutzke at an early future date. The faculty approved the procedures at a special meeting on October 13.

With the publication of the alternative plan, faculty members knew they had a choice. Under the ground rules of the Academic Program Committee, they knew exactly what the procedure would be. Although tensions remained fairly high, the atmosphere was considerably calmer than it had been in September.

While these preparations were underway, Dean Drake, President Worner, and I were engaged in quiet conversations with faculty members, especially those in the opposition. Drake and Worner had stated their support of the plan in the spring of 1969, but were not heavy handed in lobbying for the change. Even so, some of the opponents of the plan thought that the Dean and President were inappropriately partisan.

The faculty meeting on October 27 was almost anti-climactic. The debate was calm and measured. No new issues of consequence were raised. One amendment was passed to allow students to take two adjunct courses instead of one. Another amendment, by Professor Neale Reinitz of English, would have allowed faculty to teach eight of the nine blocks. After some discussion, he changed the amendment to a friendly recommendation. Another amendment, to have seven week half courses as well as ten and a half week half courses, was rejected.

In the waning minutes of the debate, Biology Professor "Doc" Stabler said that he was near retirement and thought that the "young bucks" who supported the plan should have a chance to make it work. The question was called at 6:11 p.m. A bipartisan group of faculty served as counters for the secret ballot. President Worner then announced the result. Dean Drake and I had estimated that the vote would be 70 for and 55 against. We missed by two votes we had not counted on. The final vote was 72–55. The President then asked the faculty to comment on whether this majority was sufficient to implement the plan. Professor Ray Werner, as a leading opponent, said that he thought there had been a fair fight and that the College should proceed. Professor Hans Krimm, also an opponent, made a motion to implement the plan. The voice vote was virtually unanimous. One strident "no" was cast by Eila Hanne, an economist who left the college the following year. President Worner said that he interpreted the faculty action as a decision to implement.

EPILOGUE

This narrative concludes with the faculty vote to introduce the Colorado College Plan in September, 1970. The Board of Trustees endorsed the plan with minimal discussion. For the next eleven months, faculty dedicated themselves to the formidable task of redesigning courses, changing requirements, and figuring out how they would teach under the new scheme. To help the process, the faculty put together another schedule and then practically the entire student body went through another mock registration as a means of refining the new block offerings. The administration labored mightily to find classroom space. Two enterprising students, Malcolm Ware and Jim Levison, haunted Salvation Army thrift stores in search of temporary furniture for jury-rigged classrooms. The library and bookstore braced themselves for a new way of doing business. The plan went into full operation on Labor Day, 1970, two years after the process had begun. It remains today as a centerpiece of Colorado College.

David D. Finley
Professor of Political Science and
Former Dean of the College

CHAPTER 6

Some Views from
the Dean's Office, 1987–1992:
Diversity, Civility, Scholarship

David D. Finley
Professor of Political Science and
Former Dean of the College

On a quiet July day in 1987, I was trying to get my bearings in the un-familiar Dean's office I'd just inherited from Glenn Brooks. I came upon a five page list of maxims for new deans. It ended with the following cheer-ful advice: "Remember, the kitchen is normally hot. . . . Don't give up your tenure. . . . If none of this works, run ten miles a day and marry money."

My five years as Gresham Riley's dean of the faculty and college were busy, surprising, frustrating and rewarding, in more or less equal parts. Glenn left me a memorable artifact propped in a corner of the office that I retained for guidance. It was a ramshackle wooden cross, once painted, with shreds of moldy crepe dangling. Scrawled into the wood was the in-scription, "administration ROTS the mind." Besides begging many a fac-ulty question, the slogan kept liberal arts deaning in perspective. The only visitor to take obvious exception was a dignified German university rec-tor who clearly thought such a sentiment was inappropriate.

A number of faculty colleagues sent me notes and helpful memo-randa after Gresham Riley asked me to be dean. Among them came sev-eral copies of an article by former Harvard dean Henry Rosovsky, who compared decanal-faculty relations to Salieri's with Mozart and reviewed many ways to say no agreeably. There was also a wonderful article Ric Bradley had written for the CC alumni magazine. Among other telling vignettes, Ric remembered having found a package of pipe-cleaners in the deanery desk when he took George Drake's place. He mused that George was not a smoker; they must have been left by Ken Curran in the 1960s. Then, his telephone rang, and I guess the pipe-cleaners stayed there five more years. Omens.

My own first day on the job included a short discussion with a new alumnus, just appointed a science paraprof. The daily security office report had cited him for an encounter with a guard the previous night, while breaking into his former abode, the late Beta house, possibly under the influence. We discussed the need to recognize changing obligations associated with changing roles. We didn't discuss my own mental note to keep abstemious as dean and wear a tie more often, and of course to stay away from the Beta House.

I think it was my son who gave me a copy of *The One-Minute Manager.* It contained some good points, but I flunked one-minutism flat. Maybe college faculty are different, at least certain departments. One minute seldom got us past rolling eyes to the point, much less through it. One hour was more like par. I did make an effort to deter precipitous abuse by putting a coffee cup hospitably into visitors' hands. Occasionally I wondered if just a little sedative in the coffee might help.

But while it's one natural role of the Dean to be a lightning rod, which leads to headaches and burned feet, I found the job provides lots of little opportunities to nudge the college in directions that seem constructive. Though these sometimes had their associated headaches too, the opportunities far outweighed the routine occupational aggravations. Especially in retrospect they provide real satisfaction. In the following pages I want to concentrate on a few of the salient concerns that I identify with the latter half of the Riley years and which occupied me in the Dean's office.

A DIVERSE WORLD AND A MORE DIVERSE COLLEGE

Ethnicity and Gender. When I came to CC in 1963, I think there were four female members of the regular faculty and every professor was white. We maintained the student body at a 60/40% male/female ratio by policy. We could count the occasional ethnic minority students on one hand. Since World War II we had become a relatively expensive place, and the

socio-economic stratum of the student body had narrowed. Professors
Fred Sondermann and Tom Brandt and the Hungarian Revolution had
briefly raised our attention beyond a parochial horizon, and had leavened
the student body with a few foreign students and a "Summer Crossroads"
that brought in others for a week. But we were still mostly a WASP, mid-
dle-class, regional school.

In 1968, a year of national turmoil and self-criticism, Physics Professor
Will Wright got up in a faculty meeting and said we ought to change. The
world was different and our responsibility as a liberal arts college was different too. He personally canvassed the faculty and asked us each to start
recognizing that responsibility in a small way by pledging regular financial
support to a minority-student scholarship fund. That was one small symbol of our growing acceptance of a changed world and changed responsibility for a college that wanted a national constituency rather than local.
Looking back, by 1987 we'd come quite a distance in twenty years. But
looking out at the world, it didn't seem as though we'd moved that far.
Even ten years later, we're still a long way from where we'd like to be. But
making the college reflect the multi-cultural world became a high priority
in the 1980s, and perhaps the most enduring commitment of my years in
the administration.

Gresham Riley was the essential impulse. There was never any doubt
of Gresham's aim to diversify the student body and the faculty and staff
by gender, geography, socio-economic status, race and ethnicity. He felt
that was important not so much as a moral responsibility to those who had
not been part of CC in the past but to enrich the college community for
all of us; to bring the contemporary currents and issues of our society into
the center of CC education by gradually changing the people who composed the college. CC's continued progress depended on more variety. As
president, Gresham Riley gave a clear leadership voice to this vision.

My own part of the effort concentrated on the faculty and curriculum
and began by moving ahead on lines already established by Glenn Brooks.
We believed it was educationally desirable to broaden our academic conversation by introducing the perspectives of women and ethnic minorities,
out of their own experience, on the traditional questions of the liberal arts.
Could we serve this vision without short-changing our rich traditional

canon and without reverse discrimination against white males? Could we keep our balance as these sensitive issues engaged us in affirmative action debates and in the practical challenges of making our policies real?

When we got the chance to hire a new faculty member, being a woman or member of a minority group would be counted an asset among one's other qualifications for a position. Departments, pushed by the zeal of the Women's Concerns and Minority Concerns committees, were required to make a special effort to bring minority applicants into the pool. A good faith effort to do this, based on widespread support for the college policy, was evident. But the constraints of departmental curricular needs together with the painfully small numbers of new minority Ph.D's in many academic fields made it clear that wouldn't be enough to change our faculty's ethnic composition dramatically or soon. Better gender balance was more readily attainable. American graduate schools in the 1980s were beginning to produce almost as many highly qualified women as men, and the wretched job-market for new Ph.D's often gave the college its choice among the top tier of large applicant pools. But there were very few ethnic minority candidates among them.

CC faced other sources of frustration. Ironically, as some dimensions of our effort to diversify were successful (e.g., our attraction of more Chicano students and female faculty), the disappointing performance of other dimensions (e.g., our difficulty attracting African American students and faculty) became the basis for rancor and mistrust. Were we really trying hard enough? As the college community became in fact more diverse, our new internal constituencies spoke louder, calling for more. African American and Native American and Asian American groups compared their achievements unfavorably. Other old and new interests of the college worried that "diversity" might obscure their own legitimate priorities for limited college resources. We learned that a more diverse community implied more, often discordant, visions of institutional priorities, that competition and conflict challenged the common norms that had made a more monolithic community harmonious. It was easier to agree in the abstract that diversity would enrich our community than to really put under question comfortable old verities. We were a college microcosm of pluralism issues that students of American politics recognize throughout the life of the Republic, going back at least to the constitutional debates of Federalists and anti-Federalists.

In the departments and the dean's office our daily problems were more concrete—how to find and attract these people we wanted: paragons of appropriate disciplinary erudition, with an aptitude plus appetite for teaching undergraduates in the distinctive conditions of the Block Plan, for whom living in Colorado Springs would be agreeable, but who could bring distinctive gender, cultural and ethnic diversity to our college?

To recruit imaginatively, to balance desired qualities, to foresee on-the-job development of new scholars, to communicate fully and fairly to applicants, and to reconcile our different evaluations and choose—all these tasks placed a heavy burden on departments, significant financial costs and time obligations on faculty department chairs and faculty committees and administrative offices. We were all aware of the truism that faculty hiring is close to the heart of the college enterprise. Where faculty collectively control evolution of the curriculum, each year's new hires will largely define the ethos of the college ten years down the road. Mistaken hiring decisions come back to haunt us all. Firing is painful business on both sides and, more importantly, takes a toll on collegiality. In the 1980s and 1990s that toll has been amplified by the prevalence of our society's changing legal norms and the prospect of litigious recourse by every disappointed party.

Nothing would really prevent a college from avoiding many of these difficult challenges by simply seeking to clone itself for the future—but the faculty and administration solidly agreed that to do so would abdicate our educational integrity. Thus we took sustenance from slow progress in pursuit of CC's vision. But the successes came mixed with disappointments. Despite good-faith effort, by 1992 we had still not yet raised the proportion of regular minority faculty as high as 10%. A few special successes, as when without yielding to a bidding war we made appointments in direct competition with UCLA or the University of Minnesota, encouraged us to think that we could offer satisfying opportunities to the diverse faculty we sought.

One of our best choices along the bumpy way to ethnic diversity at CC was a program for appointing "minority scholars in residence." I think the idea first emerged at Swarthmore. We heard about it in 1988 and President Riley decided we should give it a try. Participating liberal arts colleges would invite advanced minority graduate students or new Ph.D's to apply for a one-year position, compensated at the level of a full-time junior faculty appointment. The candidate would teach one or two courses, participate in the life of the college, and have the rest of the time free to complete a dissertation or get started on post-doctoral scholarly development. A centralized application process would distribute a list of candidates by field and their resumes. Colleges could contact and consider interested applicants in a timely fashion. The idea was to give them both a leg up on their careers and a chance to try out professional life in a liberal arts environment—often an unfamiliar sort of place. No subsequent obligation was created for either the college or the scholar, but we hoped that occasionally an opportunity for a regular appointment might emerge, that the scholar might be attracted to apply for it and that the fit might be a felicitous one on both sides. We were among about twenty colleges that immediately committed resources to the program. The lively presence of these young scholars on our campus has enriched the college dialogue. Over the past decade the program has also been our most productive source of regular minority faculty appointments, a bright spot where the cards often seemed stacked heavily against us. In recent years the college has increased its commitment from one to two and now three such appointments each year.

A student-oriented parallel to "minority scholars in residence" is a summer program called "minority students and academic careers," coordinated and partially funded through our consortium, the Associated Colleges of the Midwest. In the late 1980s the college began nominating two or three mature minority students for a summer of research supervised by a CC faculty mentor. Students wishing to explore academic life as a potential career may thus immerse themselves in the sort of environment graduate study and the profession would offer. Twice the group goes to Chicago for meetings to share their work with counterparts from other participating schools and with minority faculty and graduate school role models. A modest stipend makes devoting a summer to the program instead of working a summer job financially feasible. Coordinated by

Associate Dean Victor Nelson-Cisneros, the program over the past decade has helped steer a capable stream of CC minority graduates into the slim pipeline that leads to greater diversity of faculty candidates for all schools a few years later. It was gratifying to have Min Min Lo, one of our own earlier student participants come back to teach at the college as a minority scholar in residence during 1997–98.

Visiting faculty partly compensated for our difficulty appointing minority scholars to regular positions here. The flexibility of the Block Plan for accommodating short term visitors has permitted us to take advantage of people who can spare us a month to a semester but not a year. Unfamiliarity with a strange teaching format challenges visitors, and frequent comings and goings create a logistical burden. Lack of continuity sometimes frustrates students and colleagues. But block visitors enrich the curriculum and the community greatly. As we look back at lists of visiting faculty in the 1980s, we find many who brought us racial and ethnic diversity and infused those perspectives into the curriculum.

Another approach to ethnic diversity came through taking advantage of our geographical location at the gateway of the American southwest, close to the confluence of three cultural heritages: Anglo, Native American and Mexican American. In the 1970s English Professor Joe Gordon pioneered interdisciplinary area studies at the college. He pushed and scrambled after foundation and government support for a program that would combine teaching and research opportunities. It aimed to attract, among others, minority students and minority faculty, because we could offer something important to their interests and identity that others could not.

In the early 1980s the Aspen Institute gave up its venture to establish a conference center at Baca Grande, which looks southwest from the foothills where the Sangre de Cristo mountains descend to the San Luis Valley. Would CC be interested? That brought us an opportunity to acquire a college field station at reasonable cost. With Gresham Riley's enthusiasm and the decisive financial support of Trustees Jerry McHugh and Edith Harper and the El Pomar Foundation, the Baca Campus, under stewardship of Joe Gordon's Southwest Studies Program became a major college asset, a visible commitment to our place in the southwest and to ethnic diversity.

It was inevitable that some minority faculty appointments would not work out for the long run. As with all jobs, individuals' expectations are sometimes disappointed, or departments' hopes turn out to be ill-founded. Sometimes outside factors of personal life collide with college roles. When minority faculty left the college, we felt an especially acute sense of regret, and tried to figure out what we should have done differently. I found myself very depressed when in my first year as Dean I concluded I should recommend denial of tenure in the case of an African American woman. We scrutinized the shortcomings of the collegial environment we created for minority faculty, as well as the standards and procedures by which the college evaluates faculty performance. We asked ourselves repeatedly whether we sought ethnic diversity in order to question orthodox majority outlooks, or whether, even subconsciously, we used orthodoxy as our yardstick and wanted minority views and priorities to conform and "fit in." Were traditional "standards" a hypocritical retreat from accepting unfamiliar and uncomfortable differences?

Much of the time what we hold in common, together with the open forum of reasoned conversation within our commitment to academic freedom, allows us to accommodate differences fairly and grow in the process. But old difficulties of transcending political ideology, such as those the college weathered successfully in the McCarthy era, were symptomatic of the yet greater difficulties we have confronted in making real the rhetorical commitment to cherishing ethnic diversity. Alternative labels of rudderless "political correctness" or narrow-minded "conservative bias" or just complacency have sometimes reflected internal or external impatience. But they trivialize the institutional pursuit of principled choices, in an environment aggravated by suspicions lodged deeply in American social history.

Our commitment to redress the imbalance of gender has proven less tortuous. During the 1980s, the regular faculty changed from less than 20% women to over 30%, and the momentum has continued to move us toward a rough parity. Most importantly, the strong candidate pools of young female scholars have made hiring easier. While the effort has occasionally raised ideological differences, the challenges for the most part have been to accommodate the college to new support requirements for family life. Establishing a new child-care center on campus and providing a maternal leave program as an integral part of personnel benefits were highly successful innovations of the 1980s that now we can't imagine doing without. The days when there was an essentially male faculty and a "faculty wives' club" to support social life seem quaint, but they are not that far behind us. We are proud now of a thriving women's studies interdisciplinary curriculum and the integration of feminist perspectives into most of the traditional departmental curricula.

Internationalization. Another important dimension of diversification has been international outreach. In the world shrunken by science and technology to a qualitatively new sort of interdependence, there can be no excuse for parochialism in a first-rate education. Broadening and deepening CC's international education became a crucial part of my deanly concerns in the late 1980s and early nineties. I think of this as the cultural and geographic dimension of diversity. Whereas I personally was rather typical of a generation who thought it exciting to go abroad for the first time (to Europe in the U.S. Army) in their twenties, many CC students, like my own children, grew up with childhood experiences abroad. Most of them will pursue careers that require them to be functional outside their own country and culture. All of their lives will be globally integrated economically, socially and politically. A liberal education for the twenty-first century must reflect these realities.

Internationalization in the late 1980s had several facets: developing study-abroad opportunities for our students, recruiting and supporting foreign students, attracting international visiting faculty, encouraging international experience for current faculty, and adjusting our curriculum to include more emphasis on international issues. The case of Zimbabwe allows me to touch on several of them.

CC's Zimbabwe connection actually began in 1961, when an I.I.E. scholar from Bulawayo, Southern Rhodesia, was admitted as a student. More than twenty years later, Professor Solomon Nkiwane, who had earned his graduate degrees at Central African University in Kampala and then McGill in Montreal, returned home to independent Harare, to be professor of international relations in the University of Zimbabwe.

Through his previous years in exile, Solomon had maintained ties with his CC classmates and faculty friends and had taught several times as a visitor here. Now he became the essential link in our successful efforts to encourage an ACM program in Africa. Professor Joe Pickle took the lead for CC, organizing a 1989 Summer Session institute for a group of our students in Harare. Solomon co-directed the institute on-site. Based on the success of that experience, the ACM took on Harare as its ninth consortial semester abroad in 1990. Other CC faculty followed Joe to teach and learn through this Zimbabwe program, and each year several students have made it part of their CC education. Solomon has come to CC almost every other year to design and teach up to a semester of Africa-oriented courses in political science and history. Other faculty from Harare, notably Ambrose Moyo in Religion, have joined the exchange. At least one Zimbabwean student has studied for a year at CC And at least one of our graduates, winning a Watson graduate fellowship, spent his year studying African music in Zimbabwe.

I think of the Zimbabwe program as a paradigm of the interconnected dimensions of internationalization at CC. People and events and pathways seemed to reinforce one another to add a significant asset to the college's educational resources.

But Zimbabwe is only representative. Glenn Brooks and farsighted Trustee Edith Gaylord Harper (whose family has been associated with so many good things for Colorado College over more than a century) had recognized college neglect and national neglect of the Pacific Rim, at a time when Japan and the 'Little Tigers' were making people speak of an Asian century. I fell heir to encouraging development of an Asian-Pacific interdisciplinary program that took Joe Gordon's work with the Southwest as a model. With the crucial appointment of Tim Cheek in History and first-time ventures into teaching Chinese and Japanese languages, the college began moving far east in a way that combined our priorities for international outreach, ethnic and cultural diversity. Again, the momentum proved self-reinforcing. Through a thirty year-old sister-city relationship between Colorado Springs and Fuji-Yoshida, we cultivated ties that led to Japanese support for our new Asian Languages House at the north end of the campus. The Economics Department brought the president of

Hewlett-Packard Japan to campus in the fall of 1987 and again in 1991 to co-teach a course on "the Japanese challenge to American competitiveness." The music department hired a scholar in world music who had particular interests in Balinese gamelan. In dance, we hired an accomplished instructor from Taiwan. We used the ACM program in Hong Kong to enlarge the flow of CC students to China and concluded an agreement to send our students in Japanese to Kansai-Gaidai as an alternative to the ACM arrangement with Waseda University in Tokyo. We took advantage of the Colorado -Hunan state-to-state agreement to welcome a Chinese educational delegation from Changsha in 1985. That led to a block visitor in politics from Changsha University and a reciprocal CC faculty visit to Changsha. A trickle of Chinese students began to appear in our student body. Thus our Asian Pacific Studies program set the college on a path that has more recently branched out to include collaborative agreements and active academic exchange with Fudan University in Shanghai as well as universities in Taiwan and Korea.

The dramatic breakup of the Cold War at the end of the 1980s offered other opportunities for internationalization. One of the ironies of my administrative job was that I lost most of my chance as a Soviet specialist to teach while the world I was supposed to know something about was in convulsions. But, again thanks to an imaginative trustee of the college, Harold Price, we were able to bring our first Soviet block visitor to campus in the fall of 1990. Nina Belyaeva, a lawyer and dissident activist during the decline of the Soviet system, brought an energetic style and strong opinions to her task of co-teaching Soviet politics with me. At that time it was novel indeed to be able to discuss the lingering appeals of Josef Stalin with a woman across the classroom who could explain that her grandmother had been a staunch Stalinist to her dying day despite having lost family members to the GULag. It quickly became clear that Nina would more than fill up any classtime during which I was diverted to deanly emergencies. My only administrative concern about her visit was the unanticipated fact that she arrived on campus eight months pregnant, eager that her second child should be born in the United States. Fortunately baby Inga waited until after final exams to make her debut as an American citizen. In subsequent years Nina has returned to the college several times to help students understand the travails of the new Russia.

During the 1990–91 academic year former dean Glenn Brooks and aggressive internationalist Walt Hecox in Economics chaired a task force of students, faculty and administrators to take stock of our evolving international programs and to propose a set of guidelines for their orderly development in the 1990s. The faculty adopted their thorough report. Joe Pickle became faculty director of international programs with the support of a full-time administrative office. The stage was set for a new surge of international outreach under the inspiration and with the strong encouragement of President Kathryn Mohrman and Dean Tim Fuller.

Interdisciplinary Programs. Reflecting on our efforts to diversify the college has led me to mention several interdisciplinary programs: Southwest Studies, Women's Studies and Asian-Pacific Studies. These were a curricular consequence of our international outreach and embrace of ethnic and cultural diversity in liberal learning. During the late 1980s and early 1990s the number of interdisciplinary and cross-listed courses grew to between 15% and 20% of the college curriculum. An emphasis on ethnicity, gender and other cultures raised topics and issues that crossed traditional department lines and accounted for a major portion of these disciplinary hybrids.

I take my own field of comparative and international politics as an example. The end of the Cold war brought a sense of unexpected relief from an international environment dominated for half a century by the polarized East-West axis anchored in thermonuclear stalemate. But it also accelerated an uncertain new configuration: an as yet dimly perceived world of much greater complexity. The participants and issues that composed international relations multiplied. The field no longer seemed pre-empted by interstate diplomacy resting upon levels of military threat. The frontiers of nation-states appeared to recede relatively in face of vastly increased people-to-people interchange, instant communications and an increased role of non-governmental organizations. The transnational corporation and supranational and regional organizations supplemented and encroached on the traditionally defined world of nation-states. The issues of commercial and financial interdependence, immigration, hunger, environmental degradation, economic inequality, ethnic and religious conflict, epidemic disease, nuclear proliferation, and terrorism swept across the artificial lines of national frontiers. More and more these were the issues that concerned students when they thought beyond local concerns. The challenges could be addressed through any number of the traditional disciplines which had historically demarcated the administrative divisions of the college. No single department, such as political science, could claim the field. When I came to the department in 1963, we taught two comparative courses: "modern democracies" and "modern dictatorships"—big good guys and big bad guys of the northern hemisphere—reflecting the history of the past generation. Today we've expanded, but comparisons of literature or religion might throw as much light on the intractable conflicts of the Balkans or Levant or the prospects for democratic values in post-Soviet Central Asia as conventional political science. Environmental chemistry, economics, sociology or anthropology might explain more about the socio-economic dynamics of Kazakhstan or the southern Sahara.

One of the inherent advantages of the small liberal arts college is its potential to resist the heavy hand of segmented knowledge prescribed by the German university system, enthusiastically imported to the United States in the late nineteenth century and superimposed on the New England college model from which we descended. We are less bound to the specialization of knowledge. "General Studies" has served as a reservoir not only for broad foundation courses but for focused inquiries such as the long-standing "Freedom and Authority" seminar. For thirty years the college has been a major participant in the consortial interdisciplinary semesters abroad organized through the ACM and has added its own, predominantly language-driven semesters abroad. The Block Plan adds special flexibility. Common faculty interests and common student concerns invite cross-disciplinary contamination and co-taught courses united by the problem rather than an inherited classification of knowledge. Thus interdisciplinary or, more accurately, multidisciplinary collaborations to address interdisciplinary problems have blossomed.

Interdisciplinarity is certainly not limited to the issues of ethnic diversity, gender and international outreach that absorbed the college in the late

1980s and early 1990s. Biochemistry, neuroscience, and especially environmental science were already becoming major contenders too. But multicul-
tural/international diversity issues found the vehicle of interdisciplinary
programs particularly apt. Thus to the Southwest Studies, Asian-Pacific
Studies, and Women's Studies trio, American Ethnic Studies and North
American Studies were added. Although a substantial number of new
courses appeared in these programs, many existing courses embraced new
materials and methods and were cross-listed for credit and often co-taught.
New sequences increased the popularity of interdisciplinary majors.

Such programs made sense intellectually, but they also attracted faculty energy and inevitably competed with the traditional disciplines and
their departmental administrative structures for the time of faculty, scarce
college resources and the attention of students. Departments countered
with the powerful observation that effective interdisciplinary inquiry must
rest on the disciplinary tools only the traditional departments could provide. Enthusiasm for new interdisciplinary topics could dissipate faculty
energy and short-change undergraduates on the fundamental skills they
need. Thus came more headaches for deans and wrangles for faculty
committees. But such tensions remain consequences of and catalysts for
constructive innovation, indicative of vital growth and perennial reshaping of the curriculum.

CIVILITY AND A CULTURE OF LEARNING

In the turbulent late 1960s and early 1970s Colorado College felt its share
of the waves of social protest which accompanied the nation's loss of
post-World War II innocence. Civil rights zeal followed by disillusion, tun-
ing in, lighting up and dropping out, the Kennedys and King assassina-
tions, summers of rage, Watts, Black Panthers and the Weather
Underground, the Free Speech movement, the long agony of Vietnam,
the Chicago Convention, Tet, Kent State and bombing Cambodia—a
dismaying decade of convulsions buffeted American society and tested
the validity of our institutions. But on the college campus here, unlike
many others, the rallies and protests and anger seldom seriously divided
students, faculty and administration from one another. It was arguably
Lew Worner's greatest gift to his college to transcend passions of the mo-

ment through his unchallengeable personal integrity and sense of humane decency, and to hold the college community together. Other schools suffered long-lasting scars; CC got the Block Plan.

But a college that cherishes diversity, takes the First Amendment seriously and welcomes into its vision of liberal learning the full range of social experience and cultural variety risks becoming a microcosm of the 'clash of civilizations.' A college which teaches the moral obligation of engaged citizenship and takes on the challenges of a global society for academic inquiry assures a discourse that will push the envelope of academic civility. Yet that envelope is also vital to its mission. In the late 1980s we pushed the envelope over the issue of Apartheid South Africa.

One tense moment of my tenure as Dean of Colorado College came about noon on March 11, 1988. A group of some fifty CC student protesters walked over me and my college security and administrative colleagues, demonstrating their impatience and anger before the College Board of Trustees. College investment in companies that did business in Apartheid South Africa was the issue. I had been talking with the leaders of the group at the head of a stairway in Armstrong Hall, trying to persuade them to go back down the stairs and conduct the protest without disrupting a meeting of the Board. Beyond the boardroom door, the trustees were deliberating over lunch, during their regular quarterly business session for shaping the college budget, approving personnel actions, setting tuition and similar matters. But out of hearing range as well as out of patience, the student group at the bottom of the stairs pressed upward, and the momentum pushed the rest on over us. Discussion became impossible. No one could hear, and soon no one was listening either. The college legal adviser and the director of security shared my fate. I guess we represented academic authority, the rule of law and the police power of our community respectively. None of the three was working. The first two had broken down, and we weren't about to invoke the third. We were apprehensive, and I think the student leaders were too, about what was happening at that moment to the fabric of our community. Civility failed. Inside the boardroom, I'm sure the trustees were a bit uncertain too.

As it turned out, nothing very dramatic or newsworthy occurred. There was just enough time before the wave surged up the stairs to help

a couple of frail and elderly members of the Board to the nearby elevator. The rest of the Board followed and made their way quietly to another
part of the building. A lot of people were angry, but only feelings were
hurt; nothing material was torn up. That was lucky. One could imagine a
much messier scenario. By the time the students occupied the premises,
there were no longer trustees to confront and not much more to do. We
were all conscious of being members of the same college after all. Across
the lines of controversy many of us knew one another quite well. We were
normally friendly and even sympathetic to each other's positions. I remember reflecting that a couple of the students storming my puny barri-
cade had dined congenially with my family at home earlier that week.
Armstrong Hall did not readily fit the category of the Bastille and the
Winter Palace.

Institutional authority, in the persons of the President and Chairman
of the Board, announced a modified policy applicable to South Africa the
following day. The provisions included consideration of a selective divestment procedure. That only disappointed most of the protesters, but it restored a measure of civility to the broken discourse on the issues. In retrospect, I realized I had been pretty ineffectual in my own effort to preserve
that discourse; it was not one of my finer administrative hours. I also realized how fragile the fabric of civility is, though fundamental to a college.
After two years of conversation and argument, we had come to the line
where reasoned debate yields to push and shove. The episode illuminated
for me how the dual commitments to teach moral responsibility and active
citizenship, and to maintain an open forum for reason, could collide in
such a way that good college citizens might find themselves in a destructive
confrontation well beyond the bounds of academic dialogue.

The college had a long engagement with the issues precipitated by
South African Apartheid. In 1965 a campus group expressed outraged
disagreement when a cultural attaché from the South African embassy in
Washington defended apartheid in a campus lecture. But not until the
mid–1980s did campus concern over South Africa become acute,
prompted by moral affront and political opposition to U.S. policies, which
seemed to abet a regime whose practices epitomized racial prejudice, exploitation and inhumanity. Several South African students at CC, one re-

sult of the conscious effort to diversify and internationalize our own community, helped bring the issue home. Apartheid in South Africa echoed racial discrimination and cultural intolerance in the U.S., in Colorado Springs, and in ourselves too. Many believed that we as an institution were implicated in support for apartheid through our endowment investment policies, and that apartheid was a symbol of race's legacy in our community. This perception made divestment an impassioned issue at CC as it did on campuses throughout the country.

The issue raised moral, political and constitutional questions. If liberal learning finds apartheid repugnant to its own core values, what should the college do about it? Should the college take a moral stand by condemning apartheid? Should it act politically to back up its words? If so, how should the college evaluate its political options? Who should speak for the college in such matters? How should such decisions be taken?

The initial stance of the college might be summarized thus: The college is foreclosed legally and by our educational mission from partisan political activity as an institution. We foster responsible intellectual investigation of all issues, leading individuals to make personal choices and commitments pursuant to those investigations. We foster citizenship, meaning responsible individual initiative to act politically on behalf of social justice. The spirit of John Stuart Mill hovers. But inherent in fulfilling our role is an obligation of *institutional* neutrality toward the political choices our members may freely make for themselves. Therefore, the college will endeavor to avoid politicization as an institution and maintain a nonpartisan forum, while encouraging independent political action by its members. Addressing South Africa, it seemed to follow that divestment would be a partisan choice, not the only reasonable political choice to oppose apartheid. Another might be "constructive engagement" as followed regarding the Soviet Union and later China. Opposition to divestment should not be equated with support of apartheid in South Africa. Furthermore, it was the fiduciary responsibility of the trustees of the college, pursuant to its charter, to invest college endowment funds prudently within the scope of the laws of the state and the United States. That responsibility could not be delegated to others. Accordingly, while recognizing the moral abhorrence members of the college felt toward apartheid, the trustees would not use college investments as a political instrument or yield to political pressure within the college to guide investment choices.

But this conventional reconciliation of the conflict of values came under intense scrutiny. Some contrary arguments attracted support in a college community whose growing multicultural cosmopolitanism gave the issue at hand emotional urgency. Thoughtful dissidents argued that conceiving the college as an island that could aspire to insulate itself from its political context was at best naive. The college was vitally connected to the larger society, and its choices were unavoidably political choices with political consequences. The question was whether the college would act politically in accord with its professed beliefs or not. Investment choices implied approval of companies in which one invested. To profit financially even indirectly from the exploitation of Black labor in South Africa and to contribute to the economic health of a regime that perpetrated apartheid were unconscionable choices. The trustees' decision implicated all the members of the college without their consent, in fact against the manifest views of a majority of the members of the college. Good college citizens ought to take responsibility and act on their convictions.

The disagreements approached an impasse in 1988, despite efforts to address the issues through a series of visiting speakers representing widely divergent interests and viewpoints on South African political economy and the likely consequences of alternative policies. Campus demonstrations and protests to dramatize opposition to continued holdings in four companies continued through the academic year. After the confrontation of March 1988, the Board established a committee representing all college constituencies, which was charged to hear and evaluate accusations against the activity of specific companies doing business in South Africa. The committee would bring recommendations to the trustees, who would consider the evidence and decide whether selective divestment was called for. In 1990, the committee recommended divestment from three companies, but the Board found the evidence unpersuasive.

Committee procedures grind slowly. By then the world had turned over, and South Africa was in a state of rapid transformation. Under multiple external and internal pressures, of which divestment might arguably be counted as one factor, the regime extended some political rights to

Black South Africans. Nelson Mandela was released from prison after twenty-seven years, and a year later was elected president. Elsewhere the Berlin Wall had fallen and the Cold War was ending. The most urgent international crisis for the United States appeared to be in the Persian Gulf. South African divestment lost its political relevance and its priority on campus as elsewhere. Environmental contamination, health threats from tobacco, the dangers of nuclear power generation, human rights in China and Northern Ireland—a host of other causes diffused the passions previously focused on South African investments. Eight years later the college committee continues, now broadened to a Committee on Socially Responsible Investment, but it doesn't attract much passion.

What may one say about the cluster of values that collided in the college over South Africa a decade ago? Did it reflect a dilemma that remains with us, though out of the current limelight? Does it suggest any movement away from the earlier orthodoxy by which the college had sought to reconcile the conflicts? I would propose that it allows us some conclusions and also leaves us with enduring issues on which reasonable people may and most likely will continue to disagree.

First, the establishment of a committee on socially responsible investment recognized that the college indeed cannot avoid the political consequences of its interdependence with the society that supports it. There is no escape from choices, and this case shows that those choices may often affect the core values and integrity of the college. The protesters made that point clear. But the case also showed the slippery slope of political engagement and the possibility that unrestrained politicization of the college could abridge the academic freedom that restraint from direct political action as an institution might preserve. While political issues invite resolution by majority rule, legal and moral issues do not yield either to majority rule or administrative fiat. It is always the academy's task to defend the opportunity of individuals "to think otherwise" without reprisal. An official position can have a chilling effect on dissidents.

The urgency South African apartheid acquired underscores the connection of the college's more culturally diverse community with issues of consequence everywhere on a shrunken globe. It invited us to recognize that our next century as a college will probably engage us with more rather than less controversy. That forecast suggested that while active citizenship and institutional impartiality may continue to be hard to reconcile, both demand our continued dedication. The all-important concomitants of tolerance, critical probity, and the habit of taking each other seriously while expecting each other to be serious—that is, the skeptical open mode of academic civility—must be protected and nourished.

SCHOLARSHIP, TEACHING AND THE EIGHT-BLOCK YEAR

The spring before Glenn Brooks and I traded offices, a long faculty debate had led to a proposal accepted by the administration and board of trustees to reduce the nine-block academic year to eight blocks. A year would be allowed for planning the transition. Thus, making preparations to implement the eight-block calendar became my most pressing curricular responsibility that first year.

It was a highly controversial change. Eight rather than nine blocks meant cutting from thirty-six to thirty-two the number available to students over four years without summer session or adjunct credits. It meant re-valuing each block to the equivalent of four rather than three and one-half semester hours' credit. The change appeared to reduce the total instruction and flexibility of scheduling available to students while tuition continued to rise. No wonder there was strong objection from many student leaders. Less anticipated was vehement alumni protest from active groups around the country. When CC adopted the radical Block Plan in 1970, few alumni had been consulted and fewer expressed themselves one way or another. But seventeen years later we had produced an actively engaged, militantly possessive cohort of Block Plan veterans who took a dim view of "tampering." Did the faculty just want to get paid more for teaching less?

What was behind the eight-block year and what were its implications for the quality of education at Colorado College? It was primarily an effort to redress the balance between faculty teaching and faculty scholarly growth. The college wanted to reduce the longer-than-average academic year and align the class time of CC students more closely with those of comparable schools. It also hoped to reintroduce the popular all-college symposia in January and to reduce the tendency of students to take a block off. But at the heart of the matter was a long-standing concern on the part of conscientious faculty that the intense teaching demanded by the block's immersion character led them to "spend intellectual capital," and neglect the continuing scholarly development that would make them better teachers ten years down the road.

The practical tasks of shrinking and combining curricular offerings to fit a schedule eight-ninths as long required a careful self-assessment in each department. We had to protect General Studies and interdisciplinary offerings against disproportionate reductions. We needed to estimate the effect on student choices in order to avoid bottlenecks in student majors owing to oversubscribed prerequisite classes. We wanted to retain the small class size limits which were a highly valued asset of the block plan, and we neither wanted nor could afford to increase the size of the regular faculty significantly. Department chairs played a critical role in the preparations, and we undertook a mock pre-registration among reluctant students to test and refine our estimates. But Registrar Al Johnson absorbed most of the logistical burden of the change-over. All agreed that after two years of trial, a full good-faith reassessment of the change would be necessary.

The transition went more smoothly than we sometimes feared. Gresham Riley and I survived skeptical inquisition on the alumni circuit and the indignation of Catalyst op-ed writers. The collaborative two-year review panel chaired by Tim Fuller and Max Taylor led to significant improvements, including a voluntary half-block for topical short courses in January and one tuition-free summer session block available to each student. Ten years later, after a comprehensive review of the block plan itself, few in any college constituency would advise returning to the nine block model. But the underlying question of the best balance between faculty teaching and personal scholarship remains lively.

CC is not a university, which would bear the societal role of creating new knowledge as well as teaching undergraduate and graduate students in a full range of specialized fields of academic inquiry. Rather, as a liberal arts college, our prime mission is to educate undergraduates to live examined lives enriched by the traditions of learning to which our institution is heir and steward. The popular view sometimes oversimplifies that distinction by suggesting that research and other forms of personal scholarship are an unnecessary or inappropriate college faculty conceit which distracts from their real responsibility to teach. The late 1980s brought such prejudice to a head, under pressure both from rapidly increasing tuition charges and widespread popular suspicion of the allegedly radical or effete preoccupations of academia. Colorado College was not spared the fall-out.

Internally, pressures were very nearly the opposite. With cutbacks in higher educational funding deepening across the country (in part fueled by popular disaffection), relatively few openings for academically oriented new Ph.D.'s have been available for over a decade and a half. A buyers' market for colleges like CC fortunately accompanies this generally deplorable drought. Thus our normal faculty renewal has been able to bring in young scholars from the best graduate schools who in earlier times might have preferred the research emphasis of university positions, following the models provided by their graduate mentors. Happily, in most cases they have also come to us with both the aptitude and appetite for intense teaching. The block plan makes it clear very quickly that a new professor must relish steady interchange with undergraduates in order to be happy here. The chief consequence of our institutionally fortuitous hiring bounty has been to compose our faculty increasingly of able teachers who also set high self-expectations of personal scholarly activity. They set their own priority on research *per se*, as well as on research in the service of continued growth as teachers. And they are impatient with the prospect of falling behind their fields in a professional environment outside the college of ever-greater specialization.

As Dean, I regularly told candidates for faculty positions that they might anticipate spending up to half again as much time with their students on the block plan at CC as at a comparable liberal arts college on a conventional schedule. At other liberal arts colleges, of course, they would still be spending considerably more time with undergraduates than they would in research university positions. But the pressure of effective full-time teaching in the nine-block year while maintaining scholarly development at a high level was growing. Faculty were not leaving CC in significant numbers, but that may have had more to do with the absence of available jobs. Faculty morale stayed remarkably high, because working conditions generally were rewarding, but more and more people had begun talking about "burn-out." The vitality of the block plan format was imperiled and required adjusting the balance.

Throughout the 1980s, the college steadily increased financial support for faculty scholarship. Support for participation at professional conferences and a strong sabbatical leave program had long standing claims, but in the 1980s the college began to allocate more money through divisional research and development committees for specific scholarly projects. President Riley's discretionary funds for institutional improvement, including a Hewlett Foundation grant, sustained scholarly collaboration with colleagues elsewhere. A Mellon Foundation grant's provision for blocks relieved from teaching for scholarly projects was extended indefinitely through in-house funding. The Development Office began to provide assistance to individual faculty to find and apply for external grants. Overall, I calculated that by 1992 about $500,000 a year was supporting faculty scholarship.

Again in this area of college policy, Gresham Riley's leadership was decisive. He felt strongly that the principle of faculty scholarship "in the service of teaching" distinguished top-tier liberal arts institutions from mediocre schools. That difference between the scholarship appropriate to a liberal arts college and that of the research university was an elusive one which led to frequent misunderstandings and many a common-room rumor. When interviewing job candidates together with me, Gresham customarily tried to put the candidate at ease by opening with a question about his or her dissertation research. Often that would continue into discussion about where the research might lead in the candidate's future plans. When it came my turn, I would guide the conversation to teaching interests and aspirations. The rumor got back to us after awhile that "All Riley cares about is research, and all Finley cares about is teaching." We tried to reverse roles, but the impression persisted.

Actually we never disagreed on the matter as far as I know. It's just that "scholarship in the service of teaching" is open to various interpretations. In our minds it embraced not only the sort of scholarship that has immediate translation into the classroom. It also included the visible habit of active intellectual engagement with an academic field. This kind of scholarship conveys to the student by example what it means to ask and answer significant questions that build on prior academic inquiries in a systematic, self-critical way, or to take chances by creative pursuit of artistic media. Departments and individuals evaluate such scholarship by subtly different measures, which vary across the college and change incrementally with time. Like the quality of good teaching, the quality of scholarship is impossible to pin down finally in black and white, despite our dutiful efforts to be as clear and consistent as possible about equitable standards and objective procedures.

Overall, the 1980s did elevate the expectations of active scholarly engagement versus passive disciplinary competence. The direction of change was controversial. Some felt it might hazard accepting the image of the college as a "mini-university" or "research college" to the detriment of our primary mission. Others felt it was the necessary foundation for attaining the national eminence in American education we desired. Trying to recognize the validity of both counsels and practice a progressive balance occupied many of my deanly hours. But in my view, the eight-block year as implemented was one essential step to improve the quality of education at Colorado College.

CONCLUSION

As the college takes note of its 125th anniversary and I have the perspective to look back on my decanal interlude, I am inclined to emphasize a Burkeian sense of connection between institutional past, present and future. Like the American Supreme Court, the college conserves and conveys its own past and the cultural tradition it represents. But it also responds to all its constituencies and is constantly being reshaped by its current students and faculty. It must be open to innovation, sometimes radical innovation, to do its traditional job in new circumstances that invite new emphases. It describes itself collectively in new ways that make old catalogs and the vocabulary of old debates seem both quaint and very familiar.

The late 1980s and early 1990s were full of consequential changes for Colorado College. I might have addressed the dramatic change of computer integration into all the administrative and teaching activities of the college. Or the completion of a $50 million capital campaign that raised college development to a new level and allowed us to think bigger and to open the Barnes Science Center among other projects. Or the quantum jump in institutional financial aid as support for the need-blind admission policy we maintained proudly against severe obstacles. Or the timely acquisition of three adjacent city blocks of land to provide for later campus expansion east of Nevada Avenue. Instead, for my contribution to this collaborative volume, I have chosen to review some topics closest to my own assignments and highest priorities.

Each of my topics had a long CC prologue: our institutional response to socio-cultural difference, our responsibility to educate students effectively for life in a changing world, our mode of discourse appropriate to liberal learning, our responsibility to know something and teach it well. Each of these will also have a significant bearing on the college's future as it contemplates the new environment of the next century.

Timothy Fuller
Dean of the College and
Professor of Political Science

CHAPTER 7

My Unrehearsed
Intellectual Adventure

Timothy Fuller
Dean of the College and
Professor of Political Science

Kalah and I arrived in Colorado Springs in late August 1965, having driven from Baltimore and Johns Hopkins with brief stops to visit families in Chicago and Waterloo, Iowa. We stopped for lunch at Ruth's Oven downtown on Tejon Street, and I then called Doug Mertz, Chair of Political Science, to let him know we were here. He advised me to get in touch with Evaline McNary who was in charge of college housing, and he invited us for dinner that evening at his house, where we were to enjoy a fine meal and the company of Doug and his wife, Charlotte.

Evaline McNary was anticipating our arrival, and she offered us the first floor of the house at 14 East San Rafael—it had been made into a very spacious apartment. Professor Ayala of the Romance Languages Department lived on the second floor with his wife and son. The house is now called Mierow House, and houses the Education Department. We lived there for two years before buying the house in the North End on San Miguel Street where we have lived since 1967.

I grew up in Chicago and went east to school. I knew very little about anything west of the Mississippi, including Colorado College. I began to learn about the college when, in 1964, Jean Torcom, a recent graduate of CC, arrived at Hopkins to begin her graduate studies in American politics. She has since gone on to a successful career as a professor of political science in California. Her first year in Baltimore was my last and I was beginning to look around for teaching positions. She told me something of the college, and of her teacher, Glenn Brooks, of whom I had already heard much. He had completed his doctorate at Hopkins and come to CC to teach in 1960. When I arrived in Baltimore in 1961 he was described to us newcomers as the model graduate student. In 1964, Glenn returned to Hopkins to see his former teacher, Frank Rourke, with whom he was co-authoring a book, *The Managerial Revolution in Higher Education*, which became an important contribution to the reexamination of higher education at that time, and predicted a number of the bureaucratic features that have emerged in contemporary higher education. Glenn and I met each other through the good offices of Professor Rourke, and we spent some time talking in the Hopkins Faculty Club. It must have gone well enough because Glenn later suggested to the department at CC that I should be interviewed, and thus the process began that eventually brought me to Colorado College.

I had spent my undergraduate days at Kenyon College in Ohio where I decided after my first year, to abandon premedical studies to choose political philosophy as opposed to classics or English. In those days, premedical studies were highly prescribed as is not now the case. Throughout my first year, I felt a growing tension as I spent every afternoon in lab work while others were reading philosophy, literature and the *Kenyon Review*. In my sophomore year, I abandoned dissecting my dogfish for T.S. Eliot's *Four Quartets*.

I knew from my sophomore year that I wanted to teach, and to do so in a college like Kenyon, that is, in a traditional, undergraduate, liberal arts college. Some of my graduate school professors urged me to seek a post in a research university, but I was determined to go in a different direction, and I got much support from one Hopkins professor, Robert W. Tucker. I had several interviews for jobs in the winter and spring of 1965, but I was drawn almost instantly to CC upon my arrival for my interview in January.

I remember in particular my interview with Dean Ken Curran who was Acting President because President Worner was on sabbatical. In the hour or so we spent together, Dean Curran asked me virtually nothing about my specialty, leaving that to others, but rather about my fiction reading habits. As it turned out, he and I had tastes in common. We discussed, among other things, Bernard Malamud's *The Natural*, and C. P. Snow's *Strangers and Brothers* series of novels about the life of the intelligentsia in twentieth century Britain, and, in particular *The Masters* about the politics of an Oxbridge college seeking a new master. Later, when I did meet President Worner, we began a similar, and extended, conversation about a wide range of books, fictional, philosophical and theological, which continued until Lew's death. At any rate, my experience of the college was such that I returned to Baltimore knowing that I would accept an offer from CC if I were so lucky as to get one. I did, and I accepted.

What I had found in my visit was a vibrant and ambitious college, but also a place that was obviously choosing its own path in the pursuit of liberal learning. The Political Science Department wanted to hire someone who specialized in teaching political philosophy rather than continuing to parcel out the responsibility to several different department members. Unlike some departments at other colleges I visited that year, where what was wanted was someone who could do political philosophy as a second field in addition to something else, at CC the subject was taken seriously and was at the center of the department's curriculum. Moreover, the faculty were genuinely interested in my ideas about what to teach and how to teach it. They conveyed the sense that here was an institution which would provide opportunities for young teachers and scholars to flourish and to contribute to the sustenance and renewal of the college. There was much conversation and collegiality. One was encouraged to think that forthright expression of one's views was welcome and would be respected.

It was a faculty of impressive intellectual character, recruited by the long time chairman, Doug Mertz, a graduate of the Yale Law School who taught constitutional law and had been at CC since 1948. There was Fred Sondermann, who had come, also from Yale, in 1953, and who had become a nationally recognized scholar of international relations, Glenn Brooks from Johns Hopkins in public policy and national security policy, David Finley from Stanford in Soviet and East European politics, and Rudy Gomez from the University of Colorado in American politics. Elsewhere in the college were the internationally acclaimed Glenn Gray in philosophy and Albert Seay in music, and an array of impressive younger scholars like George Drake in history, who later became dean at CC and then president of his alma mater, Grinnell. The historic character of Colorado College—a college with roots in the New England tradition but leavened by the frontier experience of the west—which combines tradition and innovation, was manifest in these scholars. Colorado College was at once both familiar and yet original.

I was also especially attracted to the students who exemplified the characteristics of the college as a whole. They were smart and ambitious, but also relaxed and informal in a way I had not experienced in the east. In my thirty-three years at CC, I have had the privilege of teaching a steady stream of extraordinary students, including a substantial number who are now embarked on successful academic careers in some of the best colleges and universities in the country, and others who have been highly successful in business and the professions, some of whom are now members of our Board of Trustees. For one whose vocation is to teach, to think, and to write, Colorado College seemed to me then, and has proven to be, truly what Michael Oakeshott in his celebrated centennial address, the Abbott Memorial Lecture of 1974, was to call "a place of learning."

When I began to teach in the fall of 1965, I brought with me several vivid images of how to teach, but they were not systematically worked out. Kenyon was characterized by, mostly, extraordinary teachers, and I knew every member of the faculty. Now it is a coeducational school of 1,400. Then it was a college of 500 male students with a faculty of about forty-five. It is hard for students and faculty today to grasp the experience of a college small enough that one inevitably would come to know every student and every faculty member by name, where one ate everyday with the whole student body in the commons, where every student residence was in sight of every other in a single quadrangle.

The curriculum was classical and, by today's standards, limited. There was, for example, no anthropology or sociology, no department of education, no art department (although there were occasional lectures in art history), there was a music program but not a music major, and no interdisciplinary majors. When I did my stint as a teaching assistant and then assistant instructor at Hopkins, even though its undergraduate college was still all men but with increasing numbers of women in the graduate programs, I entered into an obviously wider academic environment which I found very exciting.

Yet I never had regretted the situation of my undergraduate days. In its own way, it was as fine an academic experience as any I have had since, in some ways more intensely satisfying than much of what happened later, but I accepted that the college could not continue in that pattern. I realized later that I had matriculated at the end of one era for liberal arts colleges, and the start of a new one. When I came to Colorado College, I discovered an institution that had long since begun the transformation into that new era.

I do not think the shift affected my view of classroom teaching dramatically, except that I came almost immediately to enjoy teaching both men and women for the first time. If I would not trade my undergraduate experience for anything, I also have no doubt that the way we do things now is appropriate for us. For me, what is most important persists through all the historic changes in the nature of institutions of higher learning: the opening of the human spirit to its full possibilities, transcending one's time and place, not as an alternative to concern for one's time and place, but in recognition that what is important extends far beyond ourselves, and in acknowledging that we are the trustees of an inheritance which we must receive critically in order both to make it our own and then available to those who come after us. We approach the future appraising what we already understand ourselves to have been and to have become. We may regret or affirm what we understand, but we cannot start from scratch; we must use the resources we have, preserving and changing according to judgments informed by genuine knowledge, not merely by untested prejudices or opinions.

I had already begun to develop my own ideas about the contours of the history of political thought in trying to make sense out of the alternative views of Hannah Arendt, Michael Oakeshott, Leo Strauss and Eric Voegelin, and I was intent upon imitating certain practices of several of my undergraduate and graduate teachers, some of which, I quickly learned, had seemed more effective to me as a student than to the students I was now teaching. My biggest fear was that I would arrive in class each day (this was pre-block plan; I was teaching three classes with three fifty

minute class periods each, two on Monday, Wednesday, Friday and one on
Tuesday, Thursday, Saturday at 8 AM!) with too little to say. My remedy
for this was to stay up late at night composing elaborate lectures on
American government and the history of western political thought. Each
lecture had enough material for three class periods. But then in class I
somehow felt obligated to convey everything I had prepared. I later
learned from students that they said of me, "If you put your pen down for
a minute you'll lose a century."

About the middle of the second semester of my first year, I looked up
from my lecture notes at a sea of glazed student faces. I set my lecture
aside and I walked out in front of the desk and began talking informally
about my subject with the students. I am not sure what caused me suddenly to have this insight but it was right—I could indeed engage the students more effectively and conversationally with somewhat less material—and from then on I never returned to my encyclopedic practices.

In those days, graduate programs provided little or nothing to graduate students in the way of guidance on teaching, and colleges rarely did
either. I learned whatever I know about teaching by trial and error and by
testing the various ways that I had absorbed from my own undergraduate
and graduate professors. Today at CC we consider the sink or swim approach to be a dereliction of duty. We have created the Crown-Tapper
Teaching Learning Center and an elaborate program to help faculty, both
junior and senior, to become more effective in the classroom. Again, I
think this the right thing to do so long as we remember that, in the final
analysis, a professor must discover what to profess (this is not the same
thing as lecturing), to come to a considered point of view about the disci-
pline(s) he or she teaches while, at the same time, retaining openness to
the range of views in a field of study.

What enters into my thinking about teaching, having little directly to
do with any specific subjects to be taught, is a way of thinking which informs what I do as a teacher. As I see it, a college is a great conversation
of many voices. Each of us, whether student or teacher, enters an institution in the midst of a conversation that is already in progress and has been
going for a long time, ultimately going back to the ancient conversations
of teachers and students as with Socrates and his dialectical partners.

Moreover, this conversation will continue indefinitely into the future long after we have departed. Whatever we may have done in our time at the college will be absorbed into the ethos of the place and contribute, in whatever small way, to what the college will become.

Teachers are learners, eternal students, who have moved further on the path of learning than the students they teach, but who can be overtaken and should welcome that when it happens. Students arrive from high school having ingested bits and pieces of what they need to enter into the academic conversation, but there is much in respect of both substance and coherence that can only be learned by engaging the others and finding one's own voice to add to those already present.

A college is also an interval in life wherein one is granted the opportunity, uniquely, to explore the possibilities of knowing without immediate responsibility for the world and its predicaments. It is a temporary release from the "deadliness of doing," that interminable attention to the dailiness of life no one can avoid. But what is learned here also becomes a resource for making our way through life, for it teaches us that the manner in which we conduct ourselves may be more important than the momentary victories or defeats that punctuate a life. If one considers that the typical graduating student may well live another sixty years, it is not unreasonable to say that there will be plenty of time to set out to right the wrongs of the world. What is less likely is that most will ever again have the same chance to read and to think uninterruptedly, and to do so because these are simply rewarding activities in which to engage, and because, for once, no one is imposing anything else. None of this is to suggest that we should avoid civic responsibility or become indifferent to the world. Quite to the contrary. But if one has not learned the habits of detached examination, and the capacity for skepticism when everyone else is confident, a combination of realistic appraisal of and compassion for our common human condition, one will be less well suited to taking on these challenges.

The atmosphere of the college has consistently encouraged the enjoyment of such teaching and learning. Through the eras of Presidents Benezet, Worner and Riley, and continuing in the present period with President Mohrman, Colorado College has been expanding and strengthening its operation. The renaissance of the college, as it was called by faculty who had been here since the 1950s, and the optimism about the future, were evident in all of its undertakings. Those of us who arrived in the mid 1960s were the beneficiaries of what has turned out to be more than a generation of growing strength and accomplishment, destined to continue into the next century. I have always felt my great good fortune in coming here, and in choosing to stay.

At the same time, while maintaining its historic character, the college has also transposed that character in timely ways. When I started teaching in the fall of 1965, the students, and the classroom ambiance, were not much different from my own undergraduate days. Students of the 1950s are often described as apathetic or apolitical or as the "silent generation." It was, among other things, the era of McCarthyism, the cold war and nuclear deterrence, the civil rights movement, neo-orthodoxy in religion, existentialism and the Beat Generation. There was searching criticism of "the lonely crowd," "the status seekers," "the organization man," "the man in the gray flannel suit," and so on. When I look back on it, I do not think we were apathetic, but we were not overtly political or revolutionary.

Within three years of my arrival at CC in 1965, the Vietnam War transformed the scene dramatically, with long lasting effect on the situation of higher learning in virtually all colleges and universities. Between 1968 and 1972 there was widespread disruption on campuses, and there was certainly some upheaval and commotion at CC. But, by comparison to many places, the college handled the situation adroitly. Teach-ins were held, protests were made, but without disruption of classes or violence. I have always thought about this period that, as painful and full of conflict as it often was, it was, in my experience, a time when I had as intense and profound exchanges with students as I have ever had. Nor was it solely of national and international issues that we spoke, although, of course, they were central. The students I had the privilege of teaching intensified their study of all the subjects I taught, whether those subjects had obvious connections to the questions of the day or not.

The dubious legacy of that period in higher education was the politicization of colleges and universities, leading to a decline in scholarly standards, especially regarding the capacity for detached examination and reflection; the distinction between "speeches" and "lectures" was eroded. But that was not the only or the inevitable outcome. At its best, one was encouraged to reexamine the reasons for liberal arts education, and to defend the traditions of liberal learning under adverse conditions. I took this to be a great, if often painful and tiring, opportunity.

I never felt, and do not now feel, that the traditions of liberal learning were, in principle, undermined by the political upheavals surrounding us, even while I recognize that others disagree with this conclusion. Of course, they were called into question, and it was frequently asserted that studying classic works, and study as a good in itself, were rendered irrelevant by the events of the day. But what resulted from this, at least in my experience, was a genuine debate about these matters. It is a tribute to Colorado College that this was possible when, in numerous other places of learning, such debate broke down or was willfully prevented. I well remember participating with Glenn Gray and several other faculty in a teach-in held in Olin One, reflecting on and discussing with large numbers of students, Gray's book, *The Warriors*, one of the seminal philosophic reflections on war published in our time. And, in those days, I taught two courses, one called "Contemporary Conservatism," paired with a course called "Contemporary Radicalism," and courses on the doctrine of the "just war." They each attracted much attention, but from very different groups of students.

If we consider that colleges of liberal learning are the inheritors of an ancient academic tradition, going back to the time of Plato and Aristotle, we will see that institutions for teaching and learning, "places of learning," have persisted through every form of upheaval associated with human history, through the rise and fall of nations and empires. It is of the highest importance that we have the courage to philosophize and to reflect even in the midst of traumatic upheavals for which we must assume our due responsibility, for we do not live only for the present condition, but for the possibilities of the ages, and to preserve, in the midst of destruction, what future generations should never be deprived of encountering.

In the same period, the college launched a revolution of its own—in the structure of teaching and learning—by bringing into being the

Colorado College Plan, better known as the Block Plan, in 1970. Professor Robert Loevy's new history of the college provides a detailed account of the advent of the Block Plan, as does Glenn Brooks's essay elsewhere in this volume. I am grateful to have been included in the development and implementation of the Block Plan, along with Glenn Brooks, Don Shearn, George Drake and others. Like most of the "founding generation," it afforded me the opportunity, rarely enjoyed, to cooperate in creating what has turned out to be one of the few successful, genuinely innovative approaches to teaching and learning in our time.

The question always asked about the Block Plan is, How did we manage to do it? First and foremost, one must acknowledge the courage of President Lloyd E. Worner and Dean George Drake in supporting the concept fashioned by Glenn Brooks as a result of his conducting an intensive self-study of the college. The college had never been stronger than it was at the end of the 1960s, and thus, one could argue, there was hardly any incentive to tinker radically with an already highly successful program. It is true that this was a time of openness to experiment in higher education, and this, no doubt, helped. But if one surveys what was actually done by most institutions at the time, Colorado College emerges as one of a handful of institutions of higher learning that did anything that could be called memorable a generation later. I believe myself that this is a clear indication of how unusual a college we really are for our willingness to go our own way in fulfilling the historic commitment—which we did not abandon— to liberal arts education. In this sense, the answer to the question may always be somewhat mysterious. Yet the answer seems to be that there was at this moment a unique convergence of circumstances and individuals which could not have been predicted in advance, and could not be easily reproduced, although a number of colleges have since followed our lead.

The inspiration was to do what other colleges were not doing: to focus on altering the formal structure of the classroom experience, but not to tinker with its content. It was more typical then to alter the curriculum and leave the traditional structure of teaching and learning intact. We assumed that if we implemented this radically different framework for teaching and learning that the faculty would gradually alter the curriculum to make our program effective in new and unanticipated ways. This is what has happened over the nearly thirty years of the plan's operation. Many new interdisciplinary courses and programs have emerged, and continue to emerge, and there is a great deal of team teaching. With George Drake and others, I helped to create a three-block, team taught course for new students, Renaissance Culture, which continues now, twenty-five years later as an introduction to liberal arts education and which, since 1983, also has satisfied our AP:A or Western Civilization re-quirement. Other three-block, team taught courses such as Perspectives on the Western Tradition and Patterns in Nature were developed then. A fine two-block course called "The Idea of a Liberal Arts Education" was introduced, and, in my view, should now be revived for a new generation of students. A capstone course was created, "Liberal Learning and the Human Imagination," taken by seniors in the last block of their last year, taught variously by George Drake, Gilbert Johns, Will Wright and Max Taylor.

At the request of Gilbert Johns, Dean of the Summer Session during the 1970s, I invented an interdisciplinary, team taught course for Summer Start students. The idea was to provide in the summer an opportunity for students to take an interdisciplinary, team-taught course, equivalent to those mentioned above, introducing them to an integrated approach to liberal learning. This was called "The Conversation of Mankind," a phrase borrowed from Michael Oakeshott, and it included study of methodological assumptions of the humanities, social sciences and sci-ences for we thought that students should look at the assumptions of dis-ciplines and how they reached the substance of their findings, and we thought that faculty should engage themselves in such discussion about their work with each other and with their students.

At different times, historians, art historians, literature teachers and philosophers co-taught with me. Always, there was a physicist because a substantial section of the course every summer was about classical and me-dieval ideas and the change wrought by the scientific revolution, with an emphasis on Copernicus, Galileo and Newton, and its impact on modern thought. This summer institute lasted for quite a few years. In the mean-time, other team taught summer programs were added to the summer curriculum. Later, in the 1980s, I participated in founding the interdisciplinary major, Classics/History/Politics, which continues today and which has graduated outstanding students, including two of the college's Rhodes Scholars, Todd Breyfogle ('88) and Greg Criste ('98). By my estimate, I have taught with at least twenty-five different members of the CC faculty.

CC also has many other interdisciplinary programs of note such as Southwest Studies, Comparative Literature, Asian Studies, American Ethnic Studies, Women's Studies, North American Studies and Environmental Science. There are also numerous interdepartmental majors such as Neuroscience, Biochemistry, and Political Economy. In English, there are, in addition to the traditional English major, creative writing and film studies tracks. And there is more. We have reached a stage in the development of such programs requiring of us a careful appraisal of what we have done and how much further we should or can travel down this road. The installation of the Block Plan was a powerful catalyst that continues to show its effect in these ways.

Since 1992, when President Riley appointed me, I have had the honor and privilege of being Dean of the Faculty and Dean of the College. It has been a remarkable experience during which I have learned a great deal about the true complexity of an institution of liberal learning. In working with the faculty as a whole, I have come to appreciate more than I ever had how challenging and demanding it is to pursue teaching and scholarship at a high level over many years, and to do these things in the block plan context. Of course, I was familiar with this from my own experience as a teacher and scholar, but I have now come to see the wide variety of demands and the diverse forms of creative work of the faculty.

Colorado College, in enjoying a long period of sustained growth, has also become sufficiently multifaceted that one may well ask whether this traditional liberal arts college has in spirit transformed itself into a small university. We have by no means abandoned our defining mission to teach undergraduates. We are not planning to develop any graduate programs beyond our existing Master of Arts in Teaching summer program. We expect faculty to be active scholars but we have not adopted a publish or perish policy regarding tenure and promotion. Nonetheless, we have encouraged a wide variety of programmatic initiatives, and we continue to do so. As we approach a full generation of experience with the block plan, we need to reflect carefully on the implications of what we have done and are attempting to do now.

II

Here I want to remember Michael Oakeshott, a name familiar to many of my students and colleagues. I want to do so because there are two parallel tracks to my academic career, inseparable in my experience. For me, liberal learning, Colorado College and Michael Oakeshott are intertwined. I have enjoyed two academic havens, so to speak. First, is Colorado College; the other is London. I now realize that they were linked long before I could know them explicitly, but it seems to me in retrospect that, from the time I chose to go to Kenyon College, a direction was set in place, and I embarked on a path in advance of any knowledge of its destination. It was and is what Oakeshott would have called an unrehearsed intellectual adventure. I think there is nothing better, and I hope that other students in colleges like ours will be so fortunate as to have their version of the experience.

One of my goals when I came to CC was to make it an important center for political philosophy by bringing to the college the most distinguished scholars in the field. With generous support from the college, and in collaboration with other faculty, many distinguished scholars of political philosophy visited throughout the 1970s and 1980s, and do still today, among them: Hannah Arendt, Benjamin Barber, Allan Bloom, Joseph Cropsey, Richard Flathman, Michael Gillespie, Elie Kedourie, William and Shirley Letwin, Harvey Mansfield, Kenneth Minogue, Michael Oakeshott, J.G.A. Pocock, Arlene Saxonhouse, Judith Shklar, Robert W. Tucker, Eric Voegelin. Also, because of the number of our outstanding graduates who went on to study in places like Chicago, Duke, Harvard, Johns Hopkins, The London School of Economics, Stanford and Toronto, the college became well known as a seedbed for the field.

The highpoint for me was Michael Oakeshott's first visit in 1974. Oakeshott was the most remarkable man I have had the privilege of knowing. He was born in 1901 in Kent, England, and he died in 1990 at his cottage on the southern coast of England, as he was approaching ninety. He graduated from Cambridge University, thereafter becoming a life fellow of his college, Gonville and Caius, the second oldest college at Cambridge, founded in 1284. His portrait now hangs in his college as one of its most distinguished sons. From the late 1920s until 1949, interrupted by army service during World War II, he lectured on the history of political thought. After a brief time at Oxford, he became the Professor of Political Science at The London School of Economics in the Government Department, and there he remained, officially retiring in 1968, but continuing to teach until his early eighties.

Michael Oakeshott is, in my view, the most important political philosopher in Britain in the twentieth century. His preferred style of writing was the essay, and he was indeed a great essayist and stylist of the English language, in the tradition of British essay writing that goes back to Francis Bacon in the seventeenth century, and includes such names as David Hume and Edmund Burke in the eighteenth century, and Lord Macaulay and John Stuart Mill in the nineteenth century.

I first encountered Oakeshott through one of his most celebrated books. I was browsing in the Kenyon College library of a Saturday afternoon, I think in 1960, looking for nothing in particular but expecting to find something marvelous and unanticipated on the shelves. I had already committed myself to the study of political philosophy as my chosen profession, and I had recently been reading Hobbes and Locke. I came across an edition of Hobbes's *Leviathan* previously unknown to me. It was, as I later found out, the Blackwell's Political Texts edition, edited by someone named Michael Oakeshott. I opened it to Oakeshott's introduction and was captivated by what I later learned was a famous essay of interpretation among Hobbes scholars. As I read through it, I came increasingly to feel that this was what I wanted to write, and I expressed to myself the hope that someday I would be able to write an essay like Oakeshott's on Hobbes. I still hope someday to do it, but I cannot claim as yet to have achieved such a thing. Nevertheless, it seemed to me then, and now, that nothing less should be my ambition if I were to be serious about what I was setting out to do.

I went to my advisor in the Political Science Department, a remarkable man in his own right, Raymond English, himself a graduate of

Cambridge University with first class honors in modern history, who had come to America in the 1940s to study American history at Harvard, and then taught at Kenyon. At Cambridge he had known Oakeshott and was able to tell me something about him. As I learned then, and many times in recent conversations with old graduates of Cambridge, Oakeshott was something of a legendary lecturer to undergraduates in the history of political thought.

He was also a lover of horse racing in the 1930s and a bit of a dandy. In fact, he wrote a book with a Cambridge colleague—an ancient historian named Guy Griffiths—which they called *A Guide to the Classics or How to Pick a Derby Winner*. This was published by the distinguished firm of Faber and Faber in 1936, whose esteemed editor was T. S. Eliot. There are at least a few people who, looking hastily at the title but not at the subtitle, bought the book thinking it was an essay by two scholars on the classic great books. But closer readers who used its prescribed betting system sometimes cleaned up, and, so Oakeshott told me once, at least one such sent him, in appreciation, a case of Chateau Margaux.

Thereafter, Oakeshott hovered in the back of my mind until 1962, towards the end of my first year as a graduate student at Johns Hopkins when his collection of essays called *Rationalism in Politics* appeared. This was the book that really launched him in the United States, and remains today his most widely read book. I had the privilege of editing a new edition of it which appeared in 1991. The book was widely reviewed and soon became a staple for graduate students studying contemporary political thought. The book was also controversial because it was conservative in an era when the current success of conservative thinking in America had not yet taken place. Ironically, Oakeshott, the renowned exponent of conservatism, was the son of a man who was a charter member of the British Fabian Society, a close associate of Sydney and Beatrice Webb, and George Bernard Shaw.

Oakeshott's work gained a mixed reception even among American conservatives because it was the kind of English conservatism that we associate with the skepticism of Hume and the liberal traditionalism of Burke. American conservatism today, the leading version being what we call neo-conservatism, is really a form of chastened or restrained liberalism, and shares with the liberal outlook something of the progressive disposition that has emerged in American thought since the seventeenth and eighteenth centuries. Yet *Rationalism in Politics* was seen to be important, and it established a place for itself and has remained in place ever since.

The title essay of the volume, "Rationalism in Politics," laid out a central premise of Oakeshott's thought: That the modern world has placed too great a reliance on abstract and technical thinking in the belief that, if one could find just the right method of analysis, one could perhaps solve any problem, that all problems were technical problems, that there were no metaphysical limits to the power of human beings to take their destiny into their own hands. Oakeshott thought that this was not an ideological or partisan matter, but a matter of philosophical precision. He argued that no one can achieve such methodological power, and that the human condition is not a series of problems to be solved, but rather a recurring predicament demanding intelligent response to do the best we can under contingent and often unpredictable conditions. This is not an always welcome view in the problem-solving world of modern America. Many took Oakeshott to be a pessimist, gloomy, a cynic who found the world meaningless.

But this was a complete misunderstanding. As he said at his valedictory speech when he retired, "I have always hoped to be a philosopher, but cheerfulness kept interfering." Oakeshott's point was that politics is an activity for the purpose, as he famously said, of keeping the ship afloat on a hostile sea. It is an instrumental and secondary activity, a "necessary evil," which, when well conducted, frees us to find the meaning of life in other things that he took to be far more important: philosophy, art, poetry. In saying this, he was, in modern idiom, repeating what Plato and Aristotle had said long ago: politics is not the highest thing for human beings even if it is an important and unavoidable feature of our lives. In a society that is today highly politicized, and is the inheritor of a pragmatic, "can-do" outlook, many felt that to follow Oakeshott was to be left with nothing to do. Of course, for him doing was not everything; thought and reflection, and finding the poetic elements in the everyday life, were worthy and the most human of activities. In these respects, he transcended politics. It has never been possible to derive specific political or social programs from his writings, and what we call in America "movement conservatives" often discount Oakeshott because his way of thinking seems to impede their activism. Oakeshott was not so much expressing conservative ideas as he was returning to an ancient tradition of acknowledging limits to human power and aspiration that, he argued, apply to all human beings under all conditions.

I continued to follow his work and then the opportunity arose for us finally to meet. In 1974, the centennial year of Colorado College, I was asked by then Dean Ric Bradley to organize an academic component to our celebration. Among other things, we established a memorable series of lectures that year on liberal learning. The first, and perhaps most memorable, was given by Oakeshott in September of 1974 in the atrium of Tutt Library to an audience of about 350. It was the Abbott Memorial Lecture for the 1974–75 school year. It was called "A Place of Learning" and, for those of us who were there, it was among the most galvanizing addresses heard at the college. It was published as a special centennial issue of the *Colorado College Studies* in 1975, and later reprinted several times in journals, finally to appear in a collection of Oakeshott's essays on education, entitled *The Voice of Liberal Learning*, which I edited, and which the Yale University Press published in 1989.

Oakeshott had responded in 1974 to my invitation to come to the college despite the fact that we had not met, and he did not know me or of Colorado College. But we had mutual acquaintances who had assured him that this would be all right to do. He stayed at the college for a week, meeting with faculty and students, and it was at this point that we developed the friendship that lasted until his death in December 1990. I asked him then why he had agreed to come. He said, first, that he had had a passion for the American west ever since his childhood when an uncle of his had migrated to California to grow tomatoes; second, he was charmed by the idea of pioneers traversing the plains in covered wagons, bearing the Bible and Shakespeare, to found a place of learning at the foot of Pike's Peak. Oakeshott had, incidentally, always had many American and Canadian students at the LSE. He was quintessentially English but with a strong streak of romanticism that showed itself in his attraction to the "frontier experience."

I took him to Cripple Creek. On the way, he saw cowboys on horses punching cows. Then we clambered about the gold mines, we went to the top of Mt. Pisgah, and later had a beer at the bar of the Imperial Hotel. He loved it all and, of course, believed that all his youthful imaginings had proven true.

Thereafter, I began my regular visits to England to see him and to be introduced into the Oakeshott circle, presided over by a remarkable couple named Shirley and Bill Letwin, distinguished academics in their own right and frequent visitors in the 1980s to Colorado College. The circle included academics, writers, journalists, politicians and civil servants. It was a transforming experience, and it reached its high point when I was a visiting professor or what they call a distinguished academic visitor at The London School of Economics in 1979 and shared Oakeshott's office with him at the school. By that time, Oakeshott was long retired and participating only in the general seminar for graduate students in the history of political thought program which he had founded. He came to the school only on Tuesdays for that seminar. The rest of the week the office was mine. But often on Tuesdays, after the seminar which ran from four to six PM, he and I would go out to dinner together at one of his favorite local restaurants.

He had a flat in Covent Garden just off Trafalgar Square, but he also had a cottage on the Dorset coast overlooking the English Channel from which one could look out to the Isle of Wight. The village of about ten stone cottages in which he lived was built in the 1880s on the edge of the Purbeck marble quarries for quarrymen and their families. Purbeck marble is a special sort of grey/brown stone that one will see in many of the cathedrals of England—the interior of Salisbury Cathedral is a particularly good example.

I often visited him at his cottage where he lived most of the year, except for the academic term, called Michaelmas, from October 1 to mid-December. His village is a few miles from Dorchester in the heart of the region where Thomas Hardy set his novels. Indeed, in walking there one often felt transported back into the late nineteenth century, and I sometimes thought, as I watched the crows swooping over the plowed fields, that, at the next turn of the path, I would encounter Jude the Obscure or the Mayor of Casterbridge.

Oakeshott kept most of his books at the cottage, including many rare volumes that he was able to collect in the good old days when old books were relatively cheap and mostly bought by people who would read them rather than treat them as collectibles, antiques or investments. The cottage had no central heating, but at one end of the large main room there was a quite large fireplace that gave off much heat, at least at that end of the room. Characteristically, I would huddle at the fireplace while Oakeshott would roam the farther reaches of the room complaining that it was rather too hot. Until very late in his life, when his friends insisted, Oakeshott had no phone in the cottage, and never a television set. To the very end, he did all of his writing with a pencil or a pen, letting a secretary type up his pages for him. I never saw him use a typewriter, and the computer never existed for him. He thought most of these modern inventions had done little good for the human race.

He was an excellent cook and a gardener. One of his prized achievements was to have turned a deep cistern in his garden into a guest bedroom that one entered by climbing down a ladder about eight feet below ground where a bed awaited one. To me it seemed a little out of Edgar Allen Poe, but I never actually had to sleep there; I always got the guest room inside the cottage.

Oakeshott also owned a 1958 MG-B which he kept in Dorset and which he drove at maniacal speeds through the hedgerows. In general, he was a kind of bohemian, although you could never tell it just to see him and if you did not know him. His conservatism in practice seemed to be that you obey the basic rules of society so that you can be radically free in everything else that you do.

The cottage was a place of conversation that often lasted until late into the night. It was genuine conversation. It could be witty and frivolous, up to a point. It could be sophisticated and often philosophical. It could be literary or theological. It could be, but not often, about current politics for which Oakeshott had little taste even though he was very well informed. If you posed a serious question to him, he would often sit entranced for a time,

until you began to think he hadn't heard you and you started to speak to fill
in the void or repeat yourself when, of a sudden, a considered, precise and
elegant response would come forth, and you realized he had genuinely been
thinking about what you had stated or asked, and you realized further that,
in such moments, elapsed time had no significance for him.

In his learned brilliance, Oakeshott made shrewd, accurate judgments about people and arguments, but he was, in a way, the most un-
judgmental of all people. He was an intellectual aristocrat, but his sense
of the universal predicament of being human—what he called the ordeal
of consciousness—was authentically democratic. He was a true individu-
alist, and I mean really and truly. He spent no time worrying about
whether others had more or less than himself, he treated every encounter
with another person as a unique circumstance, a potential opportunity for
a poetic experience, he had a special enthusiasm for the young and their
dreamlike ways; and it was this, in part, that made him at eighty more effective in a seminar with students than faculty half his age. He never forgot what it is to be young even as he grew old; in this he was like Socrates,
both old and young at once. And students, even when they likely did not
understand him, were enthralled and straining to hear every word. They
sensed the poetry of it.

On the other hand, if an encounter was not fruitful, he went his way
happily, awaiting some other opportunity to present itself. He had the capacity, following Montaigne and Pascal, to sit alone in a room, to think
and to write. He certainly could be a companion to himself, and, perhaps
for that reason, he was a marvelous companion to others.

When he found himself in a conversation with someone of modest
talent and little thought, he would look up at the corner of a room, jan-
gling the coins in his pocket, and then respond, "Oh, you think that! Do
you? Do you?" His "do you's" were famous. And, at the Oakeshott
memorial meeting at the LSE in 1991, John Casey, a fellow of Oakeshott's
college at Cambridge, jokingly suggested that if God had spoken to
Oakeshott rather than Moses, saying "I am that I am," Oakeshott might
have replied, "Are you? Are you?"

Oakeshott made one more visit to Colorado College in 1982 to receive an honorary degree. He was known to turn down such offers. The

fact that he accepted this one was a sign of the affection that he had acquired for Colorado College from the time of his earlier visit in 1974. The fact that, in the 1970s and 1980s, many Colorado College students went to the London School of Economics to study in the History of Political Thought program which he had founded years before was not irrelevant. Many of those students have since become tenured professors in some of America's best colleges and universities.

Oakeshott was a teacher, but he always thought of himself as a learner, occasionally disclosing to others what he thought he had learned, interested to hear what they might think about it. Oakeshott was also a writer in the deepest sense. He wrote, so far as I can judge, every day of his life from his undergraduate days until he was well into his eighties. He kept notebooks in which he copied out quotations, wrote analyses of books he was reading, tried various opening gambits for an essay, and so on. There are about sixty of them in his archive.

When he died, he bequeathed his papers to Shirley Letwin to do with as she thought best. She and I went to his cottage in Dorset in the spring of 1991 and moved the papers to her house in London where, until a few months ago, they were stored and where she and I worked on them in our joint venture to publish his papers with the Yale University Press. They have now been moved to the archives of The London School of Economics where they will become available to scholars.

The number of papers was very large. He had written much more than anyone knew, probably more that he did not publish than he published. There were wonderful essays that had never been published, at least one completed, book length manuscript of high quality that I have edited and Yale published in 1996. From 1989 to the present five volumes of his work have been published in new form or for the first time. This project is probably drawing to a close now, but I expect to do one more publication with Yale—an Oakeshott Reader, which will be an anthology of his best writings both early and late. In remembering Oakeshott, I am also expressing my gratitude to Colorado College for the manifold opportunities that, under its auspices, have come my way as both teacher and scholar.

William A. Fischer
Professor Emeritus of Geology

CHAPTER 8

Some Thoughts About Liberal Arts, Geology, and Serendipity
William A. Fischer
Professor Emeritus of Geology

I was born and raised in a small town in northern Illinois during the era of the Great Depression and although times were difficult it was also a time when life was much simpler. My grandparents were immigrants from Germany and Denmark and, although education was stressed in our home, having a college degree was not a tradition.

During these trying financial times most of us found part time employment by mowing lawns, caddying, door to door selling, and having a paper route. Saturday night entertainment might involve a walk to the local gas station to watch somebody get an oil change and a lube job; radio was just coming on the market but few could afford to own one so instead we built crystal sets for our amusement.

This was still the era of Prohibition and as one of the "Rights of Passage" we soon discovered old Dad, the local bootlegger who manufactured two brands of booze – Kummel and Apricot Brandy at $.50 a pint. The other sign of acceptance required riding the rods on a freight train to a destination unknown. Some of my bolder friends would travel as far away as Iowa or Wisconsin and return blackened with coal soot and engage us with lurid tales of debauchery that left us drooling with envy.

A highschool diploma in these years represented a real accomplishment and for most this marked the time one entered the work force. We thought college was for brains and jocks, and I was neither. And then there followed a number of serendipitous events that altered my life forever. I decided to apply for admission to Beloit College in Beloit, Wisconsin. Tuition was $300 per year with one half waived for scholarship. One could wait tables for board, proctor for a dormitory room, and the National Youth Administration would pay $.35 per hour for janitorial work; I did all three.

All of us can remember instructors who have impacted our lives by opening doors to different branches of knowledge – the beauty of language, the excitement of scientific research, the magic of Shakespeare. I soon discovered these departments were staffed by one or two persons who were truly dedicated to the ideals of a liberal arts education. Gradually I began to understand how an institution like this could turn out men of the stature of the geologist Thomas C. Chamberlin and the explorer Roy Chapman Andrews. However, it was only natural that we would chafe under the all college requirements of chapel four times a week, two years of Biblical literature, two years of foreign language, English, history, lab science, and even physical education.

It was during my sophomore year that I wandered into a geology class, mostly out of curiosity as I had no real idea of what the subject encompassed. After the first few classes I knew that this was it as we labored through the two volume Chamberlin and Salisbury physical and historical geology text books. With field trips to outcrops of the Ordovician Platteville Dolomite, and after collecting fossil cephalopods, gastropods and trilobites, I knew there was no turning back. And then I wondered, was there possibly some way a person could use this knowledge and make a living?

For my last two years I worked as lab assistant in the department and upon graduation received a letter from the president of Beloit inviting me to return as an Instructor in the department with free room, board, tuition and a salary of $15.00 per month and the opportunity of working towards a master's degree. Here was the chance to try my wings and see if teaching had the appeal I thought it might.

Two years later with all bills paid, money in the bank, and armed with the M.S. degree I was hired by an oil company as an exploration field geologist firmly believing that the best educators are those who have known something other than the world of academia.

Shortly thereafter Hitler was on the rampage in Europe, Pearl Harbor had been bombed, and though draft exempt I felt that I should be contributing more directly to the war effort. And so I left and went to work on the ultra-secret atomic bomb project at Las Alamos, New Mexico. Living inside a barbwire enclosure on an isolated mesa with constant monitoring by FBI agents took some adapting and somehow from sheer naivete it never occurred to me that it was a bit unusual to be associating with Robert Oppenheimer, Niels Bohr, Edward Teller and Hans Bethe while at the same time working closely with Popovida, the son of Maria Martinez, the potter of the pueblo SanIldefonso. Geologists of that era were not well versed in the field of nuclear energy.

As the war progressed and with the continued loss of dear friends in the armed forces, I could finally stand it no longer and so I resigned from the project and enlisted in the U.S. Navy as Seaman 1st class, serial number 402003. After boot camp at Great Lakes Naval Training Center in Illinois, I was selected for officer training as a "ninety-day wonder," commissioned as an Ensign, and sent to Camp MacDonald at Plattsburgh, New York.

Having now completed a second boot camp it was time to go to sea and when asked by the placement officer "in what branch of the navy did I think I belonged?", without hesitation I replied "the Navy Hydrographic Office." As the shades came down it became apparent to me that he had never heard of it and the following day I received orders to report as gunnery officer aboard the USS Kishwaukee, a 100 octane gasoline tanker situated somewhere in the south Pacific Ocean. This was the closest connection the placement officer could make between oil, geology, and navy.

Once aboard ship things got lively as we progressed from Ulithi to Leyte Gulf, Palau, Babelthuap, Iwo Jima, and finally Okinawa with every island bitterly contested by fanatical Japanese.

And like any normal geologist I was dying of curiosity to set foot on a real coral atoll, especially so after our first approach to Ulithi Atoll where I sat glued to the fathometer watching it ping out a steady 10,000 foot depth and then rapidly shoal as we cruised through one of the inlets and dropped anchor in a 50 foot depth of water. Darwin was a keen observer and after his famous cruise of the Beagle and theory on the origin of atolls, he was proven correct by the post-war drilling of the atoll Eniwetok. Atolls turned out to be this country's most important secret weapon by providing the safe anchorage for amphibious assaults in the Pacific.

With around the clock Kamikaze attacks at Okinawa and days spent at general quarters, the raids gradually eased and mopping up operations were well under way when our ship received an all navy bulletin pleading for anyone in the service who had experience in mapping as they were urgently needed in the Navy Hydrographic Office in Washington, D.C. The circle had closed. Rush orders sent me back to the states just as the atomic bomb was dropped on Hiroshima, Japan.

After a short tour of duty at the Hydrographic Office I was discharged. Recently married and with a zero bank balance, a baby on the way, and lots of dreams, we moved to Boulder, Colorado to attend graduate school on the G.I. Bill. By working in the Henderson Museum, taking on a paper route, and developing film at night in a local studio, we were able to survive and with all but my dissertation finished I learned of a vacancy at Colorado College.

These were the times when one was hired with a handshake and a verbal offer of an approximate salary depending on the state of the college budget. Following an interview with President Gill, I was appointed Instructor, salary $2,900, to start in September 1949. There was no assistance for moving costs, Sabbatical leaves were unheard of, and raises we would later learn would range from $50 to $100 per year. There was an aura of mystery surrounding the subject of tenure. It was regarded as a rather vague thing that might happen sometime in the future provided one wasn't cited for immoral behavior.

During the war years the college had become almost a girls' school and in an effort to attract more men, the faculty had voted in a five year engineering program. With Don Gould as chairman and Richard Pearl as mineralogist, I was hired to implement the geological engineering program. My teaching load would consist of physical and historical geology, micropaleontology, invertebrate paleontology, stratigraphy, sedimentation, petroleum geology, subsurface geology, and well log interpretation. Classes met five and a half days a week, labs were every afternoon and enrollments ran as high as 150 students in the intro course which always met in the infamous "Pit" in Palmer Hall. Enrollment in the advanced courses averaged 15 to 20 students. We had no offices as such. Instead we had a roll-top desk in either a classroom or a laboratory, no secretary, no paraprofessionals, and best of all no telephones. One beat-up old typewriter and a hand cranked mimeograph machine served our needs, and a waste basket sufficed as a filing cabinet.

Imagine my surprise when I arrived on campus all fired up to teach my specialty micropaleontology only to learn that the department had only one dysfunctional binocular microscope and twelve students signed up for the course. An emergency appropriation was approved to purchase three microscopes and the students had to share them.

From 1937 to 1955 Don served as chairman, and it was during this period that I had the opportunity of watching a gifted teacher and talented artist at work as he would cover an entire blackboard with three-dimensional block diagrams showing the evolution of the Colorado Front Range of the Rocky Mountains. These were the years of lean departmental budgets and heavy teaching loads. When equipment couldn't be purchased Don would design and build items such as air-photo stereo viewers, miniature and full sized stadia rods, and even a table-sized relief model of the Pikes Peak region with a real and subsurface geology all portrayed. He loved the science of stratigraphy and his deep interest in the Pennsylvanian system of rocks was even displayed in Beaver Lodge cabin, where Don had constructed a stratigraphic fireplace using Precambrian rocks for the base and Pennsylvanian at the top with a hearth of Permian sandstone. Generations of geology seniors looked forward with great anticipation to their spring field trip and stay at Beaver Lodge.

Richard M. Pearl, or "Tricky Dick," as he was affectionately known by students, taught all the mineralogy and petrology courses and was constantly engaged in the writing and publication of a whole series of books that popularized geology for the layman. Often while working in the mineralogy lab and while helping students, he would lean over a lighted Bunsen burner and students kept a record of how many shirts and ties went up in smoke, thus earning him the second nickname of "Smoky Bear."

In spite of all the equipment problems and unconscionable teaching loads, we managed to offer the B.S., B.A., B.S. in G.E., and M.S. degrees. An endless procession of oil companies would begin interviewing our seniors in the fall of the year and most would be hired at starting salaries that made ours look rather ridiculous by comparison, but after all hadn't we signed "the oath of poverty"?

These were the years of descriptive geology; quantification was yet to come and geologists were notorious word smiths. For example here is a verbatim definition taken from the Glossary of Geology: "a cactolith is a quasi-horizontal chonolith composed of anastomosing ductoliths, whose distal ends curl like a harpolith, thin like a sphenolith, or bulge discordantly like an akmolith or ethnolith".

We continued to laugh at the mad Austrian meteorologist Alfred Wegner and his far-out arguments for continental drift. In graduate school required reading always included T.C. Chamberlin's classic paper "The Permanency of Continents and Ocean Basins" and nobody could offer a mechanism that would permit rigid continental crust to slide over rigid sea floor. Granted there were a few lone voices of dissent, but they came from Africa and South America and being provincial we all knew that the only "good stuff" came from north of the equator. Paleontologists, when faced with seemingly identical fossils separated by thousands of miles of open ocean, would invent new species or create imaginary island arcs to explain migration routes of the geologic past.

This also was the era of the geosyncline and every suite of rocks on the north American continent was jammed into one of a dozen different structures bearing names such as miogeosyncline, eugeosyncline, zeugogeosyncline, and if they didn't fit, rest assured that Marshal Kay of Columbia University would invent a new one.

Today, students beginning in grade school are taught the plate tectonic theory never realizing that its acceptance marked an event as profound as the time we gave up the creation story or when we accepted Darwinian evolution or Newtonian and Einsteinian physics. I will never forget the standing room only audience that packed Shove Chapel to hear J. Tuzo Wilson deliver his address on the Plate Tectonic Model. We all felt liberated having labored for decades under the dogma of the times.

In 1955 Don Gould left the department for a position in industry and we hired Trobe Grose from Stanford. After several years Trobe moved on to the Colorado School of Mines, and John Lewis from Allegheny College was added to help handle our ever burgeoning enrollments. John brought to the campus a refreshing breath of irreverence for many of the sacred cows of academia. By occasionally abandoning text books he taught students how to think, how to observe, and how to ask the right questions. Always seeking perfection, he acted as a surrogate English department by demanding, and eventually getting, reports and papers that were grammatically, logically, and geologically sound. Serving as sutler and bus driver for countless classes, his field trips became legendary and waiting lists for his intro classes set an all time college record.

During this period four things happened for which I am most grateful: the first was being selected as a Ford Foundation Post-Doctoral Fellow for a year's residency at Scripp's Institution of Oceanography; the second was having a semester's leave to investigate and publish on the effects of the 1959 Hebgen Lake Earthquake on the geologic features of Yellowstone National Park; the third was my appointment as the A.E. and Ethel Carlton Professor of Geology; and finally an invitation to present the results of my research on the Harding Formation Trace Fossils at the International Geological Congress meeting in Sydney, Australia and the subsequent designation of the Indian Springs Ranch Fossil Site at Canon City, Colorado as a National Historical Landmark.

The department has always been firmly dedicated and totally committed to the ideal of liberal arts education. What other discipline can approach geology in giving students the breadth of exposure to all the branches of science? If we view the sciences in relation to the geometric form of a tetrahedron and place physics, mathematics, chemistry, and biology on the apex of each triangle, then geology logically lies in the center as the integrator of them all.

Think what a world we might have if we could get people to value a library card more than a credit card. What if every politician had to demonstrate a knowledge of the origin and finite nature of most of our natural resources and to understand that it literally requires the destruction of an ocean basin to make ore deposits? And with an educated citizenry, how many communities would put up with the urbanization of flood plains and active fault zones and all the geological hazards that go with ignorance? And I finally would ask, how could anyone study paleontology, understand the web of life that binds us all together, and then be a racist? Geology departments have a great challenge in educating the public about the origin, past history, and wise use of the resources of this planet earth.

As the college prepares to celebrate its 125th anniversary I will celebrate the completion of my 82nd journey around the sun and my service under five Colorado College presidents. Retired now for 17 years I find it hard to let go and am pleased to have participated in numerous Southwest Studies courses, Wilderness Institutes, teacher training programs, Elder hostels, and alumni travel and education courses.

This is a great institution and a first rate department and it is with pride and gratitude that I look back over this 50 year association.

Neale Reinitz
Professor Emeritus of English

CHAPTER 9

WHOSE SPIRAL NOTEBOOK?

Neale Reinitz
Professor Emeritus of English

When I retired in 1991, I found in the back of my filing cabinet, wedged in between my Chaucer notes from Wisconsin and a seminar paper from Berkeley, a journal I'd kept in my first year at CC. In the spring of 1953, my wife, Bev, and I had been interviewed together at lunch in San Francisco (it was done that way then) by George Adams, Dean of the College. He offered me an appointment as Instructor in English. The pay was low, but I took the job: I was anxious to escape from the overheated atmosphere of graduate school and wanted to get to a small college where the emphasis was on teaching, and I wouldn't be limited to Freshman courses. Bev and I came to Colorado Springs that fall.

PAGES FROM A SPIRAL NOTEBOOK, 1953–54

September 2. Landed at the airport Monday afternoon, green from flight from Denver on Braniff DC3. Picked up rented car. Bev went to college apartment. I went to Cutler Hall to see Dean Adams. He said he hoped I would enjoy teaching here and profit from the experience—the job was good for five years. (Time limit was new to me, but kept my mouth shut.) Was directed to Hayes House, large frame building on the corner of Cascade and Cache la Poudre (what a name for a street!). Went to capacious, lived-in second-floor office of Professor Krutzke, gray-haired fiftyish man who seems to run department (he's not chairman). Krutzke told me about my classes—one Freshman English class, one Bonehead remedial, two advanced courses. Tweedy, crew-cut history professor, back from year on Ford Foundation at Harvard, walked in. Talks

153

very slow. Likes Adlai Stevenson. So far every one is friendly and open, a pleasant relief from graduate school one-upmanship.

Saturday, September 12. Yesterday was a long day. Registered students for English courses in Cossitt Hall, rambling structure attached to ruins of Greek theater. Faculty sat, department by department, at tables lined up around gym (it has small balcony for basketball games). Talked to professors from other departments: still surprised at easy-going atmosphere.

Monday, September 16. My thirtieth birthday. Met Freshman English Monday at 8:00 in one-story wooden building (Krutzke says it's temporary). Twenty-one students, attentive and neat. All wear gold beanies—Freshman hazing. I was nervous before it started but felt great in front of class. Asked them how to pronounce their names and where they were from, then gave out first assignment, 500-word theme for Friday. We are using text which matches pro and con essays. The first topic—"Is College Football Too Commercialized?"

Sunday, September 20. Busy week. Met my other classes. The Bonehead English group (Tuesday–Thursday-Saturday at 9) rather frightening. Class is no-credit. One student looks like Toulouse-Lautrec. Many speak ungrammatically, most are apathetic, some defiant. I had them write short theme—"What I Did Last Summer." Results awful. Read papers from other freshman class—they write well. Gave three A's. Have to be careful about grades—Dean Adams told me they should average C.

October 2. Read in student newspaper, *The Tiger*, that Sigma Chi house crowned queen of "Watermelon Bust" last Saturday. Is this a joke? Fraternities seem pretty important at "CC" (usual name for the College). Flowers still blooming in grass-covered center strip of Cascade Avenue. Wonder how long they'll last.

October 4. Have office in Hayes House—my name on the door! Share an enormous room, with enormous communal desk, with two colleagues— young professor doubling as assistant dean and mountain climber splitting time with a private school. Pestered Dean to get Buildings and Grounds to bring me my own desk. Room is at the front of Hayes House—giant rabbit warren—so everybody knocks on my door. They think it's office of chairman, or Dean or something. I get protection from the secretary—genteel, witty middle-aged Southern lady who runs mimeograph, retrieves blue-books, and answers only telephone in the building.

October 10. Bev and I have found a place on Wood Avenue, on the second floor of Mrs. Warren's house. Classy woman. Widow of Edward Warren, author, she told us, of *Mammals of Colorado* and *The Beaver: His Works and His Ways*. She is a Republican but hates Joe McCarthy. Has wonderful way of saying something that is funny is "killing."

November 3. I like my advanced courses. They are small, five in one and six in the other (all girls)—we have absorbing discussions on the essence of Romanticism and the nature of Tragedy. This is what I left Berkeley for—an Instructor couldn't teach this stuff in a university. The Dean's daughter is in the Tragedy course—I squirm only a little. The Freshman English class is good, too. I hate to walk over to Palmer to teach the Boneheads—the girls are full of self-improvement but the men are deadly—prep school discards, fraternity pledges. Story circulating that one of them pulled out pistol and shot car that wouldn't start—"Yuh damn dead horse!"

November 13. First meeting of English Department. Another huge Hayes House office—this one long and narrow with private bathroom. Belongs to Lewis Knapp, chairman. Except for Tom Ross, my office-mate, the English faculty are twenty to thirty years older. Knapp, tall, polite New Englander (he has book on Smollett), opened the meeting. Seemed to hope it would end right away. George McCue—small mustache, dry sense of humor (teaches History of English Language)—gave out copies of plan for re-organizing English courses. He got mild disagreement, clammed up. McCue and Amanda Ellis, only woman present, did not look at each other. She is stout lady with big hat, heavy make-up, very high heels. Krutzke calmed the waters—introduced question of whether Freshman English final should be multiple choice or true-false.

Friday after Thanksgiving. Taking the day off to leaf through dissertation—what I've written so far. Long way to go, and don't know when I can get to it. But teaching is better than graduate school.

December 3. Meeting of AAUP chapter in beat-up old house, Faculty Club. Talked to senior colleagues in other departments—Glenn Gray (philosophy), Ken Curran (magisterial econ chairman), and "LEW" Worner, historian I met in Krutzke's office (name is from his initials). Can't get over how approachable they are. They tell me they've put an end to man-to-man bargaining for raises, got the President, a retired general, to establish salary scale.

December 12. Bev and I invited to pre-Christmas dinner in Bemis Hall. Beautiful room—expect to see Henry VIII walk in with one of his wives. Girls dine graciously with tablecloths, candles, waitresses. Their dorm quad looks attractive. They lead well-bred, regulated life—sign out after dinner, must wear skirts to classes (except on Saturdays). The men, I have discovered, are on the loose. Most live in rented rooms off-campus and take meals in the primitive cafeteria in Cossitt (where everyone goes for afternoon coffee). I have seen them loading up for dinner on four hamburgers, two orange drinks.

December 20. Had a blow yesterday. Went out with Tom Ross to buy Christmas chocolates for the Dean's secretaries—candy shop is oldest house in Colorado Springs. Ross told me Dean Adams was on a terminal contract and would be gone in June. He said he didn't know why. Very unsettling.

January 31. First semester over. Stayed up all night to read final exams for four classes. Got grades in next morning. Then found out they could have been a couple of days late. With help of Bonehead English, I didn't go much above the C average.

February 1. New semester. Pretty much the same students as before, even a few more in advanced classes—I was holding my breath on that one. Dean's daughter is back for second course. Easy to like the students (in my good classes). I call them "Mr." and "Miss"—it seems to amuse them. I don't get into politics. Judging by *The Tiger*, terrible student newspaper, they care more about fraternity and sorority rush and hockey than about segregation, the bomb or McCarthy. They are mainly from plush suburbs all over U.S. Dean warned me I wouldn't be teaching "horny-handed sons of toil."

March 7. Last night we were introduced to new custom, something I'd never heard of before—chaperoning. (You can't have a student party without chaperones.) Bev and I spent the evening at the Beta house with hockey coach and wife, socializing with housemother, "Mom," in her sitting room. Room was on direct route to the first-floor bathroom—our Scrabble game was interrupted by dates racing past with pained expressions on their faces.

March 14. Getting used to teaching and liking it even more. Now we're on poetry in Freshman English. I don't even mind reading the themes and correcting them—use signs out of Perrin's *Index to English*. Don't think of the low pay too often, except when we kite checks at the end of the month. We get by with help of Bev's salary from nursery school—she still does what she did when we were in Berkeley. I'm not sure she likes it here. She's made friends but finds most faculty wives boring. At parties they sit together and talk about their children. Once a month there is a tea for Faculty Wives (hat and white gloves *de rigeur*), presided over by President's wife. (Bev says hot mushroom *hors d'oeuvres* make afternoon bearable.)

April 5. Hunt for a new Dean is now out in the open. They don't invite me to the interviews. Is this because it's my first year or because they're thinking of letting me go?

April 12. Comic but disturbing faculty meeting in room where I teach Freshman English. General-President, as usual, presided (there is rumor that he calls these meetings "formations"). He introduced new money-raiser, man who says CC is "liberal arts college with anchor in God." We will be paid in silver dollars, to show Colorado Springs what we do for local business. George McCue pointed out grammatical "howlers" in prospectus that was handed out.

May 21. My suspicions are confirmed. The yearbook says 63.5 percent of the students are Republicans, 16.5 Democrats, and 14.8 Independent.

June 7. The year is over—I made it! A new Dean has been appointed, English professor from MIT. Yesterday, after Commencement, large group of faculty and wives saw the old Dean off at the Rio Grande station. The President is retiring, too, at the end of next year. Frank Krutzke tells me it's not voluntary—says no President has ever left CC on his own. I could use the extra money, but don't want to teach summer school. I better get back to my dissertation. I'll never get another job without a degree

* * *

I never did get another job. I didn't have to. But I can remember the events of no other year at CC as vividly as I do that first one (for, to tell the truth, I didn't find the journal—I reconstructed it). Images from intervening decades crowd each other out. Our new Dean from MIT disappeared in the middle of the night; LEW Worner was appointed to take his place; the time limit on my job fell away. It took me three years to finish the dissertation, get the degree, and become an assistant professor (and a father). There were other rites of initiation: a lecture that all new faculty were required to give (mine was part of a series called "Can Modern Man Survive?"); a first beer-soaked, sun-drenched Senior Sneak; reckless resistance to the full professor who pressured me to raise his daughter's grade. For the campus as a whole, there was a jaunty infusion of confidence from Worner and Louis Benezet. When I came back from a Fulbright in Finland in 1961, I discovered, to my distress, that I was senior faculty, that younger men (still men, at that point) were knocking at the door. Sixties protests, the block plan, a department chairmanship (which included minority hiring and a harassment case): these things were a part of my personal history that I find hard to separate into chapters or untangle from the turmoil of the world outside.

The College of the 1990s seems distant in many ways from the College of a half-century ago. Looking back, I picture the institution of that time as a tweedy professor, slightly threadbare with elbow patches, driving a twelve-year-old Ford (as indeed many did), accepting the fact that he would never be too prosperous. I think of the present college as a with-it junior executive, male or female, dressed casually for academic success, well-supported with all the computer technology and fund-raising platoons that she (or he) needs, and absolutely sure that she (or he) will make the grade.

I wonder how a first-year professor will feel in 2003.

Bill Hochman
Professor of History and
Former Dean of the Summer Session

CHAPTER 10

I'M GLAD I WAS HERE

Bill Hochman
Professor of History and
Former Dean of the Summer Session

One day in the middle of the Spring semester, Colorado College President William Gill told the Dean of the College to pack his things and get out. He installed Lew Worner in the Dean's office. That night at dinner, my phone rang and Lew's slow Missouri voice asked if I could take over all his classes at Colorado College the next day. It was March 13, 1955.

Lew Worner was one of Colorado College's most popular professors. I will never forget the look of sullen resentment on his students' faces when he introduced me to them and left the room. I was already teaching two American history courses at night for the University of Colorado. Lew turned over his four courses to me. I nearly died that Spring, but I fell in love with Colorado College.

One of the courses Lew Worner bequeathed to me was Freedom and Authority, the pioneering interdisciplinary course that he, Glenn Gray of the Philosophy Department and George McCue of the English Department had established five years before. Lew handed me a pile of books for Freedom and Authority and disappeared into the Dean's office without telling me much about the course. In those days, the class met around a long table in the wood-paneled library of Hayes House, on the corner of Cascade Avenue and Cache La Poudre Street, where Packard Hall now stands. The first day, I went around the room and asked each person what the course was about. Some legendary characters sat in that class—Melon Cruthirds, Mid Gammell, Van Skilling, Debbie Brewster, Rich Hayes, Tom Pankau, John Watts, and others.

I had just finished my doctoral degree at Columbia, yet I was what might be called "university ignorant." My real education began in Freedom and Authority, but I needed help. The next fall, I asked Glenn Gray and George McCue to have lunch on Tuesdays to talk about the book we were discussing in Freedom and Authority that week. After a while, other faculty joined us. Those Freedom and Authority lunches have continued for more than forty years. Every Tuesday, a group of disputatious faculty still have lunch in the little "Exile" dining room in Bemis Hall to discuss an article, a book, or a film.

I have been at Colorado College during five presidencies (Gill, Benezet, Worner, Riley and Mohrman—that's a lot of presidents) and seven deans (Worner, Curran, Drake, Bradley, Brooks, Finley and Fuller—that's a lot of deans). Gill was my first president. He had been a Major General in the Second World War. After the war, a number of generals were invited to be leaders of colleges and universities—Dwight Eisenhower at Columbia is the most famous example. I remember Gill as a courtly, erect man, a bit uncertain about his relationship with faculty eggheads. At the end of his last faculty meeting in May, 1955, Gill told about crouching down behind a bulldozer on a South Pacific Beach when a Japanese machine gunner started to spray bullets. He said to the young soldier who operated the bulldozer: "Son, if you lower the blade, we can get down behind it and be safe from that gun." The soldier replied: "General, you're not as dumb as I thought." Those were President Gill's last formal words to the Colorado College faculty.

The Formative or Foundational Age of the modern College began when Lew Worner became Dean and Louis Benezet became President. Weeds were growing on the campus when Benezet arrived to take charge the summer of 1955. Benezet articulated a vision of excellence. He was adroit in dealing with external affairs, with alumni, foundations, and the local community. I used to think that if Albert Einstein had dropped in for a chat, Benezet would have found it possible to make a few useful points about the theory of relativity. Benezet brought vital outside support to the College—new buildings blossomed on the campus, life-nourishing gifts came from alumni, businessmen and friends.

Lew Worner was responsible for internal affairs, for revitalizing the academic program. One of his greatest talents was recruiting new faculty members. He involved himself in the hiring process in every department. He had a way of making candidates feel something important was happening or about to happen at this college, that a career teaching at a small liberal arts college, even a lesser-known college, promised excitement, satisfaction and reward. They made a good team, Benezet and Worner—President Outside and Dean Inside.

It was a heady time to be a faculty member at Colorado College. Everything seemed to be in motion all the time. Lights burned late on the second floor of Cutler Hall, where the Dean's Office was located. Walking across the campus and seeing those lights induced twinges of nervous excitement—"What exactly was going on up there now?" Lew Worner imbued the new young faculty with his energy and sense of purpose. We thought ourselves to be Young Turks then—independent, confident, sometimes brash. We worked hard and played hard. Lew had appointed us, but we were not his creatures; sometimes we disagreed with him. Yet he was our leader, not by dint of his high college office, but by the force of his character, ability and example. He stood astride the creative fault line of the deanship; between faculty and administration. Louis Benezet was the administrator, and we were faculty members. Lew was of the faculty and *also* of the administration, a unique and precarious straddle of tremendous potential for shaping the quality and future of the College.

Many of the institutions and practices of that old time no longer exist. In those days, students had to deal with a complex of college requirements. They took four or five courses simultaneously, often three on Monday, Wednesday and Friday, and two others on Tuesday, Thursday and Saturday. They had Saturday classes, and morning classes at eight o'clock. Saturday morning at eight was a gruesome time. That is when I used to quote Marcus Aurelius, Stoic philosopher and Emperor of Rome: "Is man made to stay in a warm bed on a cold morning, or is he made for better things?" I never listened for an answer. Men had to take ROTC for two years. Freshmen wore caps, called beanies, at the peril of having their heads shaved on the front steps of Palmer Hall. The women had dorm hours. Rule violators had to deal with Sally Payne Morgan, Dean of

Women, or Juan Reid, Dean of Men. Students went to see Dr. Roger
Whitney at the infirmary on the north side of San Rafael Street to have
their throats painted or receive a dose of APC pills (what did APC stand
for?). They ate "mystery meat" in the College dining rooms; they said
grace before dining; on Wednesday nights they dressed for dinner and
were served at candle-lit tables, sometimes with faculty guests. They received grades on forms filled out with pen and ink by the Registrars, Ruth
Scoggin and Blanche Hahne, in the basement of Cutler Hall. The night
before football games, they went to pep rallies with huge bonfires. At the
games they watched the Bengals and the Tiger Club perform, listened to
the CC Band led by Music Professor Earl Juhas, and sang the Colorado
College fight song:

> When Colorado College men fall in line
> We're going to win again another time
> For old CC I yell, I yell, I yell,
> and for our colors black and gold
> I yell, I yell, I yell

At Homecoming, they decorated houses and built floats with thousands
of pieces of crepe paper, and admired the beauty of campus queens.

Those hallowed practices and institutions seem quaint now. I am sure
mystery meat of uncertain origin is still consumed, but the dining rooms
are now all cafeterias, there is no table service, and nobody gets dressed
up. Of course, there are no dormitory hours; in fact the sexes are mixed
in the dormitories. There is no football band, no Tiger Club, there are no
house decs and floats, no pep rallies. Social life is less decorous; there are
no campus queens, no Christmas formals with faculty chaperons. There
isn't much ballroom dancing; now the music is often earsplitting and
dancers do not waltz.

Many college landmarks of those days are no longer standing. Gone
are Hayes House on the corner of Cascade and Cache La Poudre,
Coburn Library, and Perkins Hall, where the campus theatre was located.
Gone is Hagerman Hall, the dilapidated men's dormitory, which I was
warned never to walk past at night. Gone are South, East and West Halls,

the temporary classroom structures built during the Second World War. Gone are the old fraternity houses decorated with posters of pneumatic ladies and "borrowed" street signs, semi fire traps where robust men lived in constant peril of being burned alive.

The customs, the landscape, the faces of Colorado College have been transformed, yet Colorado College is recognizably the same institution it was forty-three years ago when I first came here. In the classrooms we continue to discuss those eternal questions at the heart of liberal education—questions of taste and judgement, of values and standards, truth and error, war and peace. We search after definitions of the cultivated, compassionate person appropriate for our time. Most important of all, the College continues to be a college-in-ferment, ever seeking new ways to fulfill its vital educational mission.

Unlike some other institutions to which we are often compared, Colorado College has never reached a plateau of rest, we have never succumbed to the seduction of assumed success, we have never said to the passing day, "Stay Thou Art So Fair" (the phrase is from Goethe's *Faust*, which I learned about in Freedom and Authority). We were then and remain today an uncontented college. This makes Colorado College an exciting place to be.

The enduring heritage from that Formative Age in the College's history, the Age of Lew Worner and Louis Benezet, was commitment to change and the search for excellence. We did not embrace change for change's sake. Lew was actually a conservative, in the tradition of Edmund Burke and John Adams, who had great respect and understanding for the past, and also a vision of the future. Our relatively small size and independent status gave us a special opportunity, indeed an obligation to be educational leaders. We sought new ways to realize the hallowed goals of the liberal arts tradition. I sometimes thought we were seeking to fulfill, in a modest way, Thomas Jefferson's famous dictum— "Earth belongs to the living, not to the dead."

Any process of change involves controversy, a continuous dialectic between what exists and what might be. Liberal education has always involved conflict and spirited, sometimes acrimonious debate. So it was at

Colorado College. The conflicts over curriculum, courses and campus life were sometimes bitter, yet they released a fruitful creative energy.

One of the early controversies involved the inauguration of a new academic calendar in which the first semester ended before Christmas, not after a short lame-duck session of classes following the holiday. A second controversial change was to accept work in Advanced Placement courses in high school for Colorado College credit. These do not appear to be monumental events, but they were debated with spirit on the floor of the Faculty Meeting and had significant consequences. The new calendar opened the way to the week-long Colorado College Symposium, a feast of lectures, discussions and films, which took place in the week before the beginning of classes in the second semester. The Symposium was one of the most innovative institutions in the College's history. By accepting Advanced Placement credits, the College made itself more attractive to the academic cream of high school students. Lew Worner was at his masterful best in bringing about these and other changes, working behind the scenes, attending departmental and division meetings, buttonholing faculty. He practiced what party politicians know: the key to success is quiet preparation prior to public voting.

A third controversial change of those formative years of the modern College was the abolition of compulsory Chapel Services. Students had traditionally been required to attend Chapel each Tuesday morning at 11 o'clock. Frank Krutzke of the English Department and I were the only faculty members who regularly were present; we were both members of the latitudinarian Unitarian Church. The Chapel was a chaotic scene on those Tuesday mornings—letters were written, card games were played, love bloomed. Very few speakers could tame that fractious audience. One of the few who did was the Nobel Prize winning Physicist, Linus Pauling, who spoke about the new field of molecular medicine, a preview of the startling understandings that were to come in biology, genetics and medicine. In 1956, the Faculty voted for a voluntary Chapel program, but only after spirited argument. That step was important in the development of an open and free intellectual community.

Meanwhile, there were changes in all-college requirements and in the structure of departmental majors. In those days, Colorado College may have been unique in welcoming younger faculty to positions of leadership.

We retained traditional faculty ranks, but there was no consciousness of rank in debating and implementing new ideas. In my very early days, I was invited to participate on prestigious committees. I quickly learned there were two kinds of department chairmen at the College. Some chairmen resented the boisterous new faculty (always spreading their seed on the ground, one said), perhaps threatened by the new atmosphere of change. Other established chairmen delighted in the energy and innovations of young colleagues. Ken Curran, Chairman of the Economics Department, Doug Mertz, Chairman of Political Science, and Frank Krutzke of the English Department were of that stripe. Mertz was always talking with gleaming eyes about what Fred Sondermann, David Finley, Glenn Brooks and Tim Fuller, the young stars of his department, were up to. I decided then if ever I attained the exalted status of department chairman, *that* was the kind I hoped I would be.

Of course, I remember with unusual clarity the issues in which I was particularly involved. One portentous controversy was over the establishment of a program for top students at the College. Some departments had Honors Programs for majors, but there was no program for extraordinarily talented entering students, who were often disappointed when they first came to college. All freshmen at that time were required to take the History of Western Civilization and Freshman English. There were many sections of each course, and the classes were large. Some of us had the idea of placing the top students in each freshman class in a special section of history and two smaller sections of English. Neal Reinitz and Tom Ross were the English teachers, and I was the designated hitter for the history course. Frank Krutzke, a graduate of the Swarthmore Honors Program, was our mentor. It seemed a fruitful idea, but it was not easily brought about. Some faculty members thought it a coup by smart-aleck Young Turks to set up an elite curriculum for able students and themselves (which in a way it was). Lew Worner's constant, quiet encouragement and support were critical. There were tense arguments, one in President Benezet's office at which sharp words were spoken, before the program was finally adopted to begin in the fall of 1961. We called it the Selected Student Program.

Some of the College's famous graduates passed through the Selected Student program—Jack Berryhill, Chuck Buxton, Judge Ray Jones, Gary

Knight, Donna Haraway, Jim Heckman, Phil LeCuyer, Tom Wolf, Terry Winograd, and many others. I had a spasm of nervous anticipation going into class with that crew each morning—a room full of students all brighter than I. I used to say I taught them everything I knew every day. I experimented in that class with the previously neglected history of science; every afternoon I went to Olin Hall for help from real scientists, and was a day ahead of the class at the most. Class sessions were embellished by talks on music by Albert Seay and Carlton Gamer, and on art by Jim Trissel and other artists. Once, Jacob Bronowski, the famed cultural historian, came to the campus and talked to the Selected Students about creativity.

One day, a striking young man visited my office. He was a Grinnell graduate and Rhodes Scholar. He was interested in the possibility of teaching history at the College. Fortunately, Lew Worner was in his office, and I took my impressive visitor over to meet him. Lew saw at once this was someone we had to have. That was how George Drake came to Colorado College, the start of his illustrious career as Professor and Dean here, and then as President of Grinnell College. He took my place as teacher of the history section of the Selected Student Program.

The Selected Student Program was part of the College's move toward academic excellence. It seemed to have a snowballing effect; talented students and Boettcher scholars were drawn to the College. Gradually many of the readings and techniques used in the Selected Student Program were incorporated in courses for the general student body—for example, topical instead of survey coverage, and the use of a series of paperbacks rather than a textbook. At the same time, the general quality of the student body rose. Forty years ago, Colorado College had the reputation for being a party school, popular with skiers, and patronized by preppies from the East who could not get into Ivy League colleges. There was some truth to that stereotype, although we always had able students here. In the 1960s, the quality of the student body dramatically improved. After that, students failed because they did not do the work, not because they could not. Because of these changes, the Selected Student Program lost some of its significance and lapsed.

I left the Selected Student program to participate in another project that had long-term consequences for the College. One of Lew's techniques of leadership was to enlist critics to undertake reforms (Lincoln and Franklin D.

Roosevelt did that too). Gilbert Johns of the Psychology Department was a vocal critic of the Summer Session. Lew made Gilbert Dean of Summer Session, and he revitalized the curriculum, established the first summer institutes, and was the impresario for glorious summer arts festivals that included concerts, opera, dance and theatre, a program I inherited as Summer Session Dean many years later. With Don Jenkins of the Music Department, Gilbert Johns founded the Colorado Opera Festival at the College, which was the foundation of the present opera organization in Colorado Springs.

I had been an outspoken critic of the shallowness of teacher education programs. In the 1960s, many of our students were interested in careers of service to community, state and nation. Many thought to become teachers, but they had no wish to pass through the traditional educational methodology courses that were widely regarded as lacking intellectual interest and rigor. One day, Lew Worner took me to lunch at the Broadmoor Golf Club, and while I was munching on a delicious pork chop, he suddenly said: "I want you to be chairman of our Teacher Education Program." I nearly choked. I had never had an education course, but I came to see it was an offer I could not refuse—a put up or shut up proposition.

The Education Department was then a little teachers' college within the College. The five Education Professors regarded me as an obviously unqualified intruder, which in many ways I was. When I moved into the Department as chairman, it was, for a while, like being camped on a hostile shore. I spent the first year studying what the best colleges and universities were doing. Ken Curran, who was Dean at the time, gave me $10,000 (a large sum then) to visit colleges and universities that were experimenting with new ways to prepare teachers, and to bring educational leaders to the campus for consultation and lectures.

Changing our program was a painful and controversial process. I persuaded college faculty members from a variety of disciplines to teach courses for prospective teachers on a regular schedule. Thus, Glenn Gray of our Philosophy Department taught the Philosophy of Education, Van Shaw of Sociology taught the Sociology of Education, Lou Geiger of the History Department taught the History of Education. Members of a number of departments went into the schools to observe what our student teachers were doing.

One of the most radical aspects of the new plan was to do away with the Education major. Henceforth, students who wanted to be teachers majored in an academic discipline, or in a new Liberal Arts for Elementary Teachers major. We abandoned the master's degree programs we had in a number of fields, and organized a new Master of Arts in Teaching program for Experienced Teachers, and a Fifth Year Master of Arts in Teaching program for liberal arts graduates who had not taken education courses as undergraduates.

Summer Session Dean Gilbert Johns collaborated in organizing summer courses and institutes for teachers that would be intellectually refreshing. We persuaded Tom Doherty, the willing Superintendent of Schools for District 11, to underwrite courses needed by teachers (in the new math, for example), and provide subsidies for teachers enrolled in our summer courses. The bellwether of these new courses was the Arts and Humanities Institute, modeled on a Humanities Institute subsidized by the John Hay Fellows Program on our campus I had taught in for several years. A galaxy of superstars on our faculty taught the teachers in the early Arts and Humanities Institute, including Dirk Baay, Doug Freed, Doug Fox, Pete Peterson, John Simons, Fred Sondermann, Jim Yaffe, and others. The Arts and Humanities Institute avoided traditional education subjects. They were devoted instead to mind-stretching themes, like Alienation, Irrationality, Morality and Values, Creativity, Love and Hate, and Evil. On the last day of each week, the faculty stars debated a book before the whole group; many other faculty and students came to see those glorious free-for-alls.

In all this, I worked closely with the Colorado Department of Education. State officials were skeptical at first, but agreed to give us latitude to establish programs that departed from the traditional patterns of teacher preparation. The guiding rationale was to find a style of teacher education appropriate to our College that drew on the unique strengths of liberal education.

The pressing issues of those days were not all academic. We understood how the tenor of campus culture affected academic life. Forty years ago, the younger faculty had close associations with the students, and were involved in campus social life as shapers and participants. The hallowed institution of Senior Sneak Day was a high point each year for the faculty. In May, the Seniors abducted faculty members to join them at a secret rendezvous, often in the mountains. Sometimes the Seniors were a bit too creative in devising modes of abduction. Once, a real policeman in full uniform burst into my Western Civilization class, and presented a warrant for my arrest. "Professor, come with me," he said, while my freshmen students sat mute and terrified. Once they took faculty on a hazardous ride to the Black Forest in thinly-tired animal cages borrowed from the Cheyenne Mountain Zoo. But it was worth those indignities to spend glorious days outdoors drinking beer and singing songs with the soon-departing seniors.

The Senior Sneak Day tradition ended after a beautiful sun-drenched day of beer and song at the Paradise Ranch near Woodland Park. At the end of the day, I drove a group of seniors down Ute Pass, including Ray Jones, Tom Wolf and Mary Sterrett Anderson. Neale Reinitz was in the car, too. (Neale and I were usually among the very last to leave Senior Sneaks.) A green sports car shot past at high speed. When we came around a turn (I think of it every time I pass that spot), we saw the little car upside down on the side of the road with a girl's legs sticking out. The driver, Art Department sculptor Herman Snyder, was dead underneath, his chest crushed by the steering wheel. The girl, Susan Allison '67, had a broken back. We held a special Commencement Ceremony for her in a room at St. Francis Hospital, complete with President, Marshals and a small choir. Susan Allison recovered, but that was the last Senior Sneak Day in the old style.

Faculty and students often joined together in political activities. The 1960s campus was not an ivory tower; the world pressed on us. One faculty meeting was scheduled just at the time President Kennedy spoke to the nation about Soviet missiles in Cuba. A television was set up in the meeting room, and we sat taut and silent thinking of nuclear Armageddon. At Noon one terrible day, I was in my office in Palmer Hall when I heard that Kennedy had been shot. I left at once to go home; the campus seemed to be covered with people running in all directions, but there were no sounds. After Walter Cronkite announced the President was dead, I wondered if I could force myself back to my 1:15 class, but knew I had to go. The classroom (Palmer 223, the room where I taught for many years) was jammed with my students, and a mass of others as well. They were bewildered and shaken, many were weeping. At first, I did not think any words would come out of my mouth. Finally, we began to talk,

and by the end of the hour we had comforted each other somewhat, in-
sofar as it is possible to be comforted at such a time.

One of the events that stirred the campus in the early 1960s was the report Harris Sherman '64 and Myles Hoper '65 gave in Perkins Hall
Theatre about an antiwar rally they attended in Washington as delegates of
the College. Their trip began the era of greater student involvement in public affairs. After four little girls were killed in the church bombing in
Birmingham, a large contingent of faculty and students marched from the
campus to City hall and stood silently on the steps, enduring taunts from
some passers- by. In 1968, many of our students were involved in the bitter
political campaigns. I was on the Credentials Committee at the Democratic
National Convention that year. Before one local meeting, I had some
Eugene McCarthy materials to prepare and asked Janet Robinson '70 if she
and a few of her friends could help stapling them. When I returned from
lunch, a mob of students filled the street in front of Cutler Hall where my
office was located, eager to staple. I used to take Janet Robinson, who had
an exquisite voice, and a guitar-playing friend of hers with me on speech
making occasions. When I finished talking, she sang the McCarthy song:

> If you love your country
> And the things for which it stands,
> Vote for Gene McCarthy
> And bring peace to this our land.

Even critical audiences of conservative local businessmen were moved by
the beauty of the young woman and her voice.

Students and faculty joined in many anti-Vietnam War demonstrations. The students held a flagpole rally *in support* of Lew Worner after he
made a strong statement in defense of academic freedom following a tu-
multuous Symposium on Violence in 1969. That may have been one of
the only *pro-administration* demonstrations in the nation in those days. It
was common in the early sixties, in the optimistic period of the Civil
Rights movement and campus opposition to the Vietnam War, to end fac-
ulty-student parties by linking arms and singing "We Shall Overcome."
Later, when the War dragged on and the Black Power movement
emerged, the songs were sadder and less hopeful.

One moving moment came on the day the Gulf War began. A dense crowd filled Shove Chapel listening to somber speeches from faculty and administrators. The Beast God war had suddenly intruded on the peaceful, joyful routines of campus life. The students sat silently, unbelieving, many were weeping.

In the 50s and 60s, a number of spirited controversies raged over aspects of campus life. At various times in those days, I was Faculty Advisor to the Publications Board, the student government, and the Honor Council. When I came in 1955, the student government was made up of one representative from each fraternity and sorority, plus one independent man and one independent woman. A group of students led by Judy Reid Finley and Andrea "Jelly" Jelstrup Corley (both of the class of 1958 and both sorority members) introduced a new governing structure composed of representatives from each class, led by elected officials.

Harris Sherman led the student body in a failed attempt to open the dormitories to visitation by members of the opposite sex. In those days, of course, there were separate men's and women's dormitories, and visits were strictly controlled. In this the College acted *in loco parentis* to a degree hard to believe today. But Lew Worner was opposed to opening the dorms, and the Trustees rejected the proposal. Lew once told me that as long as he was President, open dormitories would never exist at Colorado College. In time, he changed his mind and accommodated to new standards in male-female relationships; that kind of flexibility was one of the measures of his greatness as a leader. Harris Sherman and his friends failed in 1964, but their action pointed the way to the present coeducational dormitories.

When I came in 1955, the intramural program was confined to a fraternity league with one independent team, The Zetas, largely made up of hockey players. With Harry Booth, who was Dean of the Chapel and my best friend at the time, I organized two faculty teams, a touch football team known as the Socratic Seven, and a softball team, known as the Platonic Nine. At first, we thought of calling the football signals in Greek, but only Harry knew enough Greek. In the fall, I posted written challenges on the bulletin boards in the wings of Slocum Hall, where the freshmen lived, concluding with the incendiary phrase: "We hope the men of your wing will be equal to this occasion." The freshmen poured out to the field by Armstrong Hall for these contests, thinking to teach us lessons. I still have sore sports on my anatomy from those games. In the spring, we did the same thing for softball games. The Faculty began to wear white shirts emblazoned with a big letter "F" and the students' various colored shirts. Harry was the running back, third baseman and cleanup hitter. Once I heard an opposing player say: "Watch out for Reverend Booth, he's fast as Hell." I was sometimes the quarterback and usually the pitcher, but our best players were often former varsity athletes who had joined the college staff. One of these was Muscles Dave Fletcher '57, former varsity fullback who was an Assistant Director of Admissions. Once we beat the fraternity champions in a spirited game on Washburn Field. Once we tied the Department of History team from the Air Force Academy in a no-quarter game neither side wanted to lose. Soon there was a Slocum Hall intramural league. In time, the faculty softball team changed its name to Mind and Body, the perfect exemplification of the ancient Greek ideal. I look back on those formative days for the intramural program as one of my happiest involvements at Colorado College. My forty-year-old hope is that there will someday be adequate play spaces and a field house for recreational and intramural sports. Happily, the Campus Master Plan, adopted in 1997, calls for the addition of two major playing fields on the east side.

Needless to say, not all of the controversies and changes that occurred in the last forty years turned out as I might have wished. On three issues that were very dear to my heart, I was on the losing side. On each of those issues—the presence of ROTC on campus, the place of athletics at the College, and the role of fraternities in campus life—I confronted the formidable figure of Lew Worner. ROTC was compulsory for men when I came in 1955, but after a few years it became a voluntary program. In my view, military interests are well cared for in American life. There ought to be, I thought, some places entirely dedicated to the political, diplomatic, peaceful solution of problems; surely a liberal arts campus was such a place. I did not think the College should give academic credit for Military Science courses or facilitate student enlistment in the ROTC program. But Lew had powerful counter arguments. His view of the inevitability of power made him sensitive to the necessity for military strength. He believed a citizen army— nourished by nonprofessional officers, particularly liberally educated officers—was essential in a democratic society. He carried the faculty again and again on ROTC votes. When ROTC finally left the campus, it was because of a decline in student interest, not because faculty opponents were ever successful in argument or tactics.

I have been a sports enthusiast all my life, yet have always been dismayed by the place of big-time athletics in educational institutions. Division I teams everywhere cost immense amounts of money, and their success depends on lowering academic standards to enroll talented players. The bifurcation between the increasingly professionalized nature of big-time sports and the educational missions of our institutions of higher education is a national phenomenon.

As President and Dean, Lew Worner defended a traditional view of athletics and education. He was steeped in the old college tradition in which spectator sports had a central role in college life. He had a kind of double vision at football games, particularly when the Colorado College band (in the days when we had a band) played the C-Men Song. He saw the team on the field, but he also saw other teams and other players from many, many years. He thought that continuing the athletic tradition was essential to the vitality of the College. He knew, of course, about the excesses of intercollegiate athletics at many colleges and universities, yet he believed we could maintain an active program without sacrificing our standards. He led the way in eliminating athletic scholarships in all sports but hockey, and believed we could play hockey at the Division I level within the spirit of Division III, which was the established policy of the College.

Lew was wrong about that. We have never lived up to the Division III standard in the conduct of our Division I sports teams. A report of a Presidential Commission on Athletics in 1993 revealed that only a few of our Division I male athletes qualified for admission using the standards applied to other students (the situation has improved since then), and that an inordinate share of the varsity sports budget was spent on Division I teams. Meanwhile, a pittance was devoted to the intramural and recreational athletics in which the overwhelming number of our students participate. One of our Athletic Directors privately called Division I sports "poison ivy in the garden of athletics." I am chagrined that my College continues to be involved in the big-time athletics national scene. How can we compete against mega-universities with huge student bodies and lower academic standards without diluting our ascending aspirations for academic excellence? In my view, liberal arts colleges of our type should play at the Division III level, and place central emphasis on participatory sports for the student body-at-large.

Actually, in the last dozen years, the faculty twice voted to do away with Division I teams by a two to one margin, without effect. The reason is, of course, that other interests and influences are involved in College athletics—alumni, trustees, townspeople. It is perhaps beyond the power of any academic official or faculty body to change a deeply-rooted athletic tradition in this country today.

The third of the controversial issues that frustrated me and many faculty members is the continuing presence of fraternities and sororities on our campus, particularly fraternities. I was not opposed to fraternities when I first came here; in fact, I was invited to be advisor to the Interfraternity Council. But I soon began to think they did not play a constructive role on the campus. One particularly unpleasant issue involved discrimination against minorities practiced by Greek organizations in the 1950s, discrimination enforced by alumni representatives and national organizations. Faculty members knew about this discrimination because our students told us. Harry Booth was chairman of a commission that looked into discriminatory practices. The Commission had many painful meetings; sorority women, our own students, told us privately they wished to end discrimination but were discouraged from telling the full truth about pledging practices.

The issue was even more agonizing because the College was just then embarking on a large fund-raising drive with the alumni, many of whom were members of Greek organizations. About that time, Lew Worner asked me if I would introduce a motion to the faculty from the Committee on Undergraduate Life stating that the faculty recognized the contributions Greek organizations made to campus life, despite the discrimination issue. This was to reassure the alumni. I did introduce that resolution because I respected Lew so much and knew the pressures he had to face. I remember standing with my back to the wall in the room where the faculty met, covered with perspiration, fielding barbed questions from my surprised colleagues. After that ordeal, I was standing on the deck of my house, inhaling a glass of beer, when Lew popped in. He said: "Thank you. I know what it meant for you to do that."

In time, fraternity and sorority discriminatory practices were aban-doned. But other things continued, including mindless and juvenile haz-ing, initiation rites that bordered on the inane and sadistic, destructive drinking and illegal drug use. To many faculty members, the fraternities have seemed to be institutions that perpetuate immaturity, contrary to the College's purpose of fostering intellectual and social maturity. Of course, neither Louis Benezet nor Lew Worner had any truck with discrimination or uncivil behavior. As a student at Colorado College, Lew had been both president of the student body and president of his fraternity, the Betas. In his day, fraternity men were often campus leaders, and the houses were sometimes centers of discussion and intellectual activity. Fraternity men have been loyal supporters of the College over the years. Lew remem-bered the good things about fraternity life, and relished warm fraternity friends. He had a hard time loosening himself from memories of those days and understanding critics who thought we would never be a truly great college as long as the fraternities remain established here. Just as in Division I athletics, many interests beyond the campus are involved in the fraternity issue. Faculty members are relatively free of the outside pres-sures presidents and deans cannot avoid taking into account. It is a fact of academic life that knee-jerk liberals like me have a hard time accepting.

One other more recent development has troubled me as an ardent ad-vocate of faculty preeminence in the halls of academe. In those distant days of the 1950s, the Faculty was the center of college governance. I once made a study of lines of responsibility and authority at the College for the Committee on Undergraduate Life. Of course, in the final legal sense, ulti-mate responsibility and authority —college sovereignty it might be called—is in the Board of Trustees. But *actual* authority devolved as a matter of practice to a variety of groups and offices. The Faculty is certainly sovereign over all curriculum matters, but in practice the Faculty used to exercise significant authority in other areas as well; for example, in the design of buildings, in the allocation of financial resources, and over student life.

When I first came here, I was impressed by how involved the Faculty was in the life of the College. Faculty influence was exercised through an elaborate structure of committees. It was not unusual for a faculty mem-ber to have three and even four committee assignments. It seemed to me that this was the modern expression of the ancient liberal arts tradition—

the Faculty *was* the College and exercised a controlling influence over most important affairs.

That time has clearly passed. Now many central issues are in the hands of the rising profession of academic administrators. The Faculty role is much diminished. Now Student Personnel professionals shape the circumstances of campus life, a professional College Relations staff is the voice of the college, outside firms are contracted to plan the campus and even design the College logo. A large professional Development Staff seeks the life-giving funds that nourish our needs.

There are good reasons for these developments. The College was once a relatively small enterprise (the President's wife used to wrap and give Christmas gifts to every faculty child). Now we are a vast and complex business with a huge budget. Student facilities and services have multiplied in number and quality beyond anything imagined a few decades ago. The demand for funds is more voracious every year. These matters are beyond the capacities of faculty dreamers attired in medieval caps and gowns.

The faculty itself is partly responsible. Faculty members, tired of the burden of committee work, reduced the number of committees and concomitant committee assignments. In a sense, the faculty abdicated, leaving a vacuum to be filled by professional administrators. One reason for this abdication is probably the increasing professionalism of graduate schools that produce our young faculty members. New faculty members have specialized research interests. They are attracted to teaching, but not to administering a college.

The price of these developments is an increasing gulf between the specialized academics on the Faculty, and the professional administrators who keep the College going. It is a nationwide phenomenon. I look back with some nostalgia to the days when a more generally-interested faculty played a broader role, and there was a functioning union between the various elements that make up a living College community. In the old days, the entire faculty and administration, sometimes with children, gathered at Professor Woodson Tyree's house for smoked, barbecued turkey. Now Chief Tyree is gone and so are those warm and fruitful collegial collaborations and celebrations.

Of course, teaching is the great joy of the faculty at a liberal arts college. I have been Dean of Summer Session for eight years, long enough to know that there are no highs in administration comparable to the surge college teachers know when they enter a classroom. The enduring magic for me was combining love of subjects with the joy of sharing them with eager students. The challenge was to make the subjects come alive, that is, be relevant to their present and future lives. I used to throw everything but the kitchen sink into that effort, relating perhaps outrageous things like Socrates' argument in *The Crito* to using a fake I.D. to buy beer, or Aristotle's view of the state as an instrument of the good life to Franklin Delano Roosevelt and the New Deal. I was glad specialized experts were not in class when I embarked on some of those forays.

How privileged I have been to be a teacher at a liberal arts college rather than a focused specialist in a university! For a while, I toyed with moving to a bigger institution, like the University of California at Berkeley, where I taught for six summers; I was never actually qualified by scholarly accomplishment or inclination for a university appointment. My approach was always general rather than specialized. Glenn Gray used to say that the Freedom and Authority course was an attempt to recapture the lost unity of knowledge. I looked on all my teaching in that way. It was great fun to open new subjects with students when we were all learners together.

Only at a college like this could I have taught such a variety of compelling subjects—the History of Western Civilization, U.S. Foreign Relations, the Civil War and Reconstruction, and Twentieth Century America, as well as courses on war and peace. The trick was to keep up with exploding scholarship in so many different fields; I could not really do that, but it was mind-stretching fun to try. My central course was Recent U.S. History, which, before the Block Plan, sometimes had 75–100 students. (How did I ever read all the papers and blue books they wrote?) A student once called that course "Bend the knee to Franklin D. in Recent U.S. History"—I adopted the title with pride.

In time, my special interest came to be courses on war experience. It was certainly not military history, which is usually written about and taught as if nobody was ever hurt. I was interested in what actually happens to people in war, and how they remember it and try to make sense of it afterwards. Of course, I drew on my own experience in the Second World War, and was powerfully influenced by Glenn Gray and his book, *The Warriors,* a philosopher's meditation on a combat soldier's experience. Together, Glenn and I conceived a course we called "War, Violence and the Humanities," which dealt with the way war appears in literature, film, philosophy, history and poetry. Glenn died on a weekend before the Monday we were to begin a block of that course; the next year, Dan Tynan of the English Department joined me in expanding and teaching it. Eli Boderman of the Sociology Department and I conceived and taught a course on "Morality and War," which dealt with justifications for going to war, and moral standards in fighting. For a few years, I directed a program on War, Violence and Human Values, financed by a grant from the Luce Foundation, which brought a galaxy of noted speakers to the campus.

Students are easily seduced by vivid accounts of war and violence. I tried to avoid that seduction. I used to teach my Civil War course without dealing much with battles, and, until recently, I avoided speaking about my own war experience. I knew that if I did, if I told them, for example, about the terrible night my ship was sunk at Normandy, every eye would be on me. One day, a young woman in one of my classes said to me, "You were lucky, you had the war." That gave me a jolt, but I soon saw what she meant. The war *had* changed my life. When I came home, I had a better ideas of who I was, and I wanted to do something useful if I could, perhaps to atone for my survival when so many of my shipmates had perished. That is how I decided to become a teacher. At Colorado College, I hoped to help students find meaning and purpose in their lives without the intervening catalyst of some traumatic and terrible experience like war.

Above all, I wanted to leave my students with a sense of humane values that would sustain them in their coming lives. I came out of the war with an abiding reverence for life. I knew students could always look up the text of Article X of the League of Nations Charter, the provision of the Second Agricultural Adjustment Act, or the origins and details of Social Security. I taught them those things, but it seemed to me that what the students wanted to know, what they needed to know was how people actually lived in the past, how they confronted crises and preserved decency and culture in sometimes dreadful circumstances, and how they experienced birth, joy, suffering and death.

I wanted my student to *feel* what it was to have been a slave, bought and sold like a horse or cow, to *feel* what it was to be mired in the fetid, ghastly trenches of the First World War, to *feel* what it was for hard-working Americans to be adrift without hope in the Great Depression, to *feel* what it was to be caught in a city during a bombing raid, siege or plague. I wanted them to know why the Bill of Rights (the Fourth Amendment, for example) was vitally important, not as a political science abstraction, but for their own ability to enjoy the great boon of liberty. I wanted them to think hard about what our obligations might be to people of other races at home and of other nations abroad, and what our chances for survival might be now that the nuclear genie (the power of the stars) has been unleashed on earth. At the end of my Recent U.S. History course, I used to say I really did not care whether they became Democrats or Republicans (which was not entirely true), but I did hope they would be active participants in public life, with a sense of empathy and compassion for people less fortunate than they, who, but for the accident of birth and the Grace of God, might be themselves.

I am a former Young Turk; now I am the Very Old Guard. It went fast. The years were filled with controversy and change—new calenders, advanced placement credits, honors programs, teacher preparation schemes, intramurals and Division I sports, fraternities and sororities, compulsory Chapel, student demonstrations, dormitory rules, departmental requirements, ROTC—the engrossing spectacle of a dynamic institution. And most of all, TEACHING, TEACHING, TEACHING! I see the faces of my students, probably thousands of them by now. I have had a lifelong love affair with them. Teaching at a liberal arts college allows faculty to taste the Fountain of Youth Ponce de Leon once sought in the Florida wilderness.

When I came here forty-three years ago, I thought this would be my first job, and assumed I would soon move on to another institution. Now I give thanks every day that this was the place where I was privileged to live my life as a teacher. How lucky I am to have been what Theodore Roosevelt once called "one of those little men who teach history in College"—this college, Colorado College!

Richard G. Beidleman
Professor Emeritus of Biology

CHAPTER 11

APPRECIATION FOR COLORADO COLLEGE AND BIOLOGY TOO

Richard G. Beidleman
Professor Emeritus of Biology

I first met The Colorado College when professing at Colorado A & M College almost half a century ago. There was a regional meeting of the Independent Student Association at CC, and as ISA faculty adviser at Aggies I brought down a group of our students to Colorado Springs. Here, indeed, I encountered a quaint campus, dominated by a gigantic stone hall, with an inevitable bell-tower administration center, an impressive chapel, assorted other stone buildings including an outdoor Greek-type amphitheater, a number of temporary wooden barracks, and a library the likes of which I had never before entered. Playing hookey from ISA sessions, I simply had to explore this library, with its balconies, precarious winding stairways, towering stacks and dark basement.

Was I astounded at what my perusal turned up! Whereas at the old A&M Library the children's novel *Wind in the Willows* was catalogued among the ecology treatises, in Coburn I discovered scientific journals going back before the Monroe Doctrine, and research materials which I had used at the Bancroft and Huntington Libraries. The ISA banquet was not to be forgotten, either, up at Bruin Inn (now extinct) in Cheyenne Canyon, with a speaker who averred that his best friends were dogs. (Yes, in retrospect, it was probably Professor Frank Krutzke.)

Afflicted by the post-sabbatical-leave itch, I left the Zoology Department at Colorado Aggies in 1956 to replace my major professor

for a year at the University of Colorado. During a meeting of the
Colorado-Wyoming Academy of Science in Denver the next spring, zool-
ogist Bob Brown of Colorado College told me there was an opening at
The Colorado College—for someone to teach a new Carnegie Program
biology class for non-science majors, as well as anatomy and physiology
for nurses and a nursing microbiology course. Why should I even be interested in such a position? After all, I was a vertebrate ecologist. I only
knew the anatomy of rats and leopard frogs; my functional biology background was in plant physiology. I had never been close to an agar plate,
much less a bacteriology professor except as a neighbor.

But remembering Coburn Library, it proved inevitable that I eventually would turn up in Cutler Hall (of the bell tower) for a job interview
with The Colorado College Dean, Lloyd Worner. What a surprising interview. I'd come from "big time" institutions, where our football players
were going on to professional teams, and the only faculty home I envied
belonged to the football coach. Now Dean Worner was telling me of plans
for a new science building and a new library. But not a whisper about a
new football stadium. I'd never heard of such a thing in academia. Then
he confided, "Dr. Beidleman, you'll like the faculty and you'll like the administration. But the students will leave something to be desired. They've
been everywhere and done everything and seen everything, and nothing
you can say will make any difference." What worried me more, however,
was that Worner never asked about my background in microbiology.

To make a long story shorter, I was hired as an assistant professor,
starting in the autumn of 1957. It would be my tenth year of college
teaching. I had risen from assistant professor to assistant professor over
that span of time, and from $3000 a year to $4500 a year. My academic
success seemed assured!

As a new faculty member I got off to an excellent start. First, I missed
the special meeting for new faculty members. (I never did find out what I
would have learned.) Then there was the faculty retreat at Star Ranch. A
little shy, I was standing by myself inside the door to the meeting room,
when a very tall, dark-haired man came in, asked who I was, cordially
chatted with me, and moved on. Boy, I thought to myself, I've never met
such a friendly basketball coach before. The next time I saw the basket-

ball coach, he was presiding over the faculty retreat. It was Louis T. Benezet, President of The Colorado College. The faculty party where old faculty and administrators got to meet the newcomers also proved equally helpful to my early advancement. In my increasingly outgoing manner, I talked to one of the women at the party, told her I was joining the zoology staff, and wondered what her husband did at the college. Wouldn't you know, she turned out to be the college vice president's wife.

Palmer Hall was an experience in itself in those days. There was The Pit (for lecturing to large classes in an Edgar Allan Poe setting). On the other hand, I talked to my classes in a smaller lecture room from behind a lengthy podium too high to jump over, and, as I remember, beneath a gigantic wall mural of a tiger salamander. Well, at any rate, the salamander mural was somewhere around. True rumor had it that in eons gone by the initiation into the zoology club involved biting off the head of a live salamander. (Alums have later verified that.) The whole center of the second floor was a museum, which contained a suspended whale that eventually proved to be two different species of whales. And there was also a disturbing whisper about a voluminous attic (or perhaps more than one) which contained stuffed carnivores.

The Benezet Period was exciting. The Colorado College was, without a doubt, on the way up. We were presumably arriving among the comparable colleges. Our faculty children could attend Stanford free, and vice versa. (But I don't think it ever turned out to be vice versa). There were many new professorial and administrative faces, new academic programs such as the Carnegie science courses, new buildings being planned, including a student non-union with a bowling alley. (The latter was what had been lacking at this college, according to students, before they thought of beer-on-campus.) At every all-college conclave we anticipated announcement of some new multi-million-dollar gift. And in some cases this actually happened! At each fall convocation we could hardly wait to see the printed faculty marching order, because it seemed to reveal who was going up the salary scale faster. One autumn you were marching behind one professor, the next fall two ahead of him (rarely any "her"). I have always suspected that after Sputnik the scientists took a quantum leap.

For those of us in the sciences and mathematics, the National Science Foundation teacher institutes, starting at Colorado College the end of the 1950s, became important, and did indeed put us "on the map". Biochemist Lewis Pino directed the earliest institutes that evolved eventually into three-summer MAT programs for secondary and junior college teachers, summer institutes for high-ability high school juniors, academic-year institutes for elementary school teachers, and even an NSF summer field biology teacher institute at Aspen in conjunction with the Aspen Institute of Humanistic Studies. (The Institute probably never did comprehend those biologists, convening in their basement with butterfly nets, muddy boots and binoculars.)

When Pino left for a position with NSF in Washington, I inherited his director's job for five years. Even more exciting, I got his office in Cutler Hall, from which I could look through a window at Pikes Peak. Most exciting, though, was finding a bonafide shotgun, I think, in my office closet. My office was above the Business Office cashier window, and I thought that if the cashier were ever held up, I'd stand at the head of the stairs and fire down an heroic volley. Alas, this never materialized.

Fortunately, I had been briefed on running institutes, because in 1959 I had been put in charge of a new "Deep Springs Program" at Colorado College for high-ability elementary school students. Deep Springs was a Saturday program that exposed selected youngsters (in part selected by their parents) to the entire academic offerings of a liberal arts program. This undoubtedly became the most demanding exercise ever engaged in by our faculty. As an example, a ten year old corrected the physics professor's blackboard calculations twice in one lecture.

Our NSF institutes, especially the three-summer program, became nationally famous. We were getting thousands of requests for applications for the program each year, that involved stuffing and licking lots of envelopes and stamps. Then, there were hundreds of completed applications which had to be read by our science staff. Our NSF grants made it possible to bring in visiting scientists and science educators for a week or more—people like science innovator Paul Brandwein, Nobel-prize winner George Beadle, Harvard's George Gaylord Simpson, Berkeley's Starker Leopold, Barry Commoner, and many others. Because our programs were somewhat unique, NSF in Washington would often send foreign scientists to visit us. But best of all were the intellectual and personal relationships which developed between our staff and our participants, continuing to this day. I always remember that in my field the secondary school people arrived thinking of themselves only as biology teachers, but they left with their MAT after three summers thinking of themselves as biologists as well as teachers. Indeed, one of our participants, who first met a solpugid (don't ask) on a class field trip, in later years became one of the country's authorities on solpugids!

Two new academic buildings had appeared on campus by 1962, Olin Hall of Science and Tutt Library. Olin was architecturally unique. The innards of the building involved a double outer hollow shell, so that all kinds of internal alterations could easily be made. The faculty planned the spaces. Only biologists asked for windows. The physicists and chemists over time became very introspective about the lack of windows. Yet the physicists did have a hall running the entire length of their floor for demonstrating physical principles. Everyone has loved the Fishbowl, connected to the main building by an elevated glassed-in umbilical cord. Its auditorium has hosted many a famous visiting personage, not to mention classes and weekend cinema and, of course, the college choir. But that towering blackboard! I'll never forget the very short Indian visiting mathematician, who came in before his scheduled lecture and totally covered that board by climbing up on a stepladder. His talk was spectacular, because as he thought of additions to his blackboard notes, he would leap up in the air with his chalk, find an open section of blackboard, and hastily scribble an additional notation as he was falling back to the floor.

Tutt Library was designed by architects who did the Air Force Academy. At one time much of Tutt's main floor was to be taken up by a spiral staircase, a remainder, we suspected, left over from the architectural balance. Presumably an opening for check-out, check-in, and overdue, our meticulous librarian, Ellsworth Mason, actually found, by pouring over the architectural plans, a room in the library that had no doors (for X-rated materials?). But the shock came on a chilly morning when we of the campus library committee assembled to see what we thought would be the sample outside wall slab, supposed to be an attractive blush-red color, a blend between that of Palmer Hall and Loomis across the street. The slab actually turned out to be cement gray (though reputed to have flecks of red in it)! The architects were delighted that we turned it down, because the slabs for the entire building were already precast gray, and on their way to Colorado. They are still with us. And then there was the delightful sunken outdoor-reading courtyard extending from Tutt towards Palmer. Actually, it never materialized as a courtyard for library use and eventually had to be covered over. When it still existed, I'm sure faculty of the period remember being thrown into the excavation during senior sneak day. Just think of all the books that would have been thrown up and out of such an attraction over the years by our undergraduates and professors alike.

Speaking of moving books, probably for the first time in The Colorado College history, essentially all students and faculty handled library books. On a designated day, the books passed by a human chain from old Coburn across the campus to new Tutt. No one will ever know how many of the college's more esoteric library holdings went into the trunks of student cars during that memorable move. What happened to the proposed greenhouse roof of Tutt, which the CC Library Committee members vehemently swore would leak during a cloudburst? The skylight roof went in, as did the beautiful orange carpet on the floor beneath it. During the first cloudburst the roof performed as predicted by the Committee, and the orange carpet reacted. This was a graphic demonstration in a liberal arts college of learning by doing.

With President Worner at the helm, the physical plant continued to expand. However, the real excitement involved inventive academic programs. There was the FISP, the SSP, the SS, the no-D, the no ABCDF, the SWS, PIN, ACM, the BP . . . and several more that fortunately escape my mind. What were all of those innovations, anyway?

FISP stood for Ford Independent Study Program, underwritten by a four-year Ford Foundation grant. The purpose was to determine if a group of selected students could be let loose on a college campus for four years to "educate themselves" by using the human and physical resources of a good educational institution. We were joined by Allegheny College and Lake Forest College, each with its own group of hand-picked students. Also, each institution had a group of faculty as preceptors for the young people. The student would be examined after two and then four years across the spectrum of the liberal arts. Wow!

We had about 26 freshmen, as I remember, and faculty advisers from each of our three academic divisions. It proved to be an educational free-for-all. Some students went regularly to classes. Some sat in on one class, found the lectures dull, never showed up in that class again (who was going to tell the professor why?). Others hopped from course to course for varying lengths of time, Whitman-sampling, while many self-studied in the library. A professor might be cornered for a mini-seminar. Students attended national and regional society meetings. One freshman decided to spend his time writing the great all-American novel. (He did finally finish a novel, mailed it to a publisher without keeping a copy of the manuscript, and it was lost in the mail.). The first year we had each individual keep a daily journal, recording his or her educational activities. When I read one of my advisee's journal, I was amused to note that each day he wrote, "Tomorrow I'm going to get down to work." Eventually he did. But by the end of two years, half of the group had dropped out of the FISP and were replaced by new students with Junior standing.

After four years, pursuant to the Program guidelines, the seniors encountered judgement day, when they were examined over the entire panorama of knowledge. Faculty from the other two institutions gave orals at Colorado College, while we did the honors off-campus. I am embarrassed to remember one oral we administered at Allegheny College in the sciences. A humanities coed had been having an extended, difficult time discussing geology. It had become early evening, and there was a striking sunset beyond the classroom window. Unfortunately, I remarked to the young lady "Did you know that the dirtier the air, the more beautiful the sunset?" This proved not to be the thing to have said!

What happened to the FISPs after four years? About fifteen—surprisingly enough mostly science types—actually completed the program and proved to be well-rounded, educated individuals. A good number of these are now noteworthy professors in their own right at various institutions, one becoming president of the American Association for the Advancement of Science.

The SSP (Selected Student Program) chose high-ability freshmen and created special social science/humanities courses for their first year. Eventually there was pressure for a second year of special courses, and science was added with a Cosmology and Evolution course taught by geologist Bill Fischer and myself. We met once a week at night. At our first session, we attracted a group of about a dozen women and several sophomore men. We never saw the men again after the first session. The women came each week for the two-hour evening class with their knitting and knitting needles. As Bill and I ploughed our way through the semester, all we could think about was the imminence of the French Revolution.

The SS (Summer Session) had tough competition with our state's public institutions of higher learning because our costs were higher. But again, innovative courses and institutes were designed. There were the Hanya Holm dance program, musicals, Danforth groups, a variety of MAT institutes for teachers that especially catered regionally, and later on Elderhostels. Probably the most memorable summer innovation involved the presence of a professional football team which boarded and roomed on our campus and did its practicing in our stadium. Oh the contrast in the Rastall dining hall between the football brawns and the ballet-dancer beauties.

Bill Fischer and I had known each other from our graduate days at the University of Colorado when we both worked as assistants at the University Museum. We both had Ford Foundation grants the same year in the past. Bill and I started an eight-week geology/ecology summer institute, focusing on the Pikes Peak Region. We accumulated a big bus load of students, and we two faculty shared one salary. Bill taught geology the first four weeks and gave me his candid evaluation of the students. I taught the second four weeks, rearranging the evaluations. On occasion, the two of us handled the group together. The apparent popularity of the course seemed to demand that the Summer Session Dean invite us summer after summer to do the course. But over time we became suspicious of the so-called popularity of our course. Other summer programs, we eventually discovered, were being taught by as many as three professors getting full salaries. So much for popularity. Yet at the end of the 1990s we are still turning up doing a brief song and dance for the Summer

Session as emeritus professors who can be bought, so we suspected, at a reduced rate.

The SWS (Southwest Studies) has proven to be a natural for The Colorado College. Our location at the entrance of the Southwest is heralded by stand of candelabra cactus. The University of Colorado is too far north and Southern Colorado University is too far south! Of all the courses I have ever taught, in over fifty years, nothing equals my Southwestern Ecosystems courses, and the first one, the Pinyon-Juniper Woodland Course (1973), has never been surpassed, for what we did and with whom we did it! Nine students, Dr. Alex Vargo in her first get-acquainted block at Colorado College, and myself, in my Wagoneer and a rented van, went off into the Southwest to focus on that wonderful southwestern ecosystem, the Pinyon-Juniper woodland.

We first ventured into New Mexico, with a dozen home-made cookies for back-up, for about ten days, doing ecological analyses of this typical southwestern ecosystem. The students did inventories of the woodland; line transects for which each species of woody plant had to be reported. At one site I was up on the top of a ridge, but I could see the students below in the basin, supposedly doing their transecting. Since I had a parabolic-mirror microphone with me attached to a recording machine, just for fun I focused the microphone on the distant cluster of students while they seemed to be having a discussion. Those rascals! They were saying, "Dr. Beidleman can't see what we're doing down here. Let's just fake the results!"

After about ten days we returned to Colorado Springs, took one look at South Nevada Avenue, and two days later headed into western Colorado and Utah P-J Woodland (also known as the Peanut Butter and Jelly Woodland). This time we took 12 dozen chocolate chip cookies baked by the young women in the class. We again had two vehicles with us, one of which broke down at a rest area near Del Norte, Colorado. Taking two students and three cookies, I towed the disabled vehicle east to Alamosa and got it fixed, returning many hours later. What did the three of us find upon our return? Alex Vargo and the remaining seven students relapsed on the rest area lawn, having consumed 141 cookies! Why? We were informed that there was common fear among the group that the three of us, with the vehicles, would never return.

Over the years there has developed a variety of exciting Southwestern Studies courses, including the summer SWS MAT Program. The latter often had enough field-trip participants to put a fourth of the group in each section of the Southwest's Four Corners for a group photograph. We experienced poolroom fights, danced, sang, picked up hitchhiking CC dropouts along our route of travel, and shed tears at course's end. But best of all, we absorbed vast quantities of information in an arid environment. Enthusiastic instructors even unplugged the bus microphone and took it sans cord and speakers out onto the trail. The ultimate experience, however, occurred at Chaco Canyon one sunrise, as our Phoenix Symphony violinist-participant played *Fiddler on the Roof* from atop the sandstone cliff as the sunlight flooded our campsite.

The academic-year science course for the SWS Program was a team-taught geology and ecology of the Southwest. The extended field trips were always memorable. We traveled down the Rio Grande Rift and then west into the Sonoran Desert or east into the Chihuahuan. Inclement weather occasionally found the CC bus parked in someone's rural driveway, students' sleeping bags scattered under every overhang, the stunned host and hostess wondering what had beset their abode. After all, they were just friends of a friend of CC. The SW geology/ecology course aptly illustrated Harvard's Louis Agassiz pronouncement that one should "Study Nature, Not Books." However, what the two instructors on one occasion near Truth or Consequences, New Mexico (wouldn't you know) claimed was swelling sediments causing the bumpy bus ride, proved instead to be a flat tire!

A brief word about the provocative PIN (Patterns in Nature) program, a sequential series of science courses for non-science majors which focused on natural patterns—ecological, geological, chemical, physical, mathematical. When the program was first promoted in a faculty meeting, a notable member of the faculty declared that there were no patterns in nature. Needless to say, he proved to be dead wrong! And none who were exposed can now contemplate the Biosphere without thinking about PIN.

In passing, I am reminded that in 1969 The Colorado College joined the ACM (Associated Colleges of the Midwest), savoring its variety of academic programs such as the one in Costa Rica and in the Boundary

Waters of Minnesota where field trips were strictly by canoe. But fortunately, we objected to the suggestion that participating institutions turn over all their bound periodicals to the Newberry Library in Chicago. In this Association, we consorted with famous liberal arts colleges, which makes me wonder why, as I departed from one of the ACM committee sessions, a biologist from a distinguished sister institution followed me down the hallway, asking if we had an opening at Colorado College.

The BP? What can one say about the Block Plan after two-and-a-half decades? At the fall faculty retreat where it was first presented, Bill Fischer and I spoke out on behalf of the concept. After all, for summers we had been teaching block-type courses, one subject with one group of students for two four-week periods. Little could we have anticipated how demanding—yet how challenging—the block plan would prove to be educationally and physically. Perhaps it particularly suited those of us who taught field courses such as geology and biology. But with imaginative planning it could suit any discipline. I used to tell students, who objected to the strenuous block schedule, that it was exactly how real scientists immersed themselves professionally, enjoying every minute of it!

Over the years of my acquaintanceship, The Colorado college has seen old faculty fall by the wayside and be replaced by new faculty. New administrators have come onto the scene with new ideas. The pile of the wall-to-wall carpet in the development office has gotten deeper. A new science building became the tail wagging the Olin dog. Some of those uncertain freshmen of yore began returning to receive honorary doctor's degrees for achievements which neither we, as professors, nor they as students, could have anticipated. An adjunct campus arose in the San Luis Valley, the Baca, whose new building complex makes Taos Pueblo look like something out of a Hollywood movie set.

When I made that first visit to the CC campus back in the early Fifties, I had wondered at the time what part a small liberal arts college could possibly play in the scheme of higher education. Over the years, those doubts for me have totally evaporated. And it turns out they have evaporated for many others, as well. In 1984 Ron Capen and I, who were teaching block courses at the Bodega Bay Marine Biology Station north of San Francisco, hosted a conclave of regional CC alumni, with a group discussion on liberal arts. This was the period when a liberal education was being strongly questioned nationally. And it had become evident that our students themselves were dubious. Yet our assembled alumni, from old codgers to new recruits, enthusiastically endorsed the value of a liberal education in their respective lives. More recently we had a 25th reunion brunch at the Baca, and again the discussion concerned liberal arts. In that group only one individual made his living in the field of his CC major that happened to be chemistry. All the others were in careers unrelated to their college field of study. Why had they succeeded? To a person, they paid tribute to their Colorado College liberal education that had broadly prepared them for life—for the challenge of any career.

And where have all our many students gone from this institution of higher learning at the foot of Pikes Peak? They play many roles and wear many hats: playing a famous statesman in a Hollywood movie; a naturalist on a Clipper ship in the Lesser Antilles; writing and illustrating classics about the Southwest; receptionist at a university herbarium; ahead of you at the downtown Washington, D.C. post office, behind you in line at Heathrow Airport outside of London; passenger on a train to Denali in Alaska; professing physiology in the Antipodes; jogging along a remote red-dust road beside the Colorado River; first tenured woman professor in Colorado State University's Wildlife Biology Department; diving off the lip of the North Atlantic ice sheet as a marine biologist; featured on the cover of a St. Louis newspaper magazine supplement; in a TV wildlife special; penning mystery novels with a geological slant; international environmental lawyering; announcing a first born by a gigantic banner hung from a Seattle high rise; escorting a killer whale up the Pacific coast; in the table of contents for *Reader's Digest*; running a Costa Rica butterfly preserve; running for Congress. The bottom line is that you never know where they will inevitably turn up and what they will be doing.

When we once lived in South Kensington (London), I could sense the presence of Colorado College students in the neighborhood, though initially we never saw any. Only later did we discover that from our flat window we could spot where T. K. and Ruth Barton were living with a summer CC group. And then there was the old-time Colorado College alum who spied our field vehicle (with "Colorado College" painted on the door) at a gas station in southeastern Utah. He hobbled across the road, told us he had gone to Colorado College. He paused for a moment, reflected—it was late September—and questioned me, "Why aren't these students in class?". I replied, "They are in class." Then after I explained the block plan to him, he muttered, "Things sure weren't like that when I was in school."

For years I used to have a recurring nightmare. To wit, I dreamed I had accepted a teaching position at another institution. (But for some strange reason my new office usually turned out to be on the second floor of where I went to junior high school.) As I tried to settle into the new environment, I began kicking myself and wondering why on earth I ever left Colorado College. President Benezet, as a psychologist, long ago apparently knew that this could happen to me. In those early days (and maybe still today) the way to get ahead in academia was to take your most recent teaching offer to the administration, use it for barter, and naturally come away with higher salary or rank. I finally tried this with Benezet. I had an offer from New York State University (Albany) for head of the department and double my CC salary in my hand. Unfortunately, we were standing where I could look out a window at Pikes Peak. He said something like, "Dick, I don't think you want to leave. There are moving expenses. Your children's lives will be disrupted. You won't like the weather in upstate New York. You won't have the interesting kind of outdoors for teaching there that you have here. No, I don't think you really want to leave." I left his office without either a raise in rank or salary. But Dr. Benezet was right. I didn't really want to leave. That appreciation for The Colorado College kept me, and many others. And over the years it keeps bringing us back, whether as former students or staff. But now emeritus and more sagacious, I realize that, way back when, I would have stayed even if I had gotten a raise in rank or salary from Colorado College. This is the type of questionable thinking which develops from exposure to a liberal education.

Eli Boderman
Professor of Sociology

CHAPTER 12

WHAT A WONDERFUL LIFE

Eli Boderman
Professor of Sociology

How do you get to be a professor at Colorado College? In my case, pure and lovely chance. In 1957, I was working for the University of California Far East Extension Program, teaching sociology courses to far-flung U.S. military personnel—a heady and transforming way to be introduced to the world if you've lived all your twenty-seven years in St. Paul/Minneapolis—and done all your graduate and undergraduate work at the University of Minnesota.

The excitement of living in the Far East was hard to give up. I left graduate school and the country in 1955 to do this; in the spring of 1957 I signed up to teach for another year. But I did have my file sent to a number of places which had announced openings, including one called Colorado College (the "The" had not yet been added) in January or February of 1957. I was motivated to do so mostly, I suspect, by a Judaic-Protestant Ethic which mandated that it was more than time to be primarily concerned about my "future"—security, respectability, career. As a great depression baby, like most other young men of my class and generation, I had accepted the idea that I had to do better than my immigrant parents and attain the occupational prestige that had eluded them.

In June I got a telegram from Colorado College offering an Assistant Professorship. The Sociology Department wanted an immediate answer. As I later learned, none of the candidates they interviewed in the spring had passed muster. Desperate, the department decided to take a chance on someone overseas they could not interview and hadn't even spoken to over the phone. (A strong recommendation from the head of the

University of California Far East Extension Program who had been a candidate for the presidency of the College before Louis T. Benezet had been selected probably didn't hurt.) I walked back and forth from my living quarters in Naha, Okinawa and the telegraph office for most of half a day trying to decide what to do.

One of my teaching colleagues had once visited Colorado Springs and told me how lovely it was. He suggested that I try and buy a house near the Garden of the Gods. I didn't buy the house, but the Gods gave me so much and so easily, that I wince in pain at what prospective faculty members must now go through to secure a position.

Still, there was a downside for me: I was prepared neither by sentiment nor past experience for what I was about to encounter. I knew I was coming to a liberal arts college but I had only the vaguest idea of what a liberal arts college was. I had taken liberal arts courses as an undergraduate, but a coherent notion of what such courses were supposed to add up to escaped me. Also, my most recent educational experiences were at the graduate-professional level, where all of us were encouraged to think about our "discipline," and nothing more.

It hadn't helped that in St. Paul I lived a few blocks from another liberal arts college, Macalester. Psychologically, we could just as well have been in separate countries. For me and my hoi polloi friends Macalester was a place that only wealthy WASPS went to. We had other choices: the mega-state university, with bulging classes of five hundred plus—or nothing.

I came to Colorado Springs by over-night train. In early morning I saw the mountains and thought: I might not be leaving this place anytime soon.

INSIGHT AND INTROSPECTION

A dormant college was coming alive when I arrived in the fall of 1957. The administration, new and cocky, was hiring young faculty, reshaping departments, increasing enrollments, and raising money. The Sociology Department had recently separated from a joint Department of Economics and Sociology and, under Van Shaw, was achieving a new intellectual identity.

In a two and a half person department (Van, me, and Ruth Carter), one had to be prepared to teach virtually everything. Graduate education rarely prepares one for this sort of environment, yet the desire to teach your graduate speciality dies hard. I assumed that students in my Methods of Research class would be as intrigued as I was with conflicting philosophical arguments about the legitimacy of social science methodology. I assigned an article by a distinguished philosopher of science under whom I had studied—Herbert Feigl (pronounced F[swa]-gull). The day we discussed it, I wanted to consider whether there was a clock on the wall while my students fought to know what time it was. As I sat openly dejected at the end of class, a student who must have had enormous empathy came up to me and said, "Don't feel bad. Last year, when *he* was new, Professor Freed in the Psychology department also assigned this "Fee-gull" article." Doug Freed and I now refer to this as the "Fee-gull" factor in undergraduate education.

I had to reeducate myself quickly, but it took me many years to absorb fully this teaching lesson: the graduate school penchant for a detailed discussion of all the arcane issues connected to a question is not the stuff out of which exciting undergraduate classes are made. My heart was still in that milieu. I wanted to impress myself and my students with how much I knew. I now know I need to discover where students are in their understanding of an issue so that I can build on it and help them to a next higher step in understanding and sophistication.

In my first years the restructuring of departments and the influx of many new people created an enormous intellectual vitality in the faculty. It was not so much within the relatively tiny departments, but between departments that this new intellectual tension and vibrancy could be felt most intensely. Collaborative teaching was now in the air (a subsequent tradition at the College) and the fluidity of ideas it generated gave one the sense that people were grappling with the human condition in all its guises.

Of all the departments then in the Social Science division of the College, the Psychology Department (which migrated to the Natural Science Division in 1962) became the lightning rod for argumentative discussions about the nature of human nature. The 50s and 60s were the heady days of Skinnerian psychology, and we perceived the Psychology Department as its Praetorian Guard on the Colorado College campus. Psychology sent out legions of epigones who, with maddening tenacity, argued the "cause" (the ubiquitous power of positive and negative rein-forcement) in all the courses they took. Whatever one might think about Skinnerian psychology, the Psychology Department succeeded in pump-ing hot blood into the nature-of-human-nature debate, a debate that is at the center of liberal education.

In most other respects, the College was quite conventional, not unlike other colleges at the beginning of the 60s. Who could have fathomed in advance the radical Zeitgeist that was yet to come? The faculty then was essentially a white male preserve; there were a sprinkling of Jews, myself included, a result of the erosion of anti-Semitic barriers since the end of WWII, but issues of gender and race were still dim on the horizon. Faculty wives stayed home and reared children, giving their academic husbands enormous amounts of time to immerse themselves in their ca-reers and in a variety of activities in and out of class. I'm sure students benefited, but the costs of this division of labor were simply too high. Now, dual career families with young children are much more the norm at Colorado College and teaching has a more human face. There are still costs to be paid, but they are different.

My earliest collision with the conservative ambience of the College came in the form of a reappointment letter from the President indicating that my life in the College community would be much happier if I mar-ried. Convinced that the President had strayed into commissar territory, I accosted the Dean of the College (it was still too early to accost a President) demanding an explanation. What could he say? Ingeniously, he told me that what probably happened is that the President was sitting in his office writing reappointments letters, wondering what to say to Boderman, when I must have wandered by his window alone—suggest-ing to him this bit of fatherly advice about marriage. Still suspicious about the "bit of fatherly advice," I decided to think more seriously about where I wanted to have an academic career.

The 60s were halcyon days for professors. Jobs were plentiful and, de-pending on taste and inclination, one could push for an appointment at a small liberal arts college or at an emerging mega-university. I wasn't sure yet what I wanted to do. In 1963 after six years at Colorado College, I took a year's leave of absence and accepted a position at a research organization connected with the American University in Washington D.C. There was an assumption then, and now, that unless you do formal research, you are not fulfilling yourself as an academic. I wanted to return to my graduate student roots and find out how fulfilling such a life would be for me.

COMMITMENT

How do options get transformed into commitments? What sparks the realization, "This is what I want to do?"

I left Colorado College with the possibility that I might return, but it was options that I had in mind, not commitments. My renewed immersion in planning and executing research was technically satisfying but constraining. What I started to miss was a collegial environment that allowed me to be a generalist. Graduate education had yoked me to its definition of competence—specialization. But the rewards I was capable of deriving from that definition of the academic enterprise were no longer sufficient. To borrow Isaiah Berlin's classification ("The fox knows many things, but the hedgehog knows one big thing."), I wanted to try and emulate the tradition of the foxes, not the hedgehogs. Teaching and the classroom, I now understood, were the catalysts which would allow me to roam far and wide, not only in my discipline but in the interstices between disciplines and from there into general education—the heart of the liberal arts. I wanted a setting where I could explore with colleagues and students fundamental human concerns: justice, happiness, authority, inequality, freedom. Armed with this new vision of my academic calling, I returned to Colorado College in the fall of 1964—to stay. Shortly after, I was informed that I had been given tenure. I had hardly been aware that I was up for consideration. Such insouciance about tenure would be unthinkable today.

Many of my close colleagues on the faculty were also driven by intellectual aims similar to mine. Although we all had a disciplinary self-image, our identities as teachers began increasingly to shape who and what we were, how we saw ourselves. Doing formal research still had enormous cachet, but many of us were now defining scholarship more broadly to include superb teaching and immersion in areas outside of our discipline,

especially issues at the core of general education. What should an educated person know? Could general education withstand the onslaught of
specialization? Did students really need to understand the defiance of
Antigone against the authority of the state or why Socrates chose a principled death over escape? The questions came easier than the answers.

Whatever the debate among faculty about the nature of liberal education and how the College could best prepare students for citizenship
and careers, there was a sense that we were all in this together. The academic market place in the 60s and 70s was still a seller's paradise. Most
new faculty coming to Colorado College came because they chose to do
so, not because market forces made the small, struggling liberal arts college the only available alternative for a position. I sense then, and never
in quite the same way since, that there was a commitment to the College
as such, something linking us to a set of purposes beyond our disciplinary
and departmental affiliations, purposes that we were able to feel, perhaps,
more than articulate, but that operated nonetheless as powerful motives
for our behavior. Perhaps, as my course in social psychology tries to show,
"we come to love the things for which we suffer," so long as the choice to
"suffer" is ours to make. Colorado College was struggling mightily in the
60s to become an exemplary undergraduate institution for liberal education. Struggle and adversity with a chance of success can be exciting and
powerful unifying forces. They were for us.

THE SYMPOSIUM YEARS

For those worried about the future of liberal education in the 60s, the
issue du jour was the split between literary intellectuals and scientists, documented dramatically by the English scientist-novelist C.P. Snow in his
1959 book *The Two Cultures*. Literary intellectuals, Snow argued, were not
on speaking terms with scientists and had little understanding of the value
and importance of scientific ideas. Many of my colleagues and I were
convinced that Snow was on to something, and we discussed his work in
terms of its meaning for undergraduate education, for example, how
could the study of science be made more accessible to non-science majors? We are still grappling with this issue today.

With a grant from what was then the Public Lectures Committee, I organized a three-day "Science-Humanism Symposium" which took place in March of 1961. The success of the "Science-Humanism Symposium" led to the suggestion that we have an "all-college symposium" lasting a week before the start of the second semester. Fred Sondermann of the Political Science Department (who could do more work in a day than most people could do in a week) became symposium director. The first symposium, "Contemporary Arts and the Citizen," was an extraordinary success. Each year's symposium thereafter became an intellectual cornucopia for many townspeople who looked to the College for intellectual engagement. In succeeding years symposium subjects were "The Second World War," "The New Science," "Humor," "The City," and "The American Presidency." The symposium on "The City" offended some city officials because it focused attention on blighted areas of Colorado Springs. That ruffling of local feathers, however, was a very minor disturbance compared to the brouhaha in which the next symposium was about to explode.

Fred Sondermann became increasingly involved in local politics and in 1968 I became director of what had become known as "The Colorado College Symposium." The Free Speech Movement which had spread to colleges and universities all over the country, the discontent over the war in Vietnam and the draft, the civil rights movement—all of these erupting challenges to the status quo focused everyone's attention on the cascading rhetoric of violence in American society. The format of the symposium seemed an appropriate venue for venting these rapidly accumulating tensions that were monopolizing discussion in and out of the classroom. Symposium topics were chosen through a series of meetings in which interested faculty and students came together to discuss various possibilities. Those attending meetings in the spring of 1968 quickly reached a consensus on "Violence." Shortly afterwards we saw the murder of Senator Robert F. Kennedy and Dr. Martin Luther King, Jr. and the TV spectacle of a Democratic National Convention held in the midst of violence. The 1969 symposium topic seemed even more compelling and urgent than when we had chosen it.

The "Violence Symposium" had an aura of radicalism about it, even though a number of conservatives and moderates were arrayed against liberals and radicals. But the radicals made the biggest splash in the local media, among them Dick Gregory former comedian turned social activist, who gave a two-hour talk to a jam-packed student audience in Armstrong Theater. His remark, "The American Flag moves me about as much as a pair of dirty drawers . . . to me the people under the flag are more important," was a bit inflammatory for many members of the local community. Local blood pressure rose even higher when two national leaders from Students for a Democratic Society (SDS), one of whom was a member of the "anarchist" wing of the SDS ("Up Against the Wall, Motherfucker!") ended their talk by advising students in the audience to "join us, get the hell out of the way, or fight us."

But what really started the lava of moral indignation flowing, and with Vesuvian force, was the final symposium event: a play, *Dionysus '69*, a modern adaptation of Euripides's *The Bacchae*. The play was given by an off-Broadway theater troupe from New York, directed by Richard Schechner, who was an advocate of "living theater," in which performers become part of the audience and the audience becomes part of the performance. Schechner gave a more controversial talk than we expected, urging students to "be free, abandon your inhibitions and do your own thing." This set the stage for the "performance" to come.

In New York this theater company sometimes gave parts of their play in the nude. I had asked them not to do so in their College performance because the ensuing controversy would overshadow what the symposium was trying to accomplish. They agreed. After they arrived, however, or so Schechner told me the morning *after* the performance, "the vibes at the College were so good" that the nine-member cast voted to perform two scenes in the nude, including the finale in which the audience was invited to participate.

A City Council woman left during the first nude scene, whispering to me, "This is not my cup of tea." Male and female performers weaved in and out of rows of seats asking members of the audience at crucial moments in the play to strip as well. A number of our students obliged. The overall effect of stage lighting on the naked bodies of the performers—which had been bathed in red paint to show the awful punishment that Dionysus inflicted on those who denied his divinity—created a striking final scene.

The symposium ended on a Saturday night. Sunday morning newspaper articles suggested a symposium wallowing in four-letter words (except for Dick Gregory, two members of SDS, and Performance Group director Richard Schechner, everyone's language was squeaky clean) with all students cavorting in the nude. Although most of the people who subsequently complained about the symposium had learned about it secondhand, it was clear to them that Colorado College was seeking to undermine the moral fibre of the community.

Monday morning was ballistic. I experienced the "Grand Clong," a term coined by Frank Mankiewicz. It occurs when "things get hopelessly loused up and you suddenly feel a rush of shit to the heart." Television crews invaded the campus, radio talk shows and letters to the editor in local newspapers talked of nothing else. One CC employee was quoted as saying, "When you go to the butcher shop, they're talking about the symposium." The local clergy weighed in with critical sermons. There were rumors that wills were being changed by college benefactors. And it went on for what seemed a very long time.

President Worner, whatever his private reservations about the good taste of the symposium, stood up to all of the scorn heaped on the College. For him it was a free speech issue, and he realized that a college would lose its very reason for being if it allowed those outside of the institution to decide what controversial issues could be explored or how to explore them. The College stuck out its collective neck in defense of controversy. Lew Worner proved his leadership by keeping the hatchets at bay.

But in a strange way, the College administration gained something of incalculable value because of the "Violence Symposium." At a time when most colleges and universities were being besieged by students who saw their institutions as complicit in an evil war and an evil government, Colorado College students could and did unite in defense of a college administration fighting to preserve autonomy against the criticisms of a conservative community. We had no student uprisings. I doubt we would have been so lucky had it not been for the aftermath of a turbulent (but nonvi-

olent!) Symposium which conferred a legitimacy on the College it might
not otherwise have had in the eyes of students.

There was one more symposium before the introduction of the block
plan in 1970 changed everything. It wasn't until 1988 with a new academic calender change that we were able to once again carve out time for
this yearly event. None of these subsequent symposiums generated quite
the controversy of the "Violence Symposium," although all of them got
the College into the community and the community into the college. Few
other formats have been able to capture the sustained excitement and ferment that these endeavors were able to generate at their best: "Intimacy,"
"Ethnicity and Identity," "Defending The Earth," "Spirituality and
Religion." This second round of symposiums ended in 1996.

But back to 1970 and the inception of the block plan . . .

TEACHING: THE TRANSFORMATION

The experimentalism of the block plan was infectious. Course structures
had to be reorganized in order to justify total student involvement in a single course for three and a half weeks. What to teach and how to teach it
were also up for grabs. How do you keep undergraduates involved in classes
that lasted for three or more hours? The lecture as a mode of instruction
seemed antiquated and authoritarian. It may have been for both ideological and pragmatic reasons that we explored a more Socratic mode of teaching in which we tried to reduce power and status differences between student and teacher. The tie-shirt-sport coat ensemble all male faculty I had
arrived in at CC was out. Most of us dressed more like students and
adopted a student patois as well: some, more convincingly than others,
rapped. As we struggled to achieve a more egalitarian classroom relationship with students, the counterculture environment of the 70s fueled the experimentalism of the block plan. People scrambled for formats for classes:
a debate one day, films the next, dividing up in small groups and then coming back together again for group presentations on a third, spending all day
reading a large work on a fourth, going to the Garden of the Gods to discuss it on a fifth, an observational study on the next two days, etc. But style
and structure weren't the only things that changed. However one evaluates

student radicalism of the 60s and 70s, it did force the professoriat to open up the question—"Knowledge for what and for whom?"

Beneath all the changes there was enormous vitality. We were venturesome, willing to poke our noses into the most controversial of things. How else explain the chutzpah that led me and Doug Freed to give a General Studies course, shortly after the inception of the block plan, titled "A Critical Evaluation of the Women's Liberation Movement." There were still very few women on the faculty, and we saw nothing wrong with two men taking on the task of introducing students to the Movement. Even stranger, although the class was all women, none attacked us for thinking we could or should be teaching it. We were still a few years away from the identity politics which would have made our teaching such a course laughable, or a dramatic demonstration to many of the very patriarchy the Women's Movement was designed to destroy. But there was no one else to do it.

Teaching in general studies and with colleagues from different disciplines seemed wonderful to me, and the block plan made it more possible. At its best, co-teaching models for students how to disagree, the rules for intellectual engagement: how to challenge someone's position respectfully, how to keep your sense of humor and playfulness, and how to remain respectful and friendly after the encounter. When Bill Hochman and I show students our disagreements in the General Studies Course "Morality in War" (Are moral concepts relevant to the conduct or analysis of war?), we not only show legitimate disagreement, but we convey to students why intellectual closure on specific issues is so hard to achieve. I hope we also lead students to learn to live with contradiction, to see the excitement and value in it, and to preserve their right to become committed to a particular view or course of action in the face of available alternatives.

Different kinds of people bring different things to the College enterprise. I love teaching in my discipline, but I have also come to believe that students need the sustenance of general education to achieve one of the highest goals of liberal education—the development of character. Few believe that the sole purpose of education is to impart knowledge. Very knowledgeable and intelligent people can do very evil things. How to use knowledge wisely, how to develop a moral imagination and a measure of wisdom to act on it, have always been a central preoccupation of the liberal arts. An exposure to general education does not insure wisdom, but it can facilitate the acquisition of self-conscious choices and the strength to live with them. Without this we are in danger of becoming what Max Weber, at the very end of his "The Protestant Ethic and the Spirit of Capitalism," once warned us we might all become: "Specialists without spirit, sensualists without heart."

Committed as I am to the importance of general studies, I delight in my discipline even more. The courses I teach in social psychology and human intimacy are the great loves of my teaching and intellectual life. I give them everything, and they take all I give—and more. But, for me, they *are* general studies. They are in the interdisciplinary borderland between sociology and psychology, a place ripe for cross-fertilization. The tradition in social psychology with which I most strongly identify has always been receptive to those who are committed to exploring the depth and breadth of human nature and to linking empirical findings to central social, political and philosophical issues. Bold and audacious social psychological studies on obedience to authority, love, altruism, commitment, and meaning in life have allowed me and my students to confront, and sometimes unriddle, a core set of problems that envelop everyday existence and telling moments of our lives. I can't think of anything else I'd rather do.

A WONDERFUL LIFE REDUX

We are shaped by our choices, even those we think are just momentary. I came to Colorado College thinking it would be a way station to the kind of academic career my professors in graduate school had modeled for me. But this institution gave me opportunities for educating myself and students in ways I had not fully understood before, and it gave me access to colleagues who were undergoing a similar transformation. The camaraderie we created as we found new drummers to march to has left me grateful for what it has meant to be a faculty member at this College. The richness of the regular but informal encounters I continue to have with colleagues—almost every morning at what has come to be known as "The Breakfast Club," which began many years ago at the Hub and continues now in Benjamin's, or at the Freedom & Authority Luncheon Group where the favorite sport sometimes is "Can you top this interpretation?"—leaves me looking forward to the new ways in which the College will become a collegial, inviting, and exciting place for a new generation of faculty as well as students.

Forty years of learning, teaching, and discovery at Colorado College. What a wonderful life!

Gilbert R. Johns
Professor Emeritus of Psychology and
Former Dean of the Summer Session, 1965–81

CHAPTER 13

THREE GOLDEN ERAS IN THE PERFORMING ARTS

Gilbert R. Johns
Professor Emeritus of Psychology and
Former Dean of the Summer Session

Colorado College has long been a cultural oasis in Colorado Springs, a city that prided itself mainly on its mountains, its clean, dry air and being the home of the *Pikes Peak or Bust Rodeo*. Early in its history, the College added to its mandate to offer a first-rate liberal arts education, a decision to offer its students the best in the performing arts. This decision had a powerful, transforming influence on the cultural life of the Colorado Springs community, an influence that continues unabated today. While there is a recent bronze sculpture of a cowboy in the center of downtown, community members attend performing arts events on campus in great numbers throughout the year. Many of the current performing arts organizations—the symphony, the opera, the chorale— have strong ties to the College in terms of origins, artistic focus and management.

The first golden era followed the appointment of composer and virtuoso pianist Rubin Goldmark to be director in 1894 of the just formed Colorado College Conservatory of Music. A Student of Dvorak and born in Austria, he is regarded as an American composer. He was a teacher of both Aaron Copeland and George Gershwin.

At the College, he organized mixed choruses, glee and mandolin clubs. His singing groups toured widely in Colorado and New Mexico. He brought to the campus such artists as Josef Hoffman, an internationally acclaimed pianist. The Chicago Symphony gave two concerts. All of this was tied academically to such College courses as voice, piano, composition and counterpoint.

Goldmark had a vision for the College and the community that still informs them. At the dedication of the Perkins Fine Arts Hall in 1899 (which was demolished in 1964 along with Coburn Library to make room for Armstrong Hall) Goldmark said: "The destiny of art pointed westward; art had come out of the East and its progress has been toward the West."

THE SECOND GOLDEN ERA

The years following Goldmark's departure were spent consolidating the gains (mainly within the College) that Goldmark had initiated. In 1940, the College joined forces with the Fine Arts Center in sponsoring a concert series that went on for ten years and included such artists as Robert Casadesus, Andres Segovia and Lotte Lehman. A conference on the fine arts with Frank Lloyd Wright as leader brought American composer Roy Harris and his wife, pianist Johana, to Colorado Springs, and in 1941 the arts conference under the leadership of the Harrises became a fixture of the College summer program.

Also in 1941, the College arranged a concert by the Leopold Stokowski youth Orchestra in Penrose Stadium, the venue of the Pikes Peak or Bust Rodeo.

The 1940's were glorious times for the performing arts. On the campus in the summers were the Harrises with composers such as Virgil Thomson and Paul Hindemith. Arnold Schoenberg was engaged to come for the Schoenberg Festival. He died before he was scheduled to arrive, and the Festival became a memorial concert for the composer, performed by members of the College faculty. A world-class string quartet was in place consisting of Joe Gingold and Robert Gross, violins, Ferenc Molnar, viola, and Carl Stern, cello. Bass Herbert Beattie who became a major artistic force in the College from 1970 to the present was a student at the College during this period.

The College won additional national acclaim with two, hour-long concerts broadcast over ABC and several half-hour concerts on CBS.

But the event that may have had the greatest, longest lasting and farthest reaching effect on the College's performing arts history was the

College's hiring of modern dance pioneer and choreographer Hanya Holm for the summer of 1941. Colorado College's relationship with Hanya Holm lasted untill 1983 and encompassed the tenures of five Colorado College presidents.

THE THIRD GOLDEN ERA:
THE HANYA HOLM YEARS AND THE OPERA

The account in most dance history books goes something like this: In the beginning there was Isadora Duncan. Then came Ruth St. Denis and Ted Shawn. Next came The Big Four—Doris Humphrey, Charles Weidman, Martha Graham, and Hanya Holm—who together established modern dance as a major cultural force, competitive with ballet.

Hanya was a key member of Germany's Mary Wigman Company that toured the US in 1931. Impresario Sol Hurok urged Hanya to leave Germany and come back to New York to head a Mary Wigman American company. Hanya was glad to leave Germany. As she said later: "I said, I go! Because I noticed that when I was in Munich there was something afoot in the beer halls that happened and was not kosher, right?"

She got her taste for Colorado when she was invited to the Perry Mansfield performing arts camp in Steamboat Springs in 1933. During the summers of the 1930s, she and the other members of The Big Four resided at Bennington College, often thought of as the Fertile Crescent of modern dance. During this time she created at Bennington and repeated in New York, *Trend*, which is thought of by many as the pacesetter—the signature of modern dance.

Martha Wilcox of the Colorado College Dance Department brought her to the College where she quickly attracted many students such as Alwin Nicolais, Murray Louis, Glen Tetley, and Valerie Bettis who became the next generation of modern dance innovators. Performances were frequent, and the final student performance gave the Colorado audience snippets of *Trend* including the fluid ensemble, "Entrances and Exits."

In the 1940s and 1950s Hanya expanded her career. She was choreographer and trend setter in what has been called the golden age of musicals, among them *Kiss Me, Kate, Camelot* and *My Fair Lady*. She was full of stories for students, faculty and friends. For example, she told how Rex

Harrison, timid about even rehearsing dance in a musical, asked to go to her hotel room with Julie Andrews. Hanya worked out the famous "Rain in Spain" tango by personally dancing with Harrison with Andrews watching and ready to step in when he felt comfortable. Years later Andrews reminisced about Hanya: "One is left with an impression of great strength, much sweetness. She is a lady—a very classy dame."

But there was steel. One of President Lew Worner's favorite stories involved Hanya. In 1963 the College business office cut a deal with the Houston Oilers to practice at the College. They needed to adjust to the altitude before their opening game with the Denver Broncos. They were perhaps overly attentive to the dozens of beautiful young Hanya dancers. (Hanya admitted that the pro football players might have received some encouragement from the dancers.) There were a few incidents and even a panty-raid scrimmage outside the dorms. As Lew told it, Hanya showed up at his office, dressed to kill in one of her elegant black curtain-call dresses, probably a Fortuny. Hanya's message to Lew was simple: "They go, or I go." They went.

During this period, Hanya demonstrated directing skills that the College made good use of. She directed the North American premiere of Gluck's opera *Orpheus* in Vancouver. In Central City in Colorado, she directed the world premiere of Douglas Moore's now famous opera, *The Ballad of Baby Doe*, with a Leadville, Colorado setting.

The College gave her an honorary doctorate in 1960, and the citation referred to her as "our fair lady." In 1965, then Summer Session Director Fred Sondermann arranged a dance festival in celebration of her 25th summer heading the School of Dance at the College. Many of her former students were brought in as performers and choreographers (six of them) in three nights of dance at the Fine Arts Center.

I had never given any thought to being Dean of the Summer Session— it certainly wasn't on my career wish list. My career was in experimental psychology, and in 1965 I was immersed in my government-supported research. I had made a few, of what I thought were casual, remarks to President Lew Worner about the state of the performing arts at the College and in Colorado Springs. I found out during a trip to Grinnell College in Iowa from their then acting president, Jim Stauss, that they had a string quartet in residence at what I thought was a reasonable price. Why couldn't Colorado College do the same thing and send the quartet around the state (and eventually the country) as a high prestige advertisement for us.

A few days later I was having a coffee break in the old student union, Rastall Center. Lew, a regular, was there. He asked me to wait until the other faculty had left, then asked me if I would be horrified if he asked me to be summer session dean and increase the College's summer involvement and visibility in the arts. I was horrified, but after a few days thought and some good-natured arm twisting by his Director of Development, Bob Brossman, I nervously accepted.

I was victim of one of Lew's famous ploys; if you complained about some aspect of the College, you might find yourself heading it. It was Missouri-native Lew Worner's down-home policy of put-up or shut-up. The same thing happened to Professor William Hochman. He was distressed by the teacher's college approach of the education department and the ill-prepared students we were turning out, often unversed in the Colleges' liberal arts ideas. Bill woke up one morning, still a member of the history department, to discover that Lew had appointed him head of the Education Department. Lew was right. Bill turned the department around and later spearheaded summer programs in arts and humanities with a strong performing arts component.

Before I actually started in the Summer Session, Fred Sondermann who was leaving it, invited me to a town and gown meeting run by Professor Max Lanner, head of the Music Department, virtuoso pianist and key player since 1951 in the College's commitment to the performing arts. Lanner told the group that the College was considering cutting back on the summer arts programs and particularly the summer string quartet whose players were not attracting any students. The quartet contained some fine players, but had little sense of ensemble, and its disappearance from the campus wouldn't be a great loss. One member who played with an embarrassing over-wrought, saccharin style, was referred to by cynics as the Gypsy Baron.

Community members were horrified by the prospects of the College pulling back. The summer performing arts program they said not only enriched the community, but some suggested it was the only game in town. We had a mandate to create a renaissance of the 1940's cultural ferment, and we still had the Hanya Holm School of Dance with its international reputation to serve as a centerpiece.

The first Summer Session I directed began on June 16, 1966. June 16 is Bloomsday, the day that Leopold Bloom in James Joyce's novel *Ulysses* makes his way around Dublin. I invited Ellsworth Mason, our former head librarian who oversaw the building of Tutt Library and who was a published Joyce scholar, to give the key note address that with Joycean wit he entitled, "Bloom on Rye." We played a rare recording of Joyce reading the "Anna Livia Plurabelle" section from his novel, *Finnegan's Wake*, while a slide show of his life was presented. Drama Department head, Professor William McMillen, and his students put on several scenes from the play, *Ulysses in Nighttown*. We gave a Joycean word-game name to our institution; it became Colorollege.

The Bloomsday celebration was well attended and enthusiastically received. It provided encouragement and even a mandate for a direction the College summer arts program might go. Many subsequent summers had a theme such as "The Muse Invoked," "The Estimable Festival Estival," "Holm on the (front) Range," and "Bach, Beethoven and Bartok." Each summer there were eight weeks of performing artists and visiting speakers such as theologian Martin Marty, film critic Pauline Kael, New York City mayor John Lindsay, US Education Department head Francis Keppel, and photography historian Beaumont Newhall.

The Aspen Music Festival had been in existence each summer since 1950, but the College had made scant use of its resources. Upon investigation, it became clear that many world class artists were delighted to make the 150 mile trip over the mountains to play here and earn additional income. The Aspen Festival became an ongoing source for musical artists. Over the years we had such groups as the American Brass Quintet, violinist Sergiu Luca, and brass and woodwind quintets drawn from the first-chair players in Aspen.

There were a variety of string quartets, including the Juilliard which for several summers played separate programs on two evenings. They, like most professional groups, welcomed programming suggestions. They gave the Rocky Mountain premiere of Beethoven's 1825 Opus 130 played with the last movement the composer wrote for it, Op. 133, the Grosse

Fuge. It is usually played as a separate work because of the length and difficulty of the two pieces. The audience went wild, but the reviewer for the
now defunct Colorado Free Press complained it was too long.

There was a genuine friendship between many Aspen artists and the
College. Juilliard often came near the birthdays of their founder and first violinist, Robert Mann. The birthday party took place each year at the home
of physics professor and later dean, Richard Bradley and his wife Dorry,
both accomplished and active musicians. Dorry arranged for a splendid
cake with a chocolate violin as a decoration. When Armstrong Hall opened
in 1966, the Juilliard Quartet played the inaugural concert in its auditorium.

The American Brass Quintet used some of their National Endowment
funds to bring their best students to the College to play an antiphonal brass
program with them, featuring works by Gabrieli and Schutz in Packard
Hall. They performed left-right as well as front-back antiphony, and for two
hours Packard hall was a mini-version of Venice's St. Mark Basilica, the
venue for which the works were written.

Hanya Holm, whose early training was in music, developed close
working relationships with many visiting artists such as Sergiu Luca and
the American Brass Quintet; she often requested that they play at her
dance concerts. It was an easy request to grant for Hanya often turned out
her most inspired work when she had great musicians working with her.
Hanya's dance program for several years had the largest summer enrollment. Hanya asked that it not exceed 100 since she and her staff were
having difficulty seeing down the dance lines.

Colorado College through the years didn't have enough spaces for
students who applied—we were committed to a limited enrollment. Like
all colleges, we had some attrition in January, the beginning of the second
half of the year. The College decided in 1968 to admit 60 to 70 students
to start in the summer, miss the fall and come back in January keeping
College enrollment fairly constant, admitting students who were ordinar-
ily denied for lack of space, and increasing our revenues. It was an ingenious plan that still works today.

The dominant academic feature during these years was the institute—six or eight weeks of intensive study taught by small groups of local
and visiting faculty. The summer institutes provided one of the templates

for what became the block plan. At one point there were eleven under-graduate institutes, ranging in size from 15 to 25. All of them had distin-guished visiting faculty who could be persuaded to give public lectures for the campus and the town.

Professor Robert Loevy's Urban Studies Institute was instrumental in attracting not only Mayor Lindsay, but also many prominent national figures still active today such as Richard Lugar, Neil Goldschmidt and Richard Hatcher.

While I was on leave, Professor Joseph Pickle (who had run some in-ventive summer institutes) was appointed acting dean. He arranged for a film institute, something I hadn't been able to do, that for several years had a good run. We invited film historians, an Academy Award winning documentary film maker, and active commercial film makers. The stu-dents made their own films which were shown to the campus as the Cache La Poudre Film Festival. These were the days before the camcorder, and most of the films were Super–8. As a class they made a one-reel 16mm. The high point for many of them was when Roger Brown, a visiting doc-umentary sports film maker, used them as grips on a documentary about the Pikes Peak Hill Climb.

Ben Benschneider, a Time-Life photographer, had long been the College's unofficial fine arts photographer for most of the College publi-cations. He taught a four-week photo course that showed he was a natural teacher and had a following. We designed a photography institute around him which quickly became the most sought after institute every summer in spite of the requirements of a submitted portfolio and an interview by Benschneider. His guest lists read like a who's who in photography with names like Lee Friedlander, Duane Michael, Jack Mitchell, and former Colorado College English Professor Robert Adams, a nationally known fine arts photographer, and award winning news magazine photographer David Burnett, class of 1968. The photographers were each here for sev-eral days, and Ben insisted they go out on a shoot with the students.

It was wonderful to watch Ben, patient to a fault, work with students who yearned for self-expression. (This was the 1970s.) Early in the insti-tute, Ben showed them painstakingly how to set up an exhibition-quality still life using not only a light meter but also a tape measure and a slide rule. The students quickly learned that if they were to do their own thing, they had better have technical skills to do it, including doing their own developing and printing in the Benschneider-designed dark room in Packard Hall. Later Ben made the first record of the Shove Chapel stained glass windows presented in a book called, *This Glorious and Transcendent Place*, with text by Tim Fuller.

Ben brought in W. Eugene Smith, the father of the photo essay and arguably the best at it. His photo essays such as "A Spanish Village" (originally in Life magazine) are burned into our consciousness. He was in frail health after being beaten up for his photo essay on Minimata, the Japanese fishing village where many fishermen and their families died or were maimed by mercury poisoning as a result of industrial waste being dumped into the water.

Smith was told that the average summer lecture was an hour or so, with up to twenty minutes allowed for questions and discussion. He informed us that he needed three hours for his lecture/slideshow. He said if people didn't like it, they would be mad at him, not me or the College. He was as good as his word and gave a three-hour absorbing and often soul searing illustrated account of his life's work. Tutt Library Atrium was the venue for most summer lectures (and Sunday afternoon concerts) through the good offices of head librarian George Fagan. The Atrium was packed to the walls, and I don't think more than a dozen people left before it concluded at 11:30 P.M. W. Eugene Smith died shortly after from the Minimata injuries. His presentation at Colorado College was the last he ever did.

Overseas summer institutes which became a feature of later summer sessions in the 1980s and 1990s got their start in the middle 1970s. Professor of Political Science Glenn Brooks, then architect of the Block Plan and later Dean of the College, planned and directed two African institutes. He brought in African faculty, poets, and playwrights. The institutes were so successful we decided to have an institute in Africa with a home base in Dar-es-Salaam. It was quickly subscribed.

Local arrangements were supposed to be made by one of our visiting African faculty who, as it turned out, did little. In addition, the affordable travel arrangements we had worked out for our students were not being honored. Brooks came to my office in early June, ten days or so before the institute's starting date. We had to decide what to do. We sat quietly, and I stared at the floor. Brooks finally spoke up: "I guess I'm going to Africa tonight." He did and, even though many of the arrangements were improvisational, the institute was a success. They even found time to climb Mt. Kilimanjaro.

When Brooks filed his final budget report, he listed an expenditure of $500 for bribes. (Bribery was often the only way he could rent busses, get accommodations and so forth.) I was nervous about the College's auditors seeing the item and went to Political Science Chairman, Professor Douglas Mertz, the College's attorney, for advice. He urged me to leave it in, which I did. It is somewhere in the College's records today.

There were many new institutes started during this period. For example, Anthropology Professor Marianne Stoller and English Professor Joe Gordon organized and ran a Southwest Studies Institute in which students and faculty bussed and camped all over New Mexico. The next step was our creation of a Master of Arts in Teaching in Southwest studies, modeled somewhat after the M.A.T. in Humanities.

During this period perhaps the institute that best reflected the College's educational purposes was The Conversation of Mankind, planned and run by Political Science Professor, and later Dean, Tim Fuller. It was a rigorous introduction to the College's divisions of sciences, humanities, and social science. We put in as many summer start freshman as it would hold. To this day, it is the best introduction to liberal learning that the College has ever mounted.

The largest program in the summer (besides the Hanya Holm Dance Program) was the Arts and Humanities Institute, developed by Bill Hochman and me. We based it on some of the ideas we took from both the John Hay and Danforth Foundation seminars that took place a few years earlier at CC. In its heyday, there were about one hundred teachers and administrators involved in our program. They received a six-week intensive, subject-matter course taught by some of the best faculty. Visiting art and architecture critic Franz Schulze told them jokingly that they were in "intellectual boot camp"—and they agreed, because much of their previous schooling had been in non-subject matter methods courses in very traditional education departments. They were asked to attend every performing arts event, and before each one, the artists would give a brief introduction and often a lecture-demonstration related to their upcoming performance.

We had what we were told was a unique collaboration between the College, a private institution, and District 11, the largest public school district in the state. In addition to Hochman, another frequent director of the Arts and Humanities Program was Professor of Religion Douglas Fox. Fox could successfully teach abstract philosophy with clarity and transparency to teachers. Hochman or Fox and I would go over to District 11 offices where we would present our institute to Superintendent Tom Dougherty who successfully ransacked his budget for funds to give partial scholarships to District 11 teachers and administrators.

While the College had stopped offering masters degrees, our participants told us they needed a place to put the hours earned in our program. In response, and under the leadership of Bill Hochman, we created a Master of Arts in Teaching, a graduate program with one foot firmly in liberal arts education.

While we were heavily into the arts, we had to resort mainly to outside artists for programs. There were exceptions: pianists Max Lanner and Rhea Sadowski and Professor Michael Grace's medieval band, the Collegium Musicum. The rest of the summer program depended mostly on our faculty. The chance to do our own thing came suddenly. Music Professor and choral director Donald Jenkins asked if we could begin an opera workshop program in the summer with some performance of short operas or opera scenes.

I suggested we could do better. We had two people with considerable opera experience and contacts who could be the core of our artistic staff—Hanya Holm, of course, and Herbert Beattie. Beattie with years of experience as a principal of New York City and Central City Operas was one of the great comic basses—maybe the best of his era. In Beattie's style we found what we were looking for. He had a great voice, but he was also a convincing actor who avoided wooden opera gestures.

Thus the Colorado Opera Festival began. We made the decision to be a professional company with union singers—in this case, the American Guild of Musical Artists, the opera equivalent of Actors Equity for the legitimate stage. I was the general director and Don Jenkins was conductor and musical director. Often he shared those duties with Holm, Beattie, and me.

Our wise counselor, our *eminence gris*, was Jim Stauss who had left Grinnell to become Provost at Colorado College. He was a tireless advocate of the performing arts and assisted us with administrative details, strategies, and helped us stay out of trouble.

Beattie was a gold mine of useful information and personal contact with singers who would be believable in our small proscenium, 800 seat house. The repertory for that first year was nothing if ambitious. Professor Albert Seay, Chairman of the Music Department and a world renown musicologist, had prepared from manuscript an edition of Tomasso Traeta's 1771 comic opera, *Il Cavalieri Errante*, (*The Wayward Cavalier*). One of the runaway hits of its day, it hadn't been done for over a century. We decided to do it for musical, prestige and political reasons.

We had expected Beattie to direct it, but he was wary of an opera that he thought might be a precious museum piece in the worst sense. Knowing of Hanya's background in opera, I called her in New York and offered to fly her out. Hanya, Beattie, Jenkins and I spent several hours in the music department studio while the entire score was played and bits of it sung by Beattie and Jenkins. Hanya listened intensely, remarked that it had some music reminiscent of Gluck, and without delay said: "Ja, I do it."

She found may of the arias endless so, in addition to having them shortened by Jenkins, she had the soldier guarding the captured heroine endlessly knit a long red muffler that became longer and longer as the opera went on.

A shipwreck was called for in the plot, and Hanya gave it some razzle-dazzle. Strips of translucent sea-green silk were pulled across the stage proscenium and undulated to simulate waves. Hanya put her cast, none of whom were anorexic, in vertical striped Victorian bathing costumes. Perched on stools of varying heights hidden by the silk bands, they appeared to be swimming and splashing as they sang the first act finale. The applause and laughter nearly covered the music.

Beattie directed the rest of the season which consisted of a double bill of Monteverdi's *Il Combatimento di Tancred e Clorinda* and a playful and sinister version of Stravinsky's *L'Histoire du Soldat*. Beattie made an artistic decision he has yet to live down; he cast Tancred and Clorinda as bikers who roared onto stage on their ear-shattering Harleys. When they raised the visors on their motorcycle helmets, they discovered that they had been lovers. It didn't quite work, but it gave the young Festival the reputation of having an inventive, anything-goes, style that helped us enormously in the years I was General Director, 1970 to 1978.

The last production that inaugural year, also directed by Beattie, was Verdi's final opera, *Otello*. The first season was a success both critically and in terms of attendance. Moreover, no one could accuse the Festival of choosing four easy pieces.

Audiences and music critics learned quickly that this wasn't ponderous grand opera. The opera wasn't over when the fat lady sang, because there were no fat ladies in our company. Beattie made our production of Prokofiev's *The Love for Three Oranges* into a *commedia del arte* circus. He had Virginia Starr, our lead soprano, the villainess of the piece and in circus tights, swing across the stage on a trapeze delivering high C threats to all assembled. At the end of the opera, the cast and crew dragged a surprised Jenkins out of the orchestra pit, put him on the swing and had him doing some high-flying on the swing as the curtain came down.

Three or four performances of three or four operas were done each summer. Hanya directed five and planned movement for several others. Beattie directed more than twice that number and sang major roles in several. He directed most of the five Mozart operas we did. Klaus Holm, Hanya's son, was stage designer for all of the opera and the dance productions. Several productions were directed by visitors we brought to the summer program for that reason. All of the conducting and musical preparation were done by Jenkins.

Artistic problems were usually settled easily. We decided to do Donizetti's *Don Pasquale* with some elements of the last scene of *Godfather I*. Klaus Holm designed and built a glorious garden. In the title role, Beattie who also directed was dressed in full Italian gentleman gardener clothes—floppy straw hat and all. New York City Center tenor, Gary Glaze, one of our stars and usually amiable, came to me in rehearsal and bitterly complained that Beattie was downstage killing bugs— with a 50-

year-out-of-period Flit Gun no less— while Glaze was upstage singing a major aria. Glaze made me an offer we couldn't refuse: "Get rid of Beattie's bug extermination program, or I walk." I told Jenkins, who told Beattie, who agreed, and peace was restored.

There were many highlights; the Festival was one of the first companies to do the sardonic Weill-Brecht opera, *The Rise and Fall of the City of Mahagonny*. The Met got around to doing it years later. We were one of the first companies to put on the original, pure, spare Mussorgsky version of *Boris Godunov* (with bass Arnold Voketaitus as Boris) and not the gussied up Rimsky-Korsakov version usually done.

Hanya directed an enchanting version of Ravel's *L'Enfant et les Sortileges* based on a children's story by Collette. She did her opera directing in between her morning and afternoon dance school duties, and often in the evenings after she prepared dinner for Klaus and her grandchildren. I remember coming back from lunch with her on an oppressively hot day. As soon as she came back into the rehearsal hall, she and her assistant choreographed and danced a soft shoe duet to Ravel's jazz rhythms. Later that day, they taught it to the singers who would have to perform it in the opera.

She choreographed Mahler's song cycle, *Kindertotenlieder* for Claudia Gittelman, one of the instructors on her dance staff. The text was sung by one of the opera principals, Mezzo soprano, Jeanne Piland.

In 1978 we decided to do Handel's comic opera *Xerxes*. ("Funnier than Messiah," I said in public meetings, "or your money back.") We quickly found out from opera archival sources that we were giving the first US professional stage production. The leading and powerful US music critic, Harold C. Schonberg of the New York Times, came to review our production. When he arrived, he went to my administrative assistant, Ann McGowan, for a *Xerxes* score. She had no choice but to hand him mine which detailed all of the cuts and rearrangement of arias and the elimination of most of the *da capo* repeats we had done to make the opera a workable length. Schonberg was noted for being a purist, and we feared he would be horrified by our presumptions and put off by director Patrick Bakman's zany, irreverent direction. Not to worry. He gave us a strong review: "This was a very good, stylish production, backed by some fine American singers."

Soon after, he devoted his Sunday column to the College, our festival's history, repertoire and goals, and our sold-out seasons. He commented on our *Xerxes*: "The music is gorgeous, and somehow the libretto works on stage—or it did work in the stylish tongue-in-cheek production of the Colorado Opera Festival."

We were always short of money. In fact, all opera companies are. Jenkins and I would begin the season in late spring by getting an elevator key and moving pianos into practice rooms on the second and third floors of Armstrong Hall for our singers. We found that when we did Verdi's *Macbeth*, we didn't have enough money to make costumes for all of the soldiers who were to go from Birnam Wood to Dunsinane. Our technical director John Redman, class of 1971, flooded the stage with thick chemical stage smoke which gave a good feeling of the Scottish moors while disguising the fact that Macduff had a minuscule army.

Jenkins and I went to New York each fall to audition and cast for the operas in our repertoire. One of our main sources was New York City Opera where we had connections through the good offices of some of their singers such as Glaze, Beattie and Voketaitus. Word got around quickly in the opera world that we were an inventive company that paid decent fees, had good weather, and, along with the community, were genuinely glad to have artists in our midst. Very soon we had to keep our whereabouts in New York secret, because singers' agents were after us to audition their clients, no matter how unsuitable they were for our kind of opera. Jenkins and I would come back to our hotel bar late after a day of auditions, talks with agents, and performances. We would combine our notes. I remember that Jenkins occasionally used the abbreviation BUV for a singer. It meant Big Ugly Voice, and I quickly adopted the notation.

Three of the sopranos we hired in those years were Elizabeth Hines, Maria Spacagna and Jeanne Piland, all beautiful women with voices to match, and now international stars. The Festival was a good training ground. Many members of our organization continued their opera careers after leaving Colorado Springs. John Redman, our first technical director (and the one who built some wonderfully weird Renaissance masks for Hanya's production of Puccini's *Gianni Schicchi*) now has his own stage design business in New York. Our next technical director, Drew

Landmesser, is tech director for Chicago Lyric Opera. Linda Brovsky who
started with the Festival right out of a local high school as prop girl, and
worked her way up to assistant director, is now a successful, nationally
known, opera director. Soprano Sally Stunkel who reveled in comic roles
is now a director with Aspen Opera Theatre. Cindy Layman started out
as an opera office gofer while she was still an undergraduate at the
College, worked for Chicago Lyric and is now head of press and market-
ing at the Santa Fe Opera.

In spite of our national success and the New York Times stories, (or as
some cynics suggested, because of it) Colorado College terminated its connection in 1978 with the Colorado Opera Festival, and I terminated mine.
The College had been generous with rehearsal space and a good deal of
in-service facilities and help. The Festival saw itself as a professional company in summer residence at the College. President Lloyd Worner, Vice
President Bob Brossman and some of the trustees were nervous about our
prominence and worried, half facetiously, that we might become Colorado
Opera College, weakening our mandate to provide the best undergraduate education in the country. While faculty had heavy involvement in the
Festival, undergraduate involvement, for the most part, was confined to the
chorus, the apprentice program and the production staff.

The Colorado Opera Festival then moved to the grim confines of
Palmer High School Auditorium where they scraped along until 1982
when the Pikes Peak Center was built. It is a 2000 seat house with first rate
acoustics for symphonies, but not particularly friendly to opera performance. The Colorado Springs Symphony was the financial and administrative force behind its construction.

The Pikes Peak Center changed the character of the Festival.
Financial considerations cut the season down from nine or ten performances of three or four operas to one opera with three or four performances per summer. The size of the hall often required the hiring of
more expensive Met-type voices. These circumstances forced it to put on
more popular and often less inventive standard repertoire blockbusters
such as *Rigoletto*, *Il Trovatore*, *Tosca*, *La Traviata*, and *The Merry Widow*. (In
the days at the College, the Festival had the luxury of considering Mozart
operas standard repertoire, and did five of them).

The new Festival in 1994 put on a production with unarguable world class standards—Puccini's *Turandot*, directed by Beattie, conducted by Jenkins, and featuring dramatic coloratura soprano Martile Rowland in the title role.

The summer arts program continued with Hanya still a key figure. In 1979 she directed and choreographed the Josef and Karol Capek expressionist play, *The Insect Comedy*. Besides her students, Hanya enlisted many faculty and staff to play insects which gave the campus and the town more pleasure than it should have. It was a cautionary tale, the kind of thing German-born Hanya was superb at. The play's litany: "Big fleas have little fleas/ On their backs to bite them/ Little fleas have lesser fleas/ And so— *ad infinitum*." The drum beats had always been a few milliseconds off during rehearsal but right on during performance. Backstage I found Hanya, mallets flying, playing the kettledrums herself.

Hanya's 40th consecutive summer at the College was 1980. Through some national grants, generous help from the College through Lew Worner, and her former students willing to work for reduced fees, we were able to put together eight weeks of modern dance in honor of Hanya entitled, *Holm on the (Front) Range*. We were told that it was the largest modern dance festival ever attempted. There were fourteen performing arts events in eight weeks.

We invited the Alwin Nicolais Dance Theatre, the Murray Louis Dance Company, the Nancy Hauser Dance Company, and the Don Redlich Dance Company. Walter Terry, the senior American dance critic gave a lecture, 200 Years of Dance. Jack Mitchell who had photographed Hanya many times for Dance Magazine and her awards, gave a slide lecture, "A Photographer Looks at the Performing Arts." Violinist Sergiu Luca and pianist Ann Epperson gave a recital of music inspired by dance and played for Hanya's new work. William Bolcom and Joan Morris performed songs from Broadway musicals that Hanya had been involved with. Nicolais, the multi-media magician who the New York Times called the "greatest showman in American," had so much tech equipment that he had to use a DC10 to bring everything. At that time, the Colorado Springs Airport was too small for a DC10 so we sent a stage crew and two trucks to Denver (where they could land) to bring company and gear down. Nik was Hanya's most famous student and went back the farthest. His shows were full of breathtaking razzle dazzle with light, sound, costumes projected and every state-of-the-art stage device that existed in 1980. Hanya wasn't always happy with Nik seemingly giving dance second place to high tech glitz. She said to him: "Nik, we don't want robots." He then put on one unadorned piece that was glorious and pure with little high tech. Hanya was ecstatic.

The master class those two old pros did together was a summer highlight. They walked up and down the long lines of dancers correcting arms, feet, hands, focus. Nik was troubled by the bulky leg and ankle warmers then in fashion for dancers. (It was 90 degrees in the Cossitt rehearsal hall.) Since he couldn't see ankles and knees, he went around gently tapping the offending warmers with a drumstick indicating that they be removed. He said to Hanya: "We never wore this s—, did we?" Hanya agreed they surely hadn't, and for the rest of the summer the warmers disappeared.

The College gave Nik an honorary degree in 1988, the same year he got the White House award in Lincoln Center.

Walter Terry attended Hanya's master class before he gave his lecture. At lunch he needled her for being a show-off. She gave her lengthy instructions to her students in a relevé (high up on the toes). Terry reported that many of the 20 year old students couldn't hold it, but octagenarian Hanya could. "It hurts, but I do it," she said.

Hanya's contributions to the performing arts that summer was her helping shape the student presentations and the repeat of her 1975 work *Rota* by the Redlich company and the world premiere of a witty work, again performed by Redlich. The music was Ravel's Sonata for Violin and Piano, where the second movement is called Blues. It was played by Luca and Epperson and is now called *Jocose*. It has been performed (and received rave reviews) several times in New York.

Nineteen eighty-one was the 100th anniversary of the birth of Bela Bartok, who along with Stravinsky, is regarded as the 20th century's greatest composer. It was my final year in the Summer Session office. We put together an eight-week festival, entitled *Bach, Beethoven, and Bartok.*

Carlton Gamer, Professor of Music, composer and Bartok enthusiast, gave the keynote address in which he showed how Bartok was the bridge to

20th century music. We put on a semi-staged version of Bartok's one-act opera *Bluebeard's Castle* with Voketaitus as Bluebeard and soprano Mary Lee Farris (who had sung the title role in *Xerxes* a few years earlier) as the unfortunate current (and doomed) bride of Bluebeard. John Redman rigged and lighted Shove Chapel to look like a menacing, medieval castle. Hiring a Bartok-sized orchestra was not feasible financially so pianist Sue Grace and Frank Shelton, Shove Chapel organist, modified the scores to be done on their instruments. Shelton played the ominous, almost subterranean chords while Grace delivered the fierce percussive sections.

There were several events each week. We found that, while many orchestras acknowledged the Bartok centennial, our festival was the most extensive in the US. The Concord String Quartet played all six of Bartok's quartets. In between their two concerts, they offered a rehearsal/lecture demonstration at which they illustrated that the Bartok quartets were the next musical step after the late Beethoven quartets. Luca and Epperson along with the principal clarinetist from Aspen played *Contrasts* originally commissioned by Benny Goodman.

Hanya choreographed a 45 minute work, her longest in decades, using 40 dancers. Bartok's *Cantata Profana* was her text, and she illuminated what Gamer had meant by the bridge as well as the symbolic plea for political freedom.

In 1983, Summer Session Dean, Elmer (Pete) Peterson told President Gresham Riley, that the dance programs enrollments were declining. There seemed to be a lot of intramural grumbling; perhaps Hanya and her staff were too old. Riley sent Peterson to New York in the fall to tell a totally surprised Hanya that her contract wouldn't be renewed. It was one of the worst public gaffes in recent College history. Hanya's Colorado Springs friends, some going back 43 years, were enraged. According to Barbara Yalich in the Development Office, people from around the country called and were saying, "Can't you people do anything right?" The New York dance establishment was incredulous and horrified. One long time observer said that the College firing Hanya would be like the Princeton Institute for Advanced Studies firing Albert Einstein.

The most damning criticism came from Glenn Giffin, dance and music critic for the Denver Post, and head of the Dance Library at

Denver University. After a long conversation with Riley, Giffin wondered whether there was a broad change in the College's attitude toward the arts. Riley, of course, denied it. Giffin wrote at the end of his long Sunday column: "When someone (of Hanya's accomplishment) is turned out so abruptly, the dance and art world sits up and takes notice. The notice is not to Colorado College's credit."

Hanya had described her dismissal to Giffin and others: "It was very abruptly, very ugly done . . . It was not friendly." While the damage had been done, Ric Bradley at a special pick-up-the-pieces meeting suggested that our first priority should be to do what we could to ease the pain for Hanya. Bradley, Yalich, Kathy Peterson in Public Relations, Jenkins, and many others spoke to Hanya assuring her she was still our fair lady.

The College timing couldn't have been worse. That same year she was invited to Harvard to give master classes. In 1984 she was given the Samuel L. Scripps American Dance Festival Award of $25,000 *For Lifetime Achievement in Dance* presented by Broadway legend Alfred Drake. It was the largest prize in all of the arts.

By 1993 both Hanya and Nik had died. Murray Louis put together programs honoring his mentors. After a successful run at New York's Joyce Theatre, Bill Hochman, summer session dean, brought the Louis Company for a weekend posthumous final tribute to Hanya.

Hanya was active to the end, teaching in New York at both the Nikolais-Louis School of Dance and at Juilliard. She concluded her Scripps award remarks this way: "Well, I keep on doing it as good as I can and as long as I can."

THE PRESENT

The 1980s and 1990s summer sessions went in new directions. Modern dance made very little impact, but classical ballet recently got a foothold. The Colorado Springs Symphony gives classical concerts in the Armstrong Hall quad. Partly at least to counteract the criticism that the severance of ties with the opera and the firing of Hanya showed that the College was down-playing the arts, Michael and Sue Grace founded a summer classical music conservatory with local and visiting artists. The varied chamber music concerts in terms of repertoire and quality of performance are as good as any in the world. The only complaint is that it is all too brief; there are only two weeks of concerts.

A GOLDEN EVENT

One glorious performing arts event brought the arts, the College, including the Summer Session, the opera and the community together. The College's Centennial was 1974, and Lew Worner found money for weekly informal soup lunches for planning. After several of these failed to develop any earth-shaking ideas, Dean Bradley and I hit on the idea of having the College perform J. S. Bach's *The Passion According to St. Matthew* which many think is the greatest musical work in western civilization—and it had never been done in Colorado because of its size, complexity, length and cost.

Bradley found the money in his budget, and the Opera Festival and the Summer Session Office made all of the musical and physical arrangements. Summer opera principal singers came to the College to be soloists; many didn't charge fees and came for expenses. The event took place in Shove Chapel on April 21, 1974.

There was a 200 plus double choir made up of the College Chorale, the Pikes Peak Chorale and church choirs; students, faculty, staff, alumni and friends of the College were represented. Following Bradley's example, the entire Physics Department sang. There was a 50-member children's choir and a double orchestra recruited mainly from the Colorado Springs Symphony.

Ray Devoll was the Evangelist, and there were eight more soloists. Beattie's aria, "Make Thee Clean, My Heart from Sin" was sung with a moving musical eloquence that brought tears to many eyes. Three of the Chorales were printed in the program, and Jenkins turned to the audience and conducted them while they sang with the choruses.

The more than four hour performance started at 4:15 P.M. There was a dinner break for audience and musicians, and the performance ended at 10:15 P.M.

Of all of the dozens of events that went on in that inaugural year, Lew Worner told everyone that our performance of *The Passion According to St. Matthew*, with its wide celebration, was the best thing that had happened.

Werner Heim
Professor Emeritus of Biology

CHAPTER 14

COLORADO COLLEGE AT 125 YEARS— SUBSTANCE OR FORM?

Werner Heim
Professor Emeritus of Biology

Anniversaries are occasions for retrospection. So here I will look back to that 100th anniversary in 1974 when I last wore my tuxedo, and from there to some of the changes that have since occurred.

That tuxedo was symbolic of Colorado College. It was then: made of excellent material, carefully assembled, perhaps not quite in the fashion of the day and of some considerable, though not great, age. A quarter of a century ago Colorado College had excellent human material in its faculty, staff and administration, lovingly and carefully assembled by presidents, deans and department heads (!).

Like my tuxedo, the College was not quite in fashion for several reasons. First, the wrenching conflicts of the late 1960's affected it much less than they did many institutions. Second, it had not succumbed to the vocationalism that drove many colleges away from a liberal arts orientation in the name of "relevance." And third, it had just a few years before differentiated itself from the masses by implementing the block plan.

That the block plan, with its many logistical problems and its demand to discard many traditional practices of academia, could be implemented at all was a compliment to both the faculty and the administration. The administration was still small and very nimble. Basically it consisted of a quartet of remarkable men: "Lew" Worner as president, Jim Stauss (for tragically few years) as provost, with Bob Broughton and "Bross" Brossman as vice-presidents, supplemented by a succession of able and

233

independent-minded deans (Ric Bradley at the time of the anniversary). While Lew Worner and Jim Stauss provided a quiet, steady academic leadership, the vice-presidents saw to the physical and fiscal side of the College. The faculty seldom heard an argument for or against an academically sound proposal based on money or the lack thereof. Somehow, funding always seemed to appear. Perhaps the only exception was one year when the size of the entering class fell 20 or 25 students short of expectation and a kind of musical comedy panic of minor budget cutting swept the campus.

The faculty in 1974–75 was not only equally nimble but also of top quality and willing to take chances. Its 136 regular members, with the help of a few "part-timers," taught 1,914 students. Each faculty member was supported by an income to the College of $27,874 (1967–68 dollars) in tuition and fees. Of every dollar spent, 27.46 cents went for faculty compensation. (For comparison, in 1995–96, there were 144 regular faculty, with many "part-timers," teaching 1,963 students. Each faculty member was supported by an income of $52,970 to the College from tuition and fees (1967–68 dollars) and 16.81 cents of each dollar spent by the College went to faculty compensation.) There were perhaps no superstars but quite a few stars among the faculty, people such as Tom K. Barton, Dick Beidleman, Glenn Gray and Fred Sonderman. Almost all faculty members were of high quality and those few who were not were rapidly, unceremoniously and usually informally helped to depart. The students were generally intelligent, fairly conscientious about their studies except on Monday mornings when a significant percentage seemed to show the effects of a weekend with alcohol or, sometimes, harder drugs. Relatively many were very well motivated and have gone on to brilliant careers in a wide variety of fields.

What, then, has changed in the last quarter of a century (and nearly in the last quarter of *the* century)? Is the tuxedo still a reasonable symbol? Well, yes and no. In some ways the formality represented by the tuxedo has markedly lessened. We no longer have the same degree of ceremony as before. For example, the faculty no longer marches by rank and seniority in academic processions. Dress, among faculty as well as students, is far less formal, sometimes to the point where the word "dress" is itself an overstatement. Language and forms of address, too, have lost much of their former formality.

On the other hand, a kind of legalistic formality has engulfed the campus. Then, many questions were settled informally or, perhaps more commonly, never arose because relationships and expectations among and within the constituent units of the College were well defined by tradition, collegiality, shared purpose, trust and common sense. Now such questions are often settled by recourse to manuals or other policy announcements. Furthermore, voluminous records must be kept in case the matter ever comes to an administrative or judicial hearing. This shift, in conjunction with certain other changes, has had many, sometimes perverse, consequences to which I will return later.

In many other respects, the tuxedo is still a fitting symbol. The College is still well made and of fine material. The faculty, although apparently only a little larger, has actually grown considerably by an increase of various sorts of part-timers. Sometimes this has improved the quality of instruction and the range of subject matter offered. Many departments now regularly bring in renowned experts on subjects that could not otherwise be covered. Intellectual excitement is added to campus life when a topnotch scholar, young or old, with new ideas can be brought in. Unfortunately, there is also an increased tendency to bring in part-timers for routine classes to ameliorate shortages of regular faculty. While this may not actually cause a great reduction in the quality of instruction, it transfers a significant load of advising and committee work to the remaining regular faculty and causes much extra work for department chairs. It also dilutes the continuity of campus life and lends some degree of uncertainty to academic standards. Lastly, it reduces the coherence and collegiality of the faculty because a significant proportion of it is not on campus long enough to absorb the functional ethos of the College.

On the other hand, the quality of the regular faculty is probably as high as it has ever been. Again, there are no superstars (and a good thing, too) but there are a number of stars and almost all members of the faculty are excellent, hard-working persons. (It would, of course, be both impolitic and impolite to attempt any list of current faculty stars.)

The orientation of the faculty has, however, shifted to some degree. In my opinion, the members of today's faculty are less dedicated to the institution and less dedicated to the professorate in general. They are—indeed they must be—more cognizant of and dedicated to the professional situation in their own speciality, at least until tenure has been achieved. First, the training period in the specialty has become longer, from perhaps four or five years between the bachelor's and doctor's degrees to perhaps six or seven. Second, at least in the natural sciences, some years of postdoctoral research work are practically *de rigueur*. Consequently, individuals now enter the professorate not only later but with more strongly developed ties to their professional specialty and fewer ties to the general academic profession.

Having once entered the professorate, the pressures to do and publish research in their specialties is greater than ever for at least two reasons. First, the likelihood of attaining tenure in their first faculty position is smaller now because more is demanded, because there is surplus of available persons in almost all fields and because the tenure review process has become more formalistic and pseudo-quantitative. Even at a relatively enlightened place such as Colorado College a certain degree of counting and weighing of published material is now inevitable. Consequently, the young faculty member must, for self-preservation and to maintain professional standing, devote more time and energy to research and scholarship. Since there are still only 24 hours in a day, teaching is at least as strenuous as ever and community service still absorbs a certain amount of time, the attention given to faculty governance must necessarily be less than formerly. Hence, at least the shared governance aspect of collegiality suffers. Finally, for reasons partially discussed below, good and careful work on college committees and thoughtful debate in faculty meetings yields neither the same prestige nor satisfaction as in the past.

The student body is still as good as in 1974 and perhaps somewhat better, in terms of intellectual ability, focus on matters academic, willingness to benefit by the college experience and general behavior. Alcohol is still around, but heavy drinking and drug use seem to be held in lower esteem than was once the case. Interestingly, while the diversity of political positions and philosophic orientation among the student body may have increased, that among the faculty may have shrunk. To a significant extent, liberalism seems to have displaced true intellectual diversity.

A walk around the campus will confirm that the physical facilities of the College have increased markedly. In at least some cases, such as my department (biology), this increase has a curious aspect. There is no question that it is an important, perhaps vital, qualitative improvement. Yet it is not a quantitative improvement because the increased space has been used up by increased departmental enrollments and the consequent increase in faculty. We are at least as crowded as before the construction of the Barnes Science Center.

Is it really still the same old tuxedo? Have there been no significant changes in the last quarter century or so? There have indeed, but these are changes at a deeper, more fundamental, less obvious level.

To understand these changes, it is perhaps best to go back to the origins of the colleges and universities in Western civilization. In its roots, a college was a cluster of scholars who gathered together for mutual support in their studies. Students came to learn from them. Kings and cardinals, magnates and municipalities found such colleges useful for educating youth and training future members of the "learned" professions. Such sponsorship—and, particularly in America, occasional sponsorship by small groups and even individuals not directly connected to government or church—soon led to a certain amount of outside control. In academia as elsewhere, those who pay the piper call the tune. Yet, in terms of their working arrangements and even more in terms of purely academic matters, the colleagues of the college kept most decisions in their own hand. For example, it is still generally true (with some regrettable exceptions) that it is a body of scholars that decides to admit or not admit newcomers to certain ranks within their group. We now call this "granting a degree."

Twenty-five years or so ago the faculty at Colorado College and at most similar institutions was still in this position. The faculty was clearly the nucleus of this college and most other reputable colleges; the students came to learn from them. The rest of the institution existed to serve the needs of these two groups. The staff helped with the daily chores, the administration administered to the larger needs of the enterprise and the board acted both as the buffer between the College and the greater world out there and as a conduit for the steady flow of funds.

Interestingly and importantly, the unique position of the faculty was not a hierarchal matter. By and large, each element of the College knew its place in the scheme; the occasional minor turf battles kept things interesting. Despite rare outbursts of purely personal ambition, there prevailed a general understanding that we were all working toward a common end, that we were all in the enterprise together, sink or swim. Each constituent element had its own internal organization and on most fundamental matters it was the faculty in meeting assembled and duly advised by its committees that had, at least *de facto*, the final word. Thus, because of clearly delineated roles—and not in spite of them—there was a high degree of collegiality in the College.

In part, this collegiality existed then because it was "the tradition." The similarity of a substantial fraction maintained the tradition in part of the faculty: white, protestant, children of college-educated parents, with undergraduate education at liberal arts institutions, and living just North of the campus. Many faculty members had spent considerable time in military service, often as officers, and had found a deep sense of and respect for the idea of a chain of command. To be sure, there were many (like myself) who certainly did not fit that mold but who adapted to a large part of it because it worked and because the collegiality represented an ideal to which we all aspired. In part, the collegiality existed because it was clear that the *sine qua non* of the long-range survival of the institution was the excellence of the education it provided, not the size of its endowment nor the modernity of its buildings. We understood that, for our own good and the good of the institution, doing the best we could for the students, in class and out, and making some moderate contributions to scholarship had to rank first in the personal and institutional priorities of the faculty. Both the faculty and the College had only moderate finances but both were, in a very deep sense, good.

All this is not to say that Colorado College was indistinguishable from the Garden of Eden in those days, although the occasional "streaking" student might momentarily have made it look that way. There was plenty of discussion, some controversy, even a rare confrontation or two, particularly over the grading system. But strong trust in each other and in other components of the College, a clear outline of responsibility, known and open channels of a communication and an effective though perhaps sometimes informal due process were there as guides. Deep down, the whole system rested upon a kind of civility. One knew the limits, one knew what was right and one operated within that system. Those few who went beyond the bounds of that civility changed either their behavior or their employment.

The world is different now. The world is different not just at The Colorado College but at most or all institutions of higher learning in the United States. It is different not only because of internal changes but also because the external world has changed and has imposed itself more heavily on the academy than it once did. Let us look first at these external factors.

Perhaps because they were under the sponsorship of the church or the sovereign, perhaps because they were largely composed of supposedly introverted and impractical—hence harmless—folk, college and university campuses were once rather special places where the king's writ did not run with full force. Even in this egalitarian country, the courts often held that colleges could do or could omit doing some of the things imposed by law on other, more commercial or more political institutions. In general, the collegiate institutions reciprocated by keeping their noses out of commerce and politics, by sticking essentially to matters *sub specie aeternitatis*. True, student riots, revolts and rebellions were a feature of political life from at least the Middle Ages onward, but these were considered temporary, though inconvenient, aberration. The campus of a college, such as the edifice of a church, was a sanctuary.

That sanctuary status gradually broke down. The courts gradually applied to colleges the same legal standards about work conditions, liability, civil rights and duties, accounting standards and even sometimes taxation as to General Motors or Woolworth (well, maybe Wal-Mart). Competition for the philanthropic dollar, so essential to a private college like ours, began to come from new sources such as foundations and to flow to new recipients, such as state universities. In turn, the large, organized philanthropic institutions, now called foundations, began to attach strings of various sorts to their "gifts." All over the land, the cry of "More accountability!" was heard.

The response—probably the necessary response—of this and most other colleges was gradually to reorganize its structure by adding experts of various sorts to its administration and by restructuring the scheme of governance to one where the more professionalized administration administered less and managed more. Because, in the face of these societal changes and demands, corporate models worked apparently well for commercial organizations (and perhaps in part because so many members of governing boards were comfortable with corporate models), a modified corporate model became the standard for colleges.

Few asked whether the modified corporate model was appropriate for a college. Fewer even asked whether such "obviously good things" as greater accountability suited a liberal arts college. Yet these are questions that should have been and should be asked, particularly by governing boards and by faculty because the importation of such constructs to the academy changed the nature of the academy. At least two species of such questions should be asked.

First, we should ask whether accountability, efficiency and modern management are suitable to a college. Clearly, in many areas of college operations they are. The fiscal and housekeeping aspects of a college ought to be conducted with at least the same efficiency, accountability and clear, professional management as that of any corporation because, with some, perhaps important exceptions, their operating requirements are very similar. But it does not follow that the rest of the college operations should also meet these external standards. On the contrary, original thought, real innovation and work at the legendary cutting edge of knowledge require a degree in inefficiency, a lack of accountability and a degree of freedom from the directives of "management" that will surely drive an accountant to Prozac™ if not to drink. A factory worker who produces 80% defective goods will be and ought to be fired. In the academic arena, a professor whose ideas, theorems or experiments stand up to the critical scrutiny of peers and others even 20% of the time should be hailed as a hero. Scientific and intellectual advances, much as evolutionary changes and for much of the same reasons, must come out of an inefficient process incapable of precise specification in advance. Tell me of an experiment whose results can be predicted with high confidence or of a thought whose results are clear afore hand and I'll tell you of an experiment or a thought not worth doing or thinking.

Second, we can and should ask what changes the importation of a corporate model brings about in the nature of a college, as indeed they have been brought about at this College and nearly all others in the last quarter of a century or so. On the surface, these changes are few. The same titles still exist in the faculty, the staff and the administration. We still have professors, secretaries and presidents, assistant professors, grounds keepers and deans. In general, they all still do the same sort of work (though secretaries rarely type and take no more dictation). There are a few new titles on campus reflective of the change. Such new positions may be appropriate and in any case they are at the margin of the real matter. Furthermore, most of the old structure is still in place. There still are faculty meetings and committees, making us think that nothing has changed. Making us think so until we remember that there was still a Roman Senate not only under Caesar Augustus but also under Caesar Nero and Caesar Caligula. The form is still there but the substance has changed.

Just how has the substance changed? From the point of view of a faculty member the substance has changed since about the last anniversary celebration because the old forms have become at least partially empty ones. One reason for this is the attempt to replace the old collegiality based upon trust and clearly agreed spheres of action directed to a common objective with a new, synthetic one based upon an assumed divergence rather than congruence of interests. For example, faculty committees were formerly fairly small and composed only of faculty. They would call upon persons from other areas of the institution for their specialized knowledge and viewpoints and would bring carefully crafted proposals for legislation to the floor of the faculty assembly. Now committees are often so large and contain persons with such diverse agendas and traditions of operation that little gets done and what does get done is often slipshod. One consequence is that for matters requiring real solutions, *ad hoc* committees are appointed. The standing committees, as they are increasingly reduced to irrelevancy, become increasingly less careful and creative, leading to fewer, less beneficial and less important actions by the faculty assembly. This leads to a further cycle in which that which has to be done is necessarily done either by an *ad hoc* committee, an elitist and more or less isolated Faculty Executive Committee or a professional administrator.

Another consequence of this shift from substance to form has been that the realm of subjects deemed appropriate for discussion and action by the faculty has narrowed considerably. For example, a quarter of a century ago, proposed changes in faculty status and retirement arrangements received full study by the appropriate standing committee of the faculty and were then discussed and voted upon by the assembled faculty. As we neared the 125th anniversary of the College, major changes in such arrangements were studied by an *ad hoc* committee and decided upon by the administration and the Board. The faculty now deals almost exclusively with strictly curricular matters and even then may be second-guessed by administrators and the Board. The children are allowed to play in the sandbox as long as their sand castles do not cast a shadow outside its boundaries.

Several other consequences result from this concatenation of causes, too many to be detailed here. (A wise man named Ptah-hotep said, about four thousand eight hundred anniversaries ago: "Discourse without causing weariness.") But in brief, it may be said that increasingly neither The Colorado College at its 125th anniversary, nor many another college, still has a group of scholars at its core. Yes, the scholars are still there, but now they are essentially the employees of a corporation, doing the work assigned to them by the corporation.

Have I been too harsh in this analysis? Still, the true path is often revealed only when a strong light is shining upon the surrounding swamp. Are the changes that occurred since the 100th anniversary good or bad? Only the next hundred yeas will tell.

Michael Grace
Professor of Music

CHAPTER 15

THE THIRD PARENT

Michael Grace
Professor of Music

I was blessed to have two parents who taught me important things. From my mother I learned something about the value of originality, free thought, liberalism and a willingness to be different. From my father I learned the value of stability, conservatism, and the importance of being a nice person. Whether any of these values have manifested themselves in my actions is something I would not deem to assess. I do know that an awareness of them made it possible for me to appreciate a variety of experiences and opportunities presented to me since I left home. And I was also prepared to make the difficult decision many of us face at the end of secondary education—the selection of what I call the "third parent." In my case, Colorado College has been this "third parent" for the past thirty-nine years.

I first saw Colorado College in the fall of 1958 when I ventured from Philadelphia to visit my brother, Brewster, who was a student here. I was a senior in high school and was considering applying to the College myself. I sat in on a class and went to his piano lesson with Carlton Gamer. I confess that Brewster's assets were not in his musical genes, so he regularly spent some of his lesson time discussing other areas in which his teacher was educated. And these were, I came to know later, plentiful and vast. Having been brought up as Quakers, we were often talking about war so my brother and Carlton discussed, among other things, the philosophy of non-violence. Brewster was preparing himself to make major decisions about his beliefs and his life. His piano teacher, although not that much older than he, was like a parent in the kind of personal guidance he could offer.

This, I decided, is what college should be like. I was particularly convinced when I later visited Colby and Middlebury, two other colleges I was considering attending. At Colby I remember everybody talked about "panty-raid weekend" which was fast approaching! And at Middlebury, the main topic of conversation was skiing. Now while Colby and Middlebury were and are excellent colleges, I am grateful to my real parents for preparing me to make a wise decision in the selection of a "third" parent. And I thank Colorado College for being there and for being ready to assume that role.

How can one relate the role of a college to that of a parent? So often we hear the phrase *in loco parentis*. When an 18-year-old is 2000 miles away from his or her family, the host institution does, perforce, take on a parenting role. And although we use different terminology now, colleges still fulfill this role. They punish students when they break the code of institutional conduct, and they encourage them to be a better people, to respect others, and, in short, to grow up! This is an important role for a college, particularly in dealing with students who have never lived away from home, away from the watchful eye of a real parent. Another familiar term which refers to the parenting role of the college is *alma mater*. Translated as "nourishing mother," this concept emerged in the 18th century in England and Scotland. Since it is usually applied to a college after one has been graduated, it recognizes, with the advantage of hindsight, what a caring third parent our colleges could be to us while we were there.

But this parenting role goes beyond the laws and manners of social living. The institution can and should help the student form character, values and beliefs. This is the education begun by parents and, while their offspring are still in their minority years, continued by their colleges. And it is this "parent" role that CC had in my life which I now acknowledge and for which I express my eternal gratitude. In my case the irony is that I returned to CC as a member of the faculty and endured the transition from collegiate child to collegiate parent. It is this transition which I will recall by anecdote in the following remarks.

Allow me to say at the outset, however, that "parenting" is not the primary purpose of the College. More fundamental is the faculty to impart information and ways of understanding it to students. Most of us go to college with the intention of learning a field so that we can get a job and contribute to our profession and to our society, or so that we can be prepared to go on to graduate study. Scholarship and academic pursuits are the soul of the institution and more fundamental than its capacity to build character in its students. But in the best colleges, particularly small ones like CC which pride themselves in small classes, these functions are intertwined. And many students select smaller colleges because they want to know the faculty better than they would at a large university and to benefit from a close relationship with them that goes beyond the strictly academic dimension of teaching and learning. My willingness to accept CC into my life as a guiding force really began in Brewster's piano lesson I described at the outset of these remarks. If Carlton was the kind of teacher one encountered at Colorado College, this was the kind of college I wanted to attend.

Foremost in my memories of my student years at Colorado College are the faculty giants I had the good fortune to encounter. And at the head of my memory is Albert Seay, if only because he led me into the field of music history through his subtle and not-so-subtle coercion, his wisdom, and the remarkable example of his own scholarship. I was in awe of his scholarly work and his prolific list of publications. I remember spending hours at his house, sitting next to him at his desk as he helped me transcribe 12th-century modal notation or taught me how to compose a complete sentence in my mind before putting a pencil to paper. And, of course, the post-tutorial supply of cheese and beer provided by his wife Janine eased my mind for even more persuasive mentoring. We talked about the joy of music, about Albert's knowledge of French literature and stamps, about his impressive collection of electric trains, and, ultimately, about what I was going to do with my life.

Often parents influence their children in the selection of careers. And when the "third parent" gets involved in this, a conflict may ensue. Over my years of teaching at CC, I have been contacted more than once by parents asking me not to encourage their children to major in music. Fortunately, I don't believe my parents ever called Dr. Seay and asked him to lay off; but I know that he, like me, was called often by other parents who feared that a career in music would basically ruin the life of their progeny destined to be rocket scientists.

There were, of course, many other wonderful professors, whose profound knowledge of their subjects was matched by their style, enthusiasm and educational rigor. Paul Bernard taught me the value of getting up for a Saturday-at-8:00(AM!) "Western Civ." class. If one missed, one got an F on the weekly quiz given that morning. More significantly, Darnell Rucker's fascination with the arcane beauties of medieval philosophy and Wilbur Wright's passion for the music of physics gave me the incentive to investigate, for my own satisfaction, the actual arguments of Boethius or the action of waves in ripple tanks. And Fred Sondermann's enthusiasm over my accumulation of journal and newspaper articles for a paper on the value of international cultural exchange gave me a feeling of pride in my accomplishment, something akin to the way a child feels when he first rides a two-wheeler.

And then there was life outside of class. At student parties one might stand over a keg and talk to Gilbert Johns about his experiments conditioning the giraffes at the Cheyenne Mountain Zoo or Bill Hochman about the activities of the local democratic party. Beyond the rigors of disciplined study which centered in the classroom, there was another world of interaction between student and faculty in which a different kind of mental growth fiourished. And those of us who were fortunate to pursue these opportunities, as opposed to the straightforward student beer busts which also occurred, but generally without our mentors, were richly rewarded. Through reasoned dialogue we learned to think critically. We continued, in effect at a higher level, what many of our parents had worked so hard to teach before we left home.

Other events consumed a large portion of our attention as students at Colorado College in the early 1960's. The Cuban missile crisis had a negative effect on class attendance because we regularly threw "end-of-the-world" parties, even on week nights. Curiously we could not get many faculty to come to these. And while these parties now seem amusing, if not irresponsible, in hindsight, I remember real fear, especially since the location of NORAD under Cheyenne Mountain made Colorado Springs one of the prime targets for a real Soviet missile attack.

Much more traumatic was the assassination of President Kennedy on that November day in 1963. Most of my friends really loved Kennedy and looked forward to voting for him in the next election when we would have attained voting age. At first we turned to each other and to television for solace, but when classes resumed after the weekend we turned to the faculty. Classes of all kinds addressed what had happened, and professors freely encouraged discussions in which students vented their feelings of remorse and asked questions about the social and political conditions in which the assassination took place.

It was the war in Vietnam, however, which was eventually to have the most profound effect on our lives. In 1963, the year I was graduated, the "military action" was like a dark cloud hanging over the horizon. As I recall, the draft lottery had not yet begun and student deferments for college study were standard practice. American casualties were still relatively few. We felt anxious over the developments that might ensue but were not prescient of the scope of the war which did occur nor the impact it was to have on us all just a few years later. When I returned to CC as an instructor in 1967, conditions were different. I will return to this momentarily.

So this was what my undergraduate experience was like. There was academic rigor. There was a rich co-curricular life. And there were the challenging issues forced upon us by a rapidly changing world outside our collegiate bubble. I set off to graduate school full of excitement, but like most others, feeling like I was leaving a second family behind. I imagined that I might be leaving Colorado Springs for the last time. That, however, was not to be.

Returning to CC during my graduate work was certainly one of the most fortuitous events of my life. After I had finished the requisite three years of graduate classes but had not yet begun my dissertation, Albert Seay, who was then chairman of the Music Department, called me to say that the other music historian at CC had suddenly taken a job at Yale. He virtually insisted that I take *one* year out of my graduate study and come to teach at CC on short notice. A national search would follow. As I recall, however, there was no search. President Lew Worner was on leave, Dean Kenneth Curran was acting president and Professor George Drake was acting dean. I imagine that Albert Seay, who liked to get his own way and generally did, simply advised the "acting" administrators that the Music Department had the person it wanted and that was that. However it happened, that "one" year which Albert proposed has now stretched into 32, and my position at CC remains the only full-time job I have ever had. If the shoe fits . . .

Since I had spent only three years in graduate school, and still had to write a dissertation before joining the club of "doctored" colleagues, my return to Colorado College as a member of the faculty in 1967 provided several bizarre circumstances. Among these was the dilemma of what to call my new colleagues. After four years of using the titles "professor" or "doctor" (we all did that back then), it was difficult to imagine using the first names. Even more difficult was to consider these mentors as colleagues. They had been an integral part of the institutional "parenting" and they were, for the most part, never going to be institutional siblings.

Two far more serious issues confronted me as a faculty novice. The first was teaching. My graduate studies at Yale precluded teaching, for that university steadfastly opposed the idea of graduate students teaching undergraduates. Unlike some other Ivy League universities, Yale required all its senior professors affiliated with the College or the Graduate School to teach at least one undergraduate course. So I learned to teach as a part of my first full-time faculty appointment. That made for a year I will never forget. I once thought I worked hard as a student at CC; then I thought my graduate program at Yale put me through the hoops. As it turned out, none of these presented a challenge as demanding as facing one's own class of students each and every day. In fact, it was through having to explain topics in music literature to a critical audience that I first really learned to understand many of them myself. Yet as usual, the institution came to the help of one of its progeny. We had no Teaching and Learning Center, no formal programs to help the first year instructor. But we had mentors. I recall conversations with Albert Seay, Carlton Gamer and Earl Juhas, all initiated by me, in which I received the kind of friendly guidance a son or daughter receives from a parent.

And while teaching, I had to commence research on my nascent dissertation. In this regard, I recall encountering Glenn Gray in the library and receiving his insightful advice on investigative problems and methods. And, of course, Albert Seay was always peering over my shoulder with more direct and hard-nosed scholarly advice. I could have written my dissertation in the rather gloomy environment of Yale's Sterling Library with only the commiseration of my fellow graduate students and the occasional counseling of my advisor. But the collegial environment of Colorado College was far more congenial and made the often painful process far more fulfilling. As if I were with my family, I felt at home completing this potentially unpleasant chore.

We must, however, return our attention to that continuing chain of events which were unfolding on the other side of the earth. The first two years of my teaching at CC were the years in which the war in Vietnam escalated to a pitch that was unacceptable to large portions of the population in the country, particularly those on university and college campuses. The bombings in North Vietnam, the frequent incursions into Cambodia, and the deaths at Kent State forced a serious debate about the propriety, if not the morality, of our country's actions. I was opposed to the war. And I was beginning to feel a need to discuss it with the students as a counselor, even though they were but a few years younger than I. I wanted to help them come to their own conclusions about what to do. I recall two incidents vividly which forced me to address my new identity in the College.

The first occurred when ten or twelve students and faculty decided to read the names of the war dead in front of the Draft Board office, then located just a few blocks south of the campus on Nevada Avenue. We assembled there in the evening and began the task which was to take many hours. We had noticed several police cars circulating in the neighborhood and felt some sense of security. Yet in the early morning hours, a truck pulled up and several people leaned out of the back with firearms. I had never faced a gun before. As one of the few faculty members present, I decided I had best alert the police. I walked around the corner and found one of the patrol cars almost immediately. When I reported what had happened, the officer told me that the police had more important things to do than to babysit college students. Since that was, in fact, exactly what they appeared to be doing, I suddenly realized that we were vulnerable, and I became afraid. Colorado College, my "third parent," did not seem to have much clout or respect in certain segments of the Colorado Springs Community at that time. But in addition to the fear I felt for myself, I felt a kind of parental compulsion to protect the students. In thinking about this incident later, I realized that my sense of identity at Colorado College was changing; while I still wanted to be nurtured and protected by the institution, I also wanted to help protect those newer and younger members of our college community – the students.

The second incident was triggered by the killing of four students at Kent State University during a march to protest the U.S. invasion of Cambodia. There was an effort by many of our students to close down the College in a sympathy protest. I was aware of the plans, and decided to go to the classroom where my first class was held to see what was happening and to discuss the tragic event. I was met at the door by two groups of students, one on each side, with two conflicting demands. Students in one group insisted that I should not teach that day and that I had a moral obligation to support the demonstration against the war and the violence it had spawned at home by joining the boycott. Students in the other group stated that they came to CC for an education and that the institution owed them this class. My solution, of which I am not particularly proud, was to teach some music history that day but not to count that material as a part of the course for which students would be accountable on the exam. I remember feeling respect for the reasoning on both sides of the issue and was not yet ready (grown up enough?) to act with the kind of decisiveness one expects of a parental authority figure.

These two episodes in the life of a young faculty member were very significant, for they marked the beginning of a change in my relationship to the College. As I mentioned, it had been difficult to feel like a colleague to other faculty who had, just a few years earlier, been my teachers. But as students began to look to me for counseling and advice, I, in turn, began to feel more like a mentor, like *in loco parentis* or an *alma mater* (or should I say *almus pater?*). I felt that I still had much to learn from the College and its people, but I was being forced to feel more and more like a colleague in this society of mentors we call a faculty.

Coming on the heels of the turbulent late 1960s and early 1970s, the rest of the 70s was a heady time for higher education. The College was a liberal parent indeed and allowed its innovative faculty to liberalize grading systems (by introducing the pass/fail option and getting rid of the D), to simplify general education requirements and, most notably, to create the Block Plan. We had similarly innovative students who changed the very long-standing name of the newspaper from the *Tiger* to the more provocative *Catalyst* and, along the way, forced the College to free itself from liability for what was written there by forming the independent Cutler Board. The institution was more like my liberal and progressive mother than my rather conservative father. And yet, throughout this time we all kept rigorous academic standards. In my classes, students continued to learn, for example, that music was one of the original seven liberal arts, precisely how a sonata form is constructed, and why Beethoven's aesthetics were a manifestation of Kant's "categorical imperative."

My transformation from student to faculty, from collegiate child to parent, was enabled by Colorado College and remains something for which I will always be grateful. There is, of course, not enough time for me to reminisce over my entire thirty-two years at this College. I would, however, like to mention one additional facet of my relationship with CC. Some parents wish for their children to experience as many different aspects of life as possible. Colorado College has certainly allowed me that. I have been an undergraduate student, a graduate student, and a member of the faculty. I have had the opportunity to start a *collegium musicum* and a summer music festival. I have served as Dean of the Summer Session which allowed me the privilege of working to enhance further the performing arts and to work with my academic colleagues to create an innovative academic program. This program included such marvelous institutes as Jim Yaffe's *Fiction, Reading It, Writing It*, Salvatore Bizzarro's enduring *Italian in Italy*, and Joe Pickle's summer in Zimbabwe which subsequently turned into the ACM semester program in Africa.

Another memorable opportunity came with the invitation to serve as what I called "interlude" President (the official appointment was as "interim" president) for the 1992–93 academic year. This followed the resignation of Gresham Riley and preceded the inauguration of Kathryn Mohrman. It was a wonderful year in that I did not have to worry about creating a presidential legacy for myself. I was a professor and would not make long-range policy decisions on which my tenure at CC would be evaluated. I worked with collegial and supportive friends, most notably Tim Fuller who became Dean that same year, and I tried my best to keep the College alive, vital, and moving toward the fulfillment of its goal as a prominent bastion of the liberal arts and a model institution of scholarship, teaching and learning.

Of course, the job did require that some down-to-earth decisions be made. Internal combustion ignited a few brush fires, such as a hockey coach scandal, which took an inordinate amount of time and strained my relations with many colleagues and friends in the community. The outcome of all this was, of course, the hiring of Don Lucia. And during that year the voters of Colorado passed Amendment 2 which denied protection to gays and lesbians. This vote brought the state and the city of Colorado Springs some adverse national attention. I had to assure parents of new CC students that their children were not coming to the "city of hate," but rather to the locus of serious debate on the fundamental and important issues raised by Amendment 2.

In all, the presidential experience taught me a great deal about the complexity of Colorado College. It also taught me a great deal about myself. In making decisions, I often thought back to my parents, to their progressive and conservative role models, to their adages about working hard and not being afraid to be different. I wondered what either one of them would have done in the horns of this or that dilemma. Occasionally, I had to make decisions which could effect a much larger number of people than any decisions I had made before, and I felt the weight of responsibility I used to imagine my parents had when they faced the daunting task of helping me grow up. In that interlude presidential year, my relationship with CC was very different from what it had been in the fall of 1959. But then again, thanks to CC, so was I.

Since that year, in addition to teaching I have had the opportunity to chair a campus master plan and to co-chair a capital campaign. This breadth of experience has been rich and rewarding. My *alma mater* has served me well by making an unusually broad array of opportunities available. And unlike most alumni, I have had the advantage of remaining a part of my "nourishing mother's" family far longer than most. While it is shameful to think of it this way, it almost seems that I am still living "at home," in my fifty-seventh year, both receiving and giving nourishment to my second family.

Susan A. Ashley
Professor of History

CHAPTER 16

THE SPACE OF A GENERATION

Susan A. Ashley
Professor of History

I came to CC in the fall of 1970, the same year the Block Plan began. I had written about fifty letters to colleges and universities inquiring about jobs in modern European history, not expecting or even hoping for much since I had more time on my fellowship and a dissertation to finish. Lou Geiger's invitation to replace Roger Heacock for a year reached me in Paris late in the spring. I said yes and arrived in Colorado Springs, just days before school started—no visit, no interview, no experience, no idea.

What a time to begin. I inherited all of Roger's classes: the French Revolution, European Intellectual History, Modern France, Twentieth Century Europe, and Western Civ from 800 to 1500. In the first year of the Block Plan, all of us taught nine out of nine blocks, a tall order for a beginning teacher and unimaginable now. I found myself preparing for three hours of class a day—the equivalent of a week's worth in the se-mester system—without a stock of lectures and without advice from col-leagues about Block Plan survival strategies. They didn't themselves know what to expect.

Impossible? Yes, looking back it seems that way. The shift to the Block Plan taxed—and energized—everyone. Even though it didn't change the substance of the curriculum right away, the Block Plan represented a bold and unique departure from the usual way of teaching. It forced a re-thinking of all courses in order to cram a semester's work into three and a half weeks. And because the class limit changed to just twenty-five, the Plan encouraged teachers accustomed to lecture halls to try out new teaching techniques even in introductory courses. To make it easier to innovate, "experimental class rooms" furnished with rugs and couches from Goodwill and Ross Auction replaced desks. In general, the rule that first year was to expect the unexpected. For example, when I went to my assigned classroom, Palmer 223, the first day, I found it full of pigeon cages. Very experimental. After that, I taught in Loomis Lounge or the Loomis t.v. room for a few years. The debris from the previous night created a peculiar atmosphere for class.

Novelty makes the first years on any job particularly intense. In the fall of 1970, though, everyone was something of a novice. Figuring out how to teach under the Block Plan stretched the faculty, and the effort seemed to create a sense of common purpose and unusual energy that I did not expect and found appealing. The feeling of being a part of something new and unique caught up the students, too, and it took some of the edge off the battles against authority common on campuses at the time. In fact in moments of cynicism, I used to wonder if the College hadn't invented the Block Plan to blunt student unrest. However noble or Machiavellian the reasons, the Block Plan fostered unusually active collaboration among students and faculty in its early stages.

For me, it all began on the first day when I sat down and overheard one student murmur to another, "Is THAT the teacher?" I looked and dressed pretty young, I guess, and I certainly realized how few years and how little knowledge actually separated us. I also understood how little I knew about teaching, since I lacked the usual introduction to the profession, work as a graduate teaching assistant or as a visiting part-time lecturer. Facing a class from the other side of the lectern for the first time, I could only rely on models from my own experience as a student, and these were traditional. My teachers lectured, assigned papers, and gave tests. Discussion, when it occurred in a few seminars, tended to revolve around the teacher or to degenerate into uncomfortable silences or painful exercises in student one-upmanship. Hence, I planned to assign some good books and get up there and lecture. About what exactly, I wasn't all that sure.

I learned that no matter how much you read or even write about a subject, you don't know it until you've tried to teach it. And then not until you've taught it over and over. Preparing a class involves absorbing a lot of information. Never enough to satisfy the curious I quickly discovered.

"Why were there so many Danes in Constantinople in the Middle Ages?" Absolutely no idea. In one class, Gene Tresenfeld challenged me, "Tell us something about the Bismarck (the battleship, not Bismarck, the statesman)." Again, not a clue. But I came back the next day with an overly exhaustive description of the Bismarck. (A couple of years later during the oral part of the History Department's comprehensive exam, I thought I'd get back at Gene a bit. So I asked him to tell me what he knew about the Bismarck. Obviously he anticipated the question, because he pulled a piece of paper out of his pocket and provided the full description.)

You need to learn enough to present the essential facts, to provide some arresting details, and field a few questions. Much more difficult, teaching requires figuring out how to present these facts in a structured way. That involves deciding what to include and how to organize an often chaotic mix of events and possible interpretations. Except when I wrote papers, I had usually relied on teachers to make sense of the material, and now that responsibility fell to me.

The general atmosphere favored experimentation; so did the fact that I came to teaching cold. More than I expected, students influenced the shape and even the content of classes. The Block Plan also played a part. When a small group sat in a circle of dilapidated couches for a morning, steady lecturing didn't make sense. Besides, with no other class competing for attention, students could do a lot of reading and therefore have something to talk about. The Block Plan permitted what students in the 70s wanted to do anyway: get involved. When I did lecture, students interrupted to challenge what I said and to add their views. Since lectures turned into exchanges and debates, it seemed more sensible to ask questions and let the students work out answers.

Gradually classes centered more and more on discussion. Lectures provided essential background information, but increasingly we met to talk about the reading, often at someone's house. I learned by trial and error which questions moved classes to the center of the material, and (more slowly) how to direct the discussion without killing it. In the 70s, students found the "what" questions tedious; they flew to the "whys" and the "so whats". They got to what happened at the Bastille by discussing the nature of the revolutionary crowd; they straightened out the details of

Great Power diplomacy as they talked about what caused World War I. It took less effort to provoke an exploration of the French Resistance or the Spanish Civil War. Issues of individual commitment, social conflict, political authority and more generally of causality and change made immediate, direct sense in the Vietnam era. Everyone took a stand on the war; every male faced difficult decisions about the draft. Glenn Williams, for one, lived out the dilemma. Classified a CO, he managed to continue at CC and do his alternative service on the night shift at Penrose Hospital.

In the early 70s students I met put a premium on "relevance." That meant they insisted on finding connections between what they learned and what they and society faced. They reduced the distance between their academic and personal lives by actively trying to mesh them. That approach to learning produced two results. First, students welcomed open-ended assignments. ("Read what and how much you like; just show me that you've thought about it.") And second, they often produced impressive amounts of work. The Block Plan, with its three-and-a-half-weeks = one-semester equation produced a College-wide ethos of concentrated effort. But most students seemed to work with a mission in mind. It wasn't the grade, since many of the most serious students took their classes pass-fail. They had personal agendas. For example, Larry King read all of Kierkegaard's works in Intellectual History because he wanted to understand one man's struggle with faith. Other people read more eclectically, but they too often read prodigiously—Baudelaire and Hesse, Nietzsche and Camus or about war, ethics, the lives of ordinary people and princes. Kristie Blees took this route and set a standard for what's possible that I've had a hard time forgetting.

The curricular and extra-curricular also flowed together. Faculty and students met in living rooms for class and class parties; they collaborated on projects of mutual interest; they socialized. In the 70s, the History Department, like other departments, got together for parties— three a year, two organized by the faculty, one by the students. Sometimes they featured Ina Malyshev's punch; sometimes everybody came dressed up as their favorite historical character or concept. How about two light bulbs hanging from a coat hanger? The balance of power. Or three people exchanging hats decorated with dirt, grain, or beans? Three crop rotation. Tom K. Barton handing out chocolates from a basket? Divine-right monarchy.

Now, almost thirty years later, classrooms all have proper tables and chairs; courses probably cover a quarter's rather than a semester's worth of work; and first-year faculty teach six of eight blocks, everyone else a maximum of seven but more like six. In 1970 the Block Plan was an experiment; no one knew whether or how it would work. Now it's an institution, a given. From an idea, it turned into a set of practices and procedures; from an invitation for trial and error, it settled into routines and orthodoxies. In the period of transition from semesters, courses came in many shapes—half courses, three-block interdisciplinary sequences, one-and two-block models. One by one these alternatives disappeared. A few two-block courses, especially surveys, remain, but anything other than one-block courses, taught in the mornings, now meets student and faculty resistance.

There is less inertia when it comes to subject-matter. At the beginning, the Block Plan encouraged the faculty to rethink what they taught. They adjusted old courses to fit the new format, and they invented new ones to meet the different possibilities. That pattern of academic innovation still characterizes the College. It's common to co-teach with colleagues in the department or in different disciplines, and it's easy to branch out from the survey and try a topic best studied in a seminar setting or off-campus. This freedom makes the curriculum responsive to recent scholarship, to contemporary issues, and to the personal interests of faculty members. Individuals design new courses; departments rework their offerings; the faculty put together new majors such as Women Studies, Asia-Pacific Studies, and Environmental Studies. The result is a dynamic set of courses and programs, distinguished by a positive balance between tradition and experiment.

The same openness to change characterizes approaches to teaching. The Block Plan by its nature multiplied the possibilities by limiting the size and expanding the length of class. Several different strategies work, depending on the class and in a particular class on the day. You can mix lecture and discussion, break the class up into groups, assign a film or group project in the afternoon, even schedule an extra session now and then.

Classes seem to meet more rarely at people's houses these days. But there is the cabin, and many classes pick up and go to the Baca campus for days at a time to study the ecology and economy of the San Luis Valley, to look at the stars, to talk with the monks, or just to do regular class in a different place and to a different rhythm.

The Block Plan forced change in the 70s; in the 90s it creates a context for limited innovation. These days other developments, particularly technology, promote changes in teaching. In 1970 most people used the mimeograph machine and their typewriters to do business. Now we have computers in our offices, fax machines in every department, and copying centers in every building. When you see a paper full of misspelled words these days, you don't bother with the red pen, you just write "next time use the spell check." Almost everyone uses a word processor; most everyone is on e-mail. Teachers set up class chat-rooms and ask students to exchange thoughts about the reading or submit papers electronically. "Smart" classrooms let us use laser disks and video. With classroom computers we can use presentation software for lectures, scan in or down load images to illustrate them, or hook up directly to the Web during class to look at a primary document or a painting. More and more classes establish web sites for course material with links to relevant sources on the Internet. Obviously, not everyone needs or wants to incorporate such technology into courses. But I've found it increasingly easy to find and to use visual material and primary documents that connect students to the past in ways history books and the chalkboard just cannot.

It's possible to look at the catalog and assess changes in the academic program over the last three decades, easy enough to measure the impact of technology on classroom teaching. It's more difficult to evaluate the ways faculty and students differ now. You can read about student culture in the news magazines, but what's said rarely applies exactly to selective residential liberal arts schools. How could it, when so few institutions of higher learning fit that model? Or you can rely on statistics, anecdotal evidence and your own experience to define "student culture." According to these sources, students in the 90s differ in some fairly obvious ways from their counterparts in the 70s. Not many take courses pass-fail; unlike students of the 1970s, almost no-one refuses the grade track as a matter of principle. Current students worry about their GPAs, and the student grapevine identifies the easy and hard graders. They say it's easy to get a "B" without doing much work at all, and maybe they're right. There seems to be a bigger distance between easy and hard departments and classes than before. Given the choice, more students opt for standard research papers than for open-ended reading and writing projects. When it comes to assignments, they prefer clear guidelines, familiar formulas.

Questions that used to animate discussion don't work any more. Students show far more patience working out the "whats" these days, greater hesitation about confronting the "whys" and the "so whats." It's easier to get at the causes of World War I by starting with the events leading up to it, or at the dynamics of revolution by examining the specifics of the attack on the Bastille. A discussion of the French Resistance during World War II arrives at opposite conclusions. Asked what responsibility individuals had to act in occupied France, students these days argue "leave or lie low." In the 70s most said, "resist." I used to expect someone to say "that can't be right" or "who says so?" to a fellow student or to me. It's rare these days to make an observation that provokes a direct challenge; most unlikely that someone would leap onto the table to make a point as one student did in the 70s.

More basic yet, class and leisure don't mesh well. People— faculty and students— compartmentalize their lives more. They come to class, do the work more or less thoroughly, and then get on with life. It's hard to drum up interest in departmental parties or functions, not too common to find students and faculty collaborating on non-academic projects. What counts now is getting on and getting out, getting the grades and landing the job. In the Vietnam era, students thought less about jobs in part because there were more of them. But they also read Charles Reich's The *Greening of America* and maybe Herbert Marcuse and contested Establishment values and lifestyles. Besides they faced more immediate choices: whether to go along with the war or protest, and for many draftable males whether to go or go away. These days students want practical knowledge and a competitive edge. Twenty-five years ago, they wanted answers to pressing questions about war, political action, social change, themselves. That difference in objectives helps explain the different attitudes to learning.

A similar shift in focus characterizes the faculty, it seems to me. In the early 70s, adopting the Block Plan concentrated effort and conversation on teaching. It's not so pressing now to rethink courses or methods. Faculty members do design new courses and rework old ones, but the effort follows personal rhythms and interests rather than wide scale institutional initiatives. Nor does there seem to be quite as much time for innovation, or for College life in general. Higher expectations for scholarly research in addition to strong teaching and college and community service increase demands on the faculty's time. In the case of younger faculty members, the tight job market in higher education puts a premium on publication.

More fundamental changes also affect the faculty. More women teach and more male faculty members have wives with demanding jobs outside the home. In the 70s, the tenured women faculty could fit around a small table. In a place run by (and largely for) men, we got together regularly to deal with problems and provide mutual support. There were so few women faculty and administrators the College had no maternity leave. I know, I had two children born on block breaks. With many more women on the faculty, new mothers receive a block off, and CC runs a Child Care Center. What seemed the exception in the 70s is the norm now: two career-families. As a result, most faculty members must manage work, household, and family. That makes for long days and continual balancing.

The Block Plan spans a generation and a bit more. Life on either end of these three decades clearly differs, but much resists change. Some constants promote continuity: CC was and is a small, selective, expensive, residential liberal arts college; it has the Block Plan—and the mountains. Like all colleges of this type, CC draws from a fairly restricted socio-economic base. Among those who qualify for and can afford higher education, students with strong vocational interests don't choose a liberal arts college at all; those attached to conventional learning wouldn't risk the Block Plan. To apply to CC, they must like the idea of small classes and intensive learning. They must want something different from the ordinary. And so does the College. The Admissions Office then and now looks beyond scores and GPAs for a mix of interesting people. What applicants do, where they've been, how they think about themselves or about society always matter in putting together a class. Prospective students were and are a bit off-beat and fairly independent and individualistic.

Many individual students stand out for me, so do collections of students. Let me take two groups and compare them. The first graduated in 1976 and the second in 1996. Most but not all of them majored in history, so I met them first in class. I can't claim they are typical CC students; there may not be any. For me, though, they stand for many who were neither hedonists nor drones. The students in each group knew each other well; they shared apartments and block breaks, and because they often took courses together, their academic and non-academic lives blended.

The 1976 group pushed the limit in almost every way. They exuded energy and passion for causes, for people, for ideas. They tried different lifestyles; they talked endlessly; they agonized—more about who they were than what they expected to do after graduation. Thinking about the future in fact focused attention on the present: ending the War and reforming society. The 1996 group forged their friendship rock climbing, skiing, and "hanging-out"—doing risky (and maybe risqué) things. They kept their futures in mind, but they certainly did not build their lives around their resumes.

Neither group put all their energies into class, but they did let themselves get carried away with ideas. Some issue or situation intrigued them, and they took after it. That meant they might insist on getting something straight in class, or they might take a position and hold to it until they convinced everyone else or gave in to other arguments. I remember one occasion at the Baca when I divided the class into groups and asked them to assess changes in nineteenth century visions of reality. One group planned to dispose of the task and go skiing, but they ended up spending most of the day debating. When good (but stubborn) friends nearly come to blows arguing about what defines the *fin de siècle* mind, they obviously care about the issue. Or they might take off on a tack inspired by something they learned in another class and work that out in a paper. For example, one student turned a Western Civ assignment on St. Augustine's *Confessions* into a comparison of Augustine's and Nietzsche's conception of the self.

Students in both groups got as excited about astrophysics as about Robert Frost or a history course. Since they weren't preparing for anything specific, they let their interests or whims (and, at times, convenience) dictate their choice of classes. Often they narrowed their interests to two or three subjects, such as geology and history or English and history, until forced to decide on a major. Their transcripts showed an independent approach to education very much in the spirit of liberal learning. To skeptics, the eclectic choices prepared them for nothing specific; they added up to a degree but no job.

And yet what they've done or are setting out to do shows direct connections between the education they chose and their lives beyond college. Twenty years is time enough to test the effect of a college education. Most of the first group came back for their twentieth reunion; a few saw each other regularly after graduation; others took up at Homecoming where they left off in 1976. It's hard to resume two decades; you do it the way Virginia Woolf does in *To the Lighthouse*—in terse, general phrases—live in San Francisco, got married, have two children, practice law, run a nursery. The brief summaries nonetheless tell a lot. In their 40s, they had regular lives: families, jobs, sorrows, grey hair. Yet in all the essential ways they struck me as the same—funny, intense, spontaneous, inventive. A gesture or inflection, a distinctive laugh linked the person now and then. To the extent possible these days, they set their own direction, it seemed to me. And they ended up doing unexpected and valuable things. Two of them established themselves in film; another built a career in publishing; one taught anthropology. (Scott Smith who once told me he intended to make his first million selling tubs of flavored butter, practices law, but he also paints and shows his work in galleries.) That's for the career side; on the personal side, they are also finding their ways, and rarely by the straight and narrow route. Good for them; they didn't take it at CC; they don't now.

The second group, just starting out, promises to carve the same independent trajectories. Even as seniors, they seemed unusually relaxed about getting a job. At the same time, they had specific ideas about their futures. They wanted a particular kind of life, and if it means sacrificing income and status to achieve it, fine. One spent the last two years learning carpentry and teaching skiing. He considered law school, decided against it, then chose to go after all, seeing law as a good way of building a life in a small town. Another signed on to work in Antarctica, figuring that he knew enough about bicycles to claim he could repair snowmobiles. After a season there, he and two CC friends decided to restore and rent houses in Colorado Springs, because it seems a good way to earn enough to live and travel. Still another first chose where she wanted to live, pieced together some jobs there, then decided to get her teaching certificate.

The two groups bracket a generation, yet the parallels seem evident. Individuals in both groups came to CC with a set of noteworthy adventures and accomplishments. They multiplied their interests and their exploits here, building many-faceted and enviably complete lives. Neither group left CC set on a predetermined course. The question "what do you want to be" usually means "what do you want to do?" I think both groups see the difference between the two and start with a sense of what they want to be, then fit what they do to that vision. Many other CC students have quite a precise idea of what they want to do when they leave CC. They go directly into business, say, or to professional school. But almost always, with them too, the route takes off from a number of interests and possibilities. Because it does, if they change their minds, they have the possibility and the confidence to double back and start again.

These people live out the liberal arts premise. With their openness to experience, they exploit the many possibilities CC provides. The College multiplies options, and it tries to equip students to exploit them by emphasizing process in classes and by helping them cultivate a strong enough sense of self to imagine and build lives fit to their measure. The Block Plan adds a twist to liberal learning by making intense, focused exploration the norm. I've met many students over the years who were not alive to the possibilities or who figured them out at the end or even some time afterwards. But plenty came to CC open to personal and intellectual adventure and, like these two groups of students, seized the chance.

Hired for a year in 1970, I didn't unpack my books for three years, always thinking I'd take another job. The one-year position turned into a tenure-track appointment, and I stayed. I got drawn into teaching; the Block Plan makes it hard not to. I found teaching intellectually stimulating and professionally and personally rewarding. A broad selection of courses and interdisciplinary programs makes better sense here than sequences of highly specialized classes. As a result, I almost never teach what I know most about—nineteenth century France and Italy. What I do teach I have to learn about. It's enlightening, indeed, to teach Greek history when the last time you studied it was in college. It's even more mind-stretching to teach Ideology and Power with a political scientist or Faust with a colleague from the German department. Even my own field I never knew well until I had to teach it.

More than the learning and thinking involved in preparing courses, I've valued the intellectual community here. It doesn't support my research interests; for that I rely on fellow historians of France and Italy outside the College. Instead faculty get together to develop courses and programs and to discuss larger questions, usually in an interdisciplinary way. In the context of the department, our interests cross time and continents, and our exchanges reflect that breadth. At end-of-the-block lunches where we share our research, the different perspectives produce lively conversation, full of unexpected parallels and questions.

The classroom creates another type of community. The material usually raises significant and perplexing questions. Even in courses I've repeatedly taught, discussions always vary. Every class has a distinct dynamic; every group takes a different tack on the reading. It's intriguing to see how the group approaches a question and to figure out how to get them going and get them going somewhere productive. Besides, it's positive to think again and again about certain issues. When you finish a scholarly article or a conference paper, you move on to another subject. In teaching you circle back and reconsider issues in the light of new research and the perspectives of a different set of students.

The fact that the Block Plan keeps classes small and the schedule flexible fosters a sense of camaraderie difficult to achieve in other systems. Every class comes together in some measure; a few develop the kind of solidarity that produces lasting friendships. Focusing on the same subject every day for a block or two creates one bond. Three hour discussions of some complex, ambiguous text or set of events create another. That kind of sustained conversation about important issues probably doesn't happen that much outside the college. How often does anyone grapple with Existentialism, or liberalism, or the Holocaust? How often do people get together to talk about social conflict, structures of authority, and sources of identity in the past?

In these discussions, you see not just how students approach an idea, but something of their personalities as well. This is especially true at the Baca or on field trips where you spend time together outside the classroom. It happened in spades in a class which spent a block studying in Italy in the spring of 1996. In the less formal context you discover people with unique outlooks, stories, and interests. You spend time with an amazing array of different personalities—funny, dead-serious, laid-back, gogetting, tortured, happy-go-lucky. Often they offer practical wisdom, contagious energy, refreshing optimism, and, almost always, perspective. Getting to know them, counting many as friends, is for me the most unexpected reward of teaching.

Charlotte Mendoza
Professor of Education

CHAPTER 17

ON PENDULUMS AND PASSIONS: "INTERESTING TIMES" IN THE EDUCATION DEPARTMENT

Charlotte Mendoza
Professor of Education

There is said to be a traditional Chinese curse, "May you live in interesting times and come to the attention of important people." While the statement is certainly an appropriate description of the Education Department's existence at Colorado College during the twenty-seven years since my arrival, I would prefer to consider it a blessing of sorts, rather than a "curse," however lighthearted its intention. It has been a "life" influenced by the philosophical environment, by the pendulums of its discipline and political context, and by the passions of its students and faculty. It is a Department characterized by movement, physically and symbolically, within the College itself, in the campus community, and in the national education arena. On each of these aspects I will comment briefly, returning forthwith to the Education Department's *raison d'être* at Colorado College.

The part that the Education Department plays in the larger context of a liberal arts college offers it unique opportunities and challenges. To engage liberally educated students who combine diversity of thought and background with a desire to foster the learning of others is the essence of the elementary and secondary teacher education programs at Colorado College. To communicate with faculty across disciplines to design programs that will best prepare future teachers and to interact with them on common concerns regarding concepts of teaching and learning creates

271

an intellectual vitality for each person involved in the endeavor. However, to recognize that the strength of the context is also a source of challenge, i.e., that while the Education Department can serve to link faculty and students in a common discourse on the nature and purpose of education in a democratic society, it also must focus on its own structure, scope, and fundamental purpose. In several ways, the teacher education program at Colorado College is an all-College undertaking; departments educate majors in various disciplines, and the Education Department uses students' prior knowledge as it prepares future teachers of these disciplines. In addition, various departments play a consistent role in the teacher education program by laying the historical, philosophical, and psychological foundations on which future teachers can more thoughtfully function. During the last quarter century, the all-College aspect of teacher education has evolved from a special campus committee that served as an external policy board, to having the Education Department "regularized" in accord with the operations of all other academic departments on campus. Most recently, the Education Department has initiated Education Department Seminars that bring together the foundations faculty and the education faculty to discuss their connections across disciplines, to define important issues, and to better comprehend our common endeavor. It is envisioned that these conversations will broaden the perspectives and understandings of all concerned, ultimately benefitting the Education program that we offer. I suspect that we are partially motivated by our desire to strengthen our collective impact and by our intellectual curiosity as scholars in related disciplines. As we continue in our work, Margaret Mead's words can encourage us: "Never doubt that a small group of thoughtful, committed people can change the world. Indeed, it is the only thing that ever has." We can truthfully acknowledge that our goals reach far beyond the immediate surroundings and current students.

The "life" of the Education Department is not only influenced by its context, but by the "swings" of the pendulum of the theoretical and political leaders that affect its discipline. Currently, for instance, national and state political leaders and major education researchers are embroiled in "the reading wars." When I first taught at the College, my reading course presented the most current thinking available which promoted the philosophy behind and the methodology of structured, phonics-based reading programs. We explored the popular DISTAR program, the initial teaching alphabet, and the wisdom of basal readers designed by reading experts. Then, the pendulum swung to concentrating on meaning-based approaches to reading, and we considered literature and thematic approaches as the bases for reading instruction. We turned to New Zealand and its success with whole language. Now, the pendulum has swung away from the whole language school toward phonics, with many literacy experts advocating a "balanced" approach toward both subjects and with recent legislation mandating a return to the bases of "phonological awareness." Similarly, we have witnessed "swings" to and from "new" math, bilingual education, values education, moral education, and career education. Currently, we see a "swing" toward integrated curriculum, constructivism, multiculturalism, inclusion, multiple intelligences, and school-to-work curriculum. Each of the recent trends, as with those of the past, comes complete with research bases and formidable political allies and opponents. The consequence is that the Education Department constantly revises its courses to offer the most current information possible, to encourage students to consider options and knowledge bases with a critical eye, and to prepare them to operate in and provide rational leadership for a discipline that, as a former popular song put it, "swings like a pendulum do."

Ultimately, the heart of the Education Department is found in the passions of its students and faculty. Some might question the use of the word "passion" to describe this feature, but I can assure the reader that it is accurate. For students who move from one side of the desk in a classroom to the other, the change calls for strong commitment and dedication. Indeed, the most frequent answer given by students to the question of "why teach?" is the desire to make a difference in the lives of young people. Many of them cite their own teachers of the past and present as their sources of inspiration, referring to the profound "difference" the individual had in their own development. In addition, many of them want to contribute to or give back to their society. With such noble goals, I have seen students confront reality and struggle with it accordingly. I watched Lynn enthrall young children with Sendak's *Where the Wild Things Are* while making special provisions for the blind boy in her class so that he too could contribute a textured mask to the class' silent "rumpus" that followed. I saw Jessica work successfully with at-risk first graders despite the challenge of the environment, and Lynne manages beautifully despite a continuum of third, fourth, and fifth graders in one class and the presence of children with severe emotionally and physically handicapping conditions. I learned of Eric's great success with the Iranian child who faced the difficulty of comprehending a new language and dealing with the previously unknown "freedom" found in American schools. I heard of Brian's achievement in using the "wilderness" as a component of teaching basic curriculum areas. I also witnessed Jeanne's amazing transformation into Grandma Moses, when she introduced her fifth grade to the life and art of the painter. Every child in the room sat on the edge of his/her seat, fascinated by the opportunity to interview the visiting artist! Finally, I have worked with many students who come to talk and cry (I keep a box of tissues on my desk!) about their frustrations with parents who don't support their children, with youngsters who have become "adults" too soon, with media that seems to contribute to questionable values, and with decisions that appear to be made with political rather than pedagogical considerations as their rationale. Faculty, too, are passionate about their professional dedication. We struggle to respond to new theories and materials, to deal with the impact of technology, to support students who need help, to counsel those who should withdraw from the direction they have chosen, and to encourage students to bring their knowledge, commitment, humor, and yes—their passion to a profession that desperately needs them. The fact that we have seen our graduates become "teacher of the year" in their schools/districts, "outstanding first year teacher" in national competition, and, in 1998, "principal of the year" in Colorado and winner of a Presidential Award for Excellence in Science Teaching is gratifying; to see our graduates become mentors and cooperating teachers for those who follow fosters the lifelong learning and commitment we encourage. Neither students nor faculty in the Education Department come to their tasks with anything less than passion; we would have it no other way.

Over the years, the Education Department has "moved" not only in the areas of curriculum and staff changes, but it has moved physically and symbolically as well. When I first arrived at Colorado College, the Department was located on the second floor of Cutler Hall. Its location, outside of the "academic" quadrangle, limited the frequency with which students engaged in courses or programs and constrained campus awareness of our existence. Then, Education moved to its current location, Mierow House, which brought the department closer to the social science division of which it is part, and closer to the academic center of the campus. With the new capital development campaign underway as of this writing, the future location of the Education Department is undetermined. Nevertheless, preliminary conversations indicate that Education is now recognized as a contributing academic department to the liberal arts and sciences mission of this institution. Therefore, the future determination of location is, in our judgement, both physical and symbolic; consequently, we expect to be actively involved in the decision to be made.

Beyond the Education Department's role in the College's academic operation, it also plays an important role in the community at large. The Department administers four Master of Arts in Teaching programs for graduates of liberal arts institutions; three of the programs (elementary, secondary mathematics, and secondary science) lead to teaching licenses. The fourth program, in integrated sciences, enrolls licensed K–12 teachers. Since the Department advertises the programs nationally, chairs the respective admissions committees, organizes the related curriculum for each, deals with financial aid, teaches basic courses, maintains its own library, and operates the Teacher Placement Center, it acts as a microcosm of the College itself. Moreover, the Education Department brings hundreds of children to campus to participate in the Summer Program for Gifted Children and in the Whiz Bang Science Program. The first floor of Palmer Hall undergoes massive change to accommodate the children, their teachers, and the Master of Arts in Teaching candidates who work with them. In this way, the prospective teachers gain from working under the guidance of master teachers from the area with "hands on – minds on" curricula, children gain from active engagement in wonderful educational programs, and the community benefits from an environment that emphasizes teaching and learning at its best.

Beyond the immediate surroundings, the Education Department has had impact on the scholarship and teaching of other higher education institutions and professional organizations. Both Professor Kuerbis and I have presented programs at national conferences consistently for the past quarter century. We have proposed new ways of preparing teachers, organizing instruction, and working with professional colleagues. On the state level, I was a founding member of the Colorado Council of Deans of Education, which regularly brings all of the State's deans and department chairs in education together to discuss mutually important issues. Since its beginning, I have been elected as its co-chair (serving with a public institution's dean) for more than twenty years. Both Professor Kuerbis and I have been recognized nationally and been elected to the leadership of several professional organizations. Last year, Professor Kuerbis served as President of the Association for the Education of Teachers in Science, while I served as President of the Association of Independent Liberal Arts Colleges for Teacher Education. The conferences, boards, and committees that we have participated in or led have served to enable us to provide "cutting edge" thinking for our programs, to broaden our frame of reference and perspective, and to offer leadership to our discipline. Our active involvement continues, and we expect that it will influence future departmental and program directions to benefit all concerned. Indeed, our experiences nationally and internationally have brought us and Colorado College's teacher education programs, "to the attention of important people."

The "interesting times" of the Education Department have presented challenges and extraordinary experiences in recent decades. As I look back, I can appreciate more fully the statement made by Henry Adams, "A teacher can never be sure of his influence." In effect, our commitment to teaching and learning is the bond we have with our faculty colleagues and students; it has been my personal and professional privilege to be part of this environment. In my opinion, it is imperative that an institution that values teaching and learning encourages its "best and brightest" students to become the intellectual and inspirational models so profoundly needed by our society. There are, obviously, many ways in which Colorado College graduates can fulfill the "civic responsibility" goal of a liberal arts education described by former President Gresham Riley, and the "community service" strategic priority of Colorado College articulated by current President Kathryn Mohrman. Certainly, educating and encouraging our students to "touch the future," as the late Christa McAullife described teaching, is and must continue to be an extremely compelling option. As it appears that in the Education Department, as elsewhere, "the past is prologue," I look forward to continuing to provide balance among the pendulums, empathy for the passions, and receptivity to the "interesting times" that undoubtedly lie ahead.

Dick Wood
Director Emeritus of Admissions

CHAPTER 18

How I Got to CC

Richard Wood
Director Emeritus of Admissions

It seems that most Colorado College people have a special story about how they were drawn to the "College at the foot of Pikes Peak." Without my realizing it, CC beckoned me during my final semester at Dickinson College in Pennsylvania eight years before I came here to work. I was being counseled by a dean who helped the "G.I. Bill" veterans. He was basically a cross between CC's Ed Matthias and Juan Reid. Like many of the vets, I was a little confused about choosing a career. Dean Horlacher suggested that I was probably not suited for sales, accounting, engineering or preaching. He recommended that I go into education, which is where one went in those days when one couldn't find anything better to do.

The dean told me about a friend who had graduated earlier and gone to Columbia Teachers College in NY, and who had then gotten a job as a dean at a small college "somewhere out west." Following his advice, I went to Teacher's College and got a masters degree in counseling a year later. That qualified me for an admissions job at Pratt Institute in Brooklyn, which led to a job in alumni relations (fund raising). After five years in Brooklyn, I moved to the University of Denver. While there, I began reading about exciting things going on at Colorado College. The more I read, the more I wanted to work there some day.

Two years later, CC's Bob Brossman invited me to lunch to talk about a new opening in the Development Office. Wow! "Bross" happened to be one of the top two or three development people in the country, and here he was asking me if I'd be interested in working at a college that was now making the national news, not just the Denver Post. The meeting went well because I was asked to come to Colorado Springs for an interview with his boss, President Louis T. Benezet. Bross had also forgotten his money, and I had to pay the check!

One of the things I remember about my Cutler Hall interview with President Benezet was his interest in my admissions office experience at Pratt Institute. It seems that he, too, had been a recruiter early in his career (at Knox College.) Benezet, by the way, referred to admissions officers as "Traffic cops in tweeds." He also talked about an outstanding young redhead named Vickie Hahn who had just finished a stint in the Dean of Women's office and noted that she had attended my alma mater in Pennsylvania. Destiny! It was because I had followed Vickie, who had gone on to a job at "some small college out West," that I was sitting there being interviewed for a job at CC!

I also remember Benezet's reference to the CC faculty. "A distinguished bunch," he said, with degrees from prestigious universities in various liberal arts fields. Therefore, he advised that I soft-peddle my Teacher's College training and emphasize instead my Dickinson background in philosophy, religion and English. (His Ph.D. was also from Teacher's College; he had already learned that academic rather than administrative training was more likely to impress the CC faculty.)

Louis T. Benezet and Bob Brossman were two of the smartest and wisest college administrators in the United States, and I'm grateful to them and to Assistant Dean of Women Vickie Hahn for bringing me to Colorado College.

THE SIXTIES:
THINGS GET TURNED AROUND AT CC

When I arrived at CC, the Benezet/Brossman team had already landed some big gifts, such as the huge grant from the Ford Foundation.

Colorado Springs was also giving support to the college, especially the El Pomar Foundation. Benezet knew where the college needed to be headed and, when he switched me from fund raising to Director of Admission two years later, he had clear instructions ready. "For one thing," he told me, "we need better visibility in Colorado." He was correct. I remembered my acquaintances in Denver knew little about CC beyond the fact that it made the news a lot. Only a few knew anyone who attended and most presumed that it was a place for out-of-state students only. He suggested that we spend less time recruiting in New England and the Chicago suburbs and concentrate more on such places as the Arkansas Valley, the Western Slope and the public schools of Denver and Pueblo. Benezet also said that we needed better qualified male students as well as more students from the region. We therefore assigned some of the Ford Foundation money, supplemented with gifts from people like Trustee Jack Cheley, specifically to recruit these students.

As of July, 1961, when I became Director of Admission, the freshman class had not been filled, which was not unusual in those days. There was always an "Admission Office Table" at registration in Cossitt Hall Gymnasium should there be any last minute "walk-in" enrollees. So the new two-person admission office staff went right to work to find a few more candidates for September.

The following year saw us publicizing the *Ford Regional Scholarships* which brought us some outstanding male candidates, many of whom happened to be good athletes. Other things were put into effect that helped us in the competition for better students. We decided to use the College Board's *Writing Sample* which required that applicants for admission submit an original essay. Although many applicants disliked the added chore, it helped identify students who wrote well despite undistinguished grades or poor test scores. The *Writing Sample* also linked Colorado College with some very distinguished institutions. (Among them were Amherst, Harvard and Swarthmore.) Colorado College was then invited to be a founding member of the *Common Application Method*, which is now accepted by more than two hundred colleges and universities in the U.S. Again, CC's name was joined with academically renown places like Carleton, Pomona and Williams. This was good exposure!

Colorado College faculty members also played a key role in our efforts to attract able students in the sixties. They won grants from the National Science Foundation to bring high school science teachers to the campus in the summers in order to increase their teaching skills and to earn a master's degree. Not surprisingly, they became enthusiastic about the CC science program and began sending us their good students. Soon, this summer program was expanded to attract smart "sciency" high school juniors to our *NSF Scholars Program*. Most of these top students were from the region and many showed up later as enthusiastic members of the freshman class.

The faculty of CC also put a lot of energy into starting the *Advanced Placement Program* in the Colorado high schools, in which college-credit courses would be taught by specially qualified teachers to very able 11th and 12th graders. The faculty traveled regularly to high schools to help train these teachers and to give lectures to their classes. In turn, the teachers brought their Advanced Placement classes to the campus for a day, where they were exposed to the good teaching and stimulating atmosphere at Colorado College. As we expected, many of them would enroll later at CC, with college credit already earned, of course.

Other innovative programs had their influence on the able and ambitious students we wanted to attract. The *Selected Students Program*, The *Adviser Program* and the *Ford Independent Student Program*, (better known then as "FISP") are examples.

Of course, the Admission Office staff spent many weeks on the road visiting schools and interviewing students. While we traveled to nearly all of the states, we made it a point to appear at every "College Night" program in Colorado, including rural Nucla or Eads where we rarely expected to see a future CC freshman.

These and other efforts paid off. In only a few years, our best applicants came from Colorado and the region. In fact, a growing number of strong candidates with first-choice interest in CC applied as early admission candidates. Teachers, counselors, prospective students and their parents were now aware of Colorado College's national reputation. Application numbers were on the rise. We experienced the largest number of applicants in our history during the last year of the Sixties. And news of the Block Plan hadn't even gotten out by then!

Maxwell Taylor
Former Vice President for Student Life and
Associate Professor of Religion

CHAPTER 19

2001—
An End and a Beginning

Maxwell Taylor

Former Vice President for Student Life and
Associate Professor of Religion

Some years ago, it dawned on me that my official retirement year would be 2001. I quickly embraced the view that 2001, and not 2000, is the official beginning of the new millennium. For someone like me who teaches religion, 2001 is fraught with theological meaning. It calls to mind *eschata*—the last things signaling both an end and a new beginning.. On the basis of what I've been reading in various evangelical publications these days, I can only hope that 2001 won't be a year of apocalypse as well! On a less esoteric level, when I retire from CC in 2001, I'll probably just watch again the 1968 Stanley Kubrick movie *2001—A Space Odyssey* since I've always seen my journey through the marvelous world of liberal arts and sciences education as a type of personal odyssey as well. This memoir gives me an opportunity to reflect back on some of my experiences as a member of the faculty and administration of Colorado College for the past twenty-nine years. Let's see. I have worn a number of hats: Assistant Dean of the College, Associate Dean of the College, Dean of Students, Vice President for Student Life, Director of Athletics, Lecturer in Religion, and Adjunct Associate Professor of Religion. It is not an easy task to try to convey something of the flavor of my years at this place of learning, but let me try anyway. I'll start at the beginning which is also an ending.

285

Recruitment CC Style

Eventually all graduate students decide it is time to begin looking for a job. In my case, that time was the 1968 summer session at Emory University in Atlanta, Georgia where I was a Ph.D. candidate. I could at last see the light at the end of the graduate school tunnel. I had passed my area Ph.D. exams and immersed myself deeply in research on my dissertation entitled, *The influence of Religion on White Attitudes Toward Indians in the Early Settlement of Virginia.* My wife and I made up our minds that we wanted to move to the West for a new start in a part of the country where life would be kinder and gentler, far removed from the tensions of the Civil Rights Movement. Let's say that we were rather naive about what the West was really like, but that's another story. I thumbed through catalogues in the reference section of the Emory library and compiled a list of eighty or so institutions that I thought would be delighted to hire me. My selections included mostly liberal arts colleges and a few small private universities. I dutifully mailed out letters to various deans and department chairs pointing out my qualifications to teach either religion or history. I had earned a BA in history from Vanderbilt University (1958), a BD from Candler Theological School at Emory (1961), and my expected Ph.D. combined my theological and historical interests nicely—or so I thought at that time. At the top of my list was a small liberal arts college in Colorado Springs. I was amused that it called itself "The Colorado College." My search was not aided by the fact that 1968 and 1969 were years of Ph.D. surplus in the educational marketplace. But in a moment either of genius or perhaps sheer insanity born of desperation, I included in my letters a sentence to the effect that I might also consider an *administrative* appointment.

Those deans who bothered to respond at all to my search sent courteous, carefully worded form letters stating that there were "no openings available or anticipated." I did manage to turn up the possibility of one or two one-year replacement opportunities in places like Portland, Oregon and Mt. Vernon, Iowa. The Westminster Schools, a local private school, K through 12, where I had previously taught for three years, wanted me to return as chair of the boys' high school history department. I at least had a job in hand and was considering the offer when quite unexpectedly in the fall of 1968 I received a letter from George Drake, the acting academic dean at The Colorado College. Dean Drake's letter was personal—not a form letter at last! He informed me that there really were no academic openings at CC for someone with my background. Then almost as an aside, he mentioned the possibility that I might be considered as a candidate for the assistant academic dean position that the College was seeking to fill in conjunction with his pending appointment as the new Dean of the College. He pointed out, however, that other candidates were already being interviewed and that my academic background was perhaps too similar to his for my candidacy to go anywhere. He asked me to let him know if I would be interested should anything develop. I wrote back immediately that I was interested, wryly observing that, although we both had degrees in history and theology, I somehow had missed out on the Rhodes Scholarship. (George Drake, I noted from the CC catalogue, had won a Rhodes as a Grinnell College student.) I did not hear back from the dean until late March of 1969. By then, the College's search for an assistant dean had not panned out, and Dean Drake invited me for an interview.

My April interview at CC was an experience I won't forget. It was 1969. Opposition to the war in Vietnam was moving into high gear on college and university campuses, and Colorado College had been under fire from the local community as a result of its Symposium on Violence. New demands for student rights were on the table—death to *in loco parentis*, proposals for coed dormitories, debates over new forms of campus government, calls for free speech and so forth. And on top of all this the campus was abuzz about something called a "a new master plan" being developed by a young political science professor, Glenn Brooks. Any new dean at CC had to pass musters before a virtual phalanx of faculty, students and other administrators. George Drake put together a thorough interview schedule that left me exhausted, intimidated and nearly starved at the end of three very long days. Most of my interviews were organized around meals. My interrogators grilled me with a nonstop volley of questions leaving me no time even to sample my food. I have vivid memories of one session in which Doug Freed of the Psychology Department challenged my rather fuzzy comprehension of just what liberal arts was all about by asking me how I would design the College's curriculum if I had *carte blanche* to do so. I am sure that my stammering response was inadequate at best, but I came away from that particular session determined to figure it all out regardless of the fate of my candidacy. Representatives from the departments of history and religion did not seem all that impressed by my preparation to teach in their respective areas. In fact, the one thing in my background that seemed to catch the attention of some students and faculty was my 1967 role in helping to establish Operation Upstream. This summer program, funded by a grant from the Department of Education, provided a wilderness, survival experience for a racially mixed group of inter-city high school males from Atlanta. One student confided to me at the end of one session that he was relieved to discover that I wasn't one of those southern bigots who had opposed civil rights.

I left CC following my interviews convinced I had no chance to be appointed to the assistant dean's position. When George Drake called me a week later and made me an offer to join the administration with part-time teaching responsibilities in the Religion Department, I was both surprised and flattered. I later decided that I got the appointment, not because of my impressive candidacy, but because George Drake and President Lloyd Worner saw in me potential and decided to gamble that I would work out all right. I also suspect that everyone had simply tired of an interminable assistant dean search. At any rate I was grateful. I accepted and arrived at Colorado College in July of 1969.

ILLEGITIMIS NON CARBORUNDUM

My first year as an administrator at CC featured several commitments—completing within a year my doctorate at Emory University as expected, learning the complexities of an administrative role in an academically demanding liberal arts college, and preparing to teach my first course in the second semester. (In the spring of 1970, I stumbled through a survey of religion in America with 86 students crammed into Armstrong 300.) I succeeded in completing my Ph.D. dissertation the following summer, 1970. I've spent the rest of my career learning what it is like to have the privilege of being an integral member of a liberal arts and sciences academic community.

That first year (1969–70) as the Assistant Academic Dean was what one would call a learning experience to say the least. I realized early on that the faculty wanted me to succeed in my new role. A steady stream of well wishers dropped by my first week on the job to offer encouragement. Kenneth Curran, the retiring Dean of the College, assured me that, although I might feel like a fifth wheel in the administration initially, in all too short order I'd be in the thick of things. Fred Sondermann of the Political Science Department fired off a memorandum welcoming me, dropped by to say hello, and sent another memorandum saying he had enjoyed seeing me—all in the space of one morning. Doc Stabler of the Biology Department came over to size me up both as a dean and, as I later learned, as a potential challenger to his title as the faculty's best flyfisherman. Glenn Brooks dropped by early to bring me up to speed on the new block calendar scheduled for a vote by the faculty later in the fall. Glenn also passed on to me a couple of aphorisms that helped me keep my administrative career in proper perspective over the years. One was written on an old wooden cross that he kept in his office as the president's faculty planning office assistant and later as Dean of the College. It read, "Administration Rots the Mind!" The other I still keep on a card attached to the lamp on my desk. It states, "Illegitimis Non Carborundum," that is, "Don't Let the Bastards Grind You Down." George Drake, after a few days of patient orientation, simply threw me into the administrative pool with orders to start swimming. I discovered that I had been appointed to no less than six standing committees of the College. By the time students returned for the 1969 fall semester, I thought I was ready for whatever walked through my door. Not a chance! I learned quickly that there were indeed forces and people out there ready to *grind down* a greenhorn assistant dean.

Within that first week, I had landed in the midst of controversy. A reporter from *The Catalyst* interviewed me as one of the newest members of the administration. In addition to the usual background materials, he finally got around to asking me what I thought about the new block calendar being readied for consideration by the faculty. My careful response was something like this, "It sounds like a fascinating idea, and I hope to learn more soon." Honestly that's all I said. Nevertheless the article that appeared the next Friday in *The Catalyst* featured the headline: NEW ASSISTANT DEAN SUPPORTS BLOCK PLAN. The reporter, a history major, received a summons to the office of that department's chair who happened to be a staunch opponent of any change in the traditional semester system. The professor accused the reporter of giving unfair publicity to the nonsense being planned by Brooks and, as was later relayed to me by the student, ended his tirade with the rhetorical question, "What do those boy deans in Armstrong think they know about education anyway?" Well, I couldn't speak for George Drake, of course, but in my case at that point in my young career "not much" seemed an accurate enough response. I was stunned by the ease with which I had stumbled into my first controversy. The President and Dean met with me, smiled, and basically said welcome to the unpredictable world of campus newspaper journalism and faculty politics. Over the next quarter of a century, I learned to read *The Catalyst* carefully each week, since the administration viewed it as a measuring stick of our success or failure in relating to CC students.

A second controversy occurred when the leaders of the Students for a Democratic Society came to the Dean of the College's office and demanded a hearing. George Drake asked me to sit in on the meeting. The SDS wanted the College to take a stand on the war issue by declaring a moratorium on classes as a show of support for the war protest movement. The atmosphere of our session intensified as it became clear that the Dean was not going to accede fully to their wishes. President Worner had set the tone for CC. Peaceful, constructive protest of the war had a place at the College, but no one was to interrupt the academic program by coercing the participation of others in programs and activities. The SDS leaders intimated that they might have to occupy the administrative wing of Armstrong and not allow any administrator to go home that day. Finally, the Dean asked me what I thought we should do in view of this impasse and threat. I had no solution, but one of us at precisely the right moment of tension responded, "In view of these threats, we can't let any of you students leave this office alive!" A moment of stunned silence. Then the entire group broke into chuckles over the absurdity of the statement. After that, we worked out a compromise that confirmed the rights of all students and faculty to participate voluntarily in protests and not be penalized for missing classes. In that confrontation, I learned the value of humor in administering a liberal arts college. On many occasions humor would prove itself as a useful tool for relieving tension in college administration, and I would spend a lot of time laughing during the next twenty-six or so years!

During my first twelve years in the administration I served as a member of Lew Worner's team. At first the team included George Drake, the Dean; Bob Brossman, Vice President for Development; Bob Broughton, Vice President for Business and Finance; Jim Stauss, Vice President and Provost; Ronald E. Ohl, Dean of Student Affairs. Bross resigned not too long after my arrival, but returned as Vice President following the sad death of Jim Stauss in the mid-seventies. When Dean Ohl resigned in 1974 to return to graduate school, President Worner asked me to take on the added responsibilities of Dean of Students. I had already received a promotion to Associate Dean of the College with continuing responsibilities for overseeing the internal evaluation of the Block Plan. (In reality, two marvelously talented CC grads, Malcolm Ware followed by Jim Levison, designed and implemented the evaluation program from 1970 to 1974.) In addition, I continued a myriad of other academic responsibilities plus teaching a course each semester in the Religion Department. My new title was Associate Dean of the College and Dean of Students, and I became a regular member of the President's senior staff. President Worner had been made uneasy by the direction that student affairs had taken since the previous Dean of Men and Dean of Women positions had been eliminated in 1968 with the retirement of J. Juan Reid and hiring of Dean Ohl. Christine Moon, the Dean of Women, had been given a new title, Associate Dean of Student Affairs and Dean of Women. Dean Reid had been named the College's first true Director of Alumni Affairs. But the President had always believed in the classical model of liberal arts college administration. He took the title "Dean of the College" seriously and believed that all administrators involved with the lives of students outside of the classroom should report to the Dean of the College. Thus, my appointment was seen as an adjustment to an administrative structure that was off balance in the President's opinion. But the die had been cast. With the rapid changes in student life on college campuses, further alterations to the administrative structure of the College emerged. Some of these changes began under President Worner's administration; others were implemented by his successor, Gresham Riley who took office in 1981. By 1982, I would find myself in the new role of Vice President for Student Life with responsibilities for a new administrative division.

But I get ahead of myself. The 1970s featured a number of ongoing developments that necessitated further expansion of administrative staff in support of student concerns. Coed living and the elimination of restrictive hours for women presented new challenges in the areas of security and programming. Greek organizations confronted the challenge of reaffirming their place on the campus of an academically demanding liberal arts college. The drug culture emerged with a vengeance on campuses, and controlling student use of alcohol continued to be the major challenge for campuses around the nation. Concerns about student health issues intensified during the early years of the Block Plan, necessitating an ongoing review of the role of Boettcher Health Center in the life of the College. The role of athletics in an academically demanding block plan college came to the forefront of the faculty's agenda time and again. The real grinding had begun.

OF PRIMARY STUDENT CONCERN

Between 1974 and 1980, CC students continued to push for full recognition of their rights to participate in decisions that affected their educational destinies. A new form of multicameral campus government, the Colorado College Campus Association, had emerged after the intense debates surrounding free speech and student rights in 1968. It replaced the old Colorado Student Association that most students saw as powerless. The CCCA gave expression to a new ideal for decision-making—students, faculty, and administration would share responsibility for campus governance. The organization's charter included the fateful statement that students would have the right to decide matters "of primary student concern." For some of the more radical students on campus, that little phrase empowered them with the right to decide all kinds of explosive issues—coeducational housing, expanded student health services, and a variety of academic matters such as the grading system. (During one four-year period in the late 1960s and early 1970s, CC changed its grading system four times.) Of course, the administration, the Board of Trustees and the faculty had different opinions about the definition of student rights in the governance of the College.

The student activists staked out three major areas to test the principle of their rights as spelled out in the charter of the CCCA: (1) Coeducational housing, (2) Gynecological services for women in Boettcher Health Center, and (3) student voting rights on College standing committees. The administration divided over a 1977 student proposal to make coeducational living the norm at the College. The residence hall staff that reported to me supported the student proposal. The President's staff on balance resisted, and the matter ultimately went before the Board of Trustees for a hearing. When representatives of the Board arrived at Rastall Center for a meeting with the student proponents in November of 1977, they walked by a sculpture adorned with a sign that read, EVEN THE KREMLIN NEGOTIATES! Feelings ran high, but CC joined the national trend toward widespread coeducational living arrangements.

Two years later, a similar outcome followed a student proposal for expanding gynecological services for women at Boettcher Health Center. Dr. Hugh Rodman whose loyalty and commitment to CC students and athletic teams have never been surpassed could not accept the new directions. He resigned. His replacement, CC graduate Dr. Judith Reynolds, introduced programs of wellness and expanded health education to the campus health center.

Finally, in 1979 the faculty with the administration concurring opened up virtually all of the standing committees of the College to student members. In the boldest move of all, students gained equal voting power on the Committee on Instruction that had responsibility for determining course proposals and other major academic matters. (I've often wondered if there is another college anywhere that has gone as far with regard to the empowering of the student voice in the academic process.) Faculty opponents expressed fears of block voting by students and a compromising of the College's educational mission. These fears have never been borne out. Indeed, student members of committees over the years have proved to be responsible, able and exceptionally committed to maintaining the integrity of the College's distinctive character.

President Worner approved my request in 1974 to hire the first three professionally trained hall directors—Eleanor Milroy, Dana Khoury (later Dana Wilson), and Paul Reville. These directors had responsibility for running our large resident halls including educational programming, but they also assumed specific roles in such diverse areas as security education, liaison work with Greek organizations, and illegal drugs/alcohol programming. All three went on to distinguished careers, and Paul Reville received an honorary doctorate from his Colorado College alma mater in the fall of 1997 as a result of his special accomplishments in the field of education. We also expanded the role of the person who directed the old student center, Rastall Center. Don Smith was hired to be Director of Rastall, Assistant Dean of Students and Director of the new Leisure Program spawned by the new Block Plan.

More important, these expansions, and others that followed, gave expression to the Block Plan's goal of creating a more coherent community of learning at the College. Glenn Brooks, from the beginning of his role in planning for the changes that were adopted in 1969, generated considerable discussion of cultural, residential, extracurricular, recreational, and athletic programs as important areas in a quality liberal education. The Residential Program, a newly structured Leisure Program and a Shove Chapel program of religious studies were seen as vital support areas for the central academic mission of the College. (Program support in the areas of minority student concerns, international programs, community service and career services were added in the 1980s and 1990s and continued the expansion of the College's educational support outside of the classroom.) For more than twenty-eight years now, the Block Plan has provided special opportunities to achieve more effective connections between academic life and the myriad of educational opportunities that go on outside of the classroom. When I look at the vast array of co-curricular programs provided to its students by Colorado College, I marvel, but over the years I've often wondered about the percentage of students who really take advantage of the rich opportunities to expand their education beyond the classroom.

OF CRIME AND SECURITY

Since Colorado College is basically an urban campus, concern over campus crime and security issues became increasingly important in the 1970s. Early in the 1970s, the College had abandoned its contract with a local security provider and begun hiring its own security personnel. The timing could not have been better. Campus unrest over Vietnam was peaking. Student protests of the war intensified after the killings at Kent State and the extension of U.S. bombing into Cambodia. The campus drug culture was also on the rise. I was summoned by local police authorities on several occasions to be warned about drug dealers among our students. James Crossey, a retired Army colonel, had been appointed Director of the Physical Plant in 1969. Jim Crossey and his associate, Claude Cowart, who later succeeded him, were to do many wonderful things for the campus. Arguably Crossey's most important early decision was to recruit Mr. Lee Parks to be head of the College's security operations. Lee Parks, himself a retired Master Sargent, must be remembered as one of the great people in the College's life. When I first met Lee Parks he struck me as being, well, *military*. He wore a campus security uniform, was clean-shaven, and had short hair in the days of campus long hair and beards everywhere. I remember wondering if this new approach to security would work any better than the old one. I discovered quickly that this man was a remarkable combination of firmness and gentleness—he knew when to be tough and when to be patient and tractable. His eyes could soften in a merry twinkle or, if warranted, burn right through you. And he had a special gift for selecting precisely the right kind of people for our campus security staff. Lee seemed almost instinctively to know what a college campus was all about. He genuinely cared about Colorado College students, faculty, and staff. During my years as Associate Dean of the College/Dean of Students and later as Vice president for Student Life, I depended a great deal on Lee Parks. His hunches always seemed to be right whether we were trying to solve the puzzle of a campus crime or determining best how to cooperate with local authorities in dealing with campus drugs or simply trying to confirm with students that CC security was there for their protection.

Of the many special stories that I could tell about Lee Parks and his special role at CC, I choose one of my favorites. Not long after Lee took over his duties, he and his security staff discovered a rather large cache of marijuana in the recesses of the CC heating plant. Someone was covertly drying the stuff for later distribution. With strong reservations, Lee dutifully followed orders from higher up and supervised the burning of the discovery in the campus incinerator, resulting in a rather aromatic column of smoke. The smoke attracted a local police car that pulled up to inquire about the activity. When asked by the police what was being burned, Lee answer with truthful, but mischievous candor, "We're burning *grass*." Lee retired in 1992 after twenty years of service. He received special and well-deserved recognition at that spring's Honors Convocation for his service to CC students, faculty and staff.

THE TAR BABY FACTOR

I suppose I should comment about two areas that have been the focus of intense scrutiny at the college—Greek organizations and athletics. Critics of these CC traditions have used the Joel Chandler Harris metaphor of the tar baby to describe the twin dilemmas from which Colorado College has been unable to free itself for a long period of time. Debate intensified in the late 1960s and early 1970s within the faculty and student body over whether or not Division I men's ice hockey and fraternities and sororities belonged at a liberal arts college of academic distinction. The debate was driven by the tenor of the times—the war in Vietnam, the Civil Rights movement accompanied by demands to diversify the student body, and the escalating cost of private school education. But it is a debate that will continue probably throughout the College's history.

BEING AWARE OF GREEKS

I had been a member of a fraternity during my 1950s undergraduate days, and I still stay in touch with many of my fraternity brothers. We shared a lot of good times together, and the memories are warm if not at times rather selective. At the same time when I look back on that experience, I am reminded that I was a part of a national system that discriminated against minorities and Jews in its membership policies. I despised those policies and the black ball system that sustained them, but I am ashamed that I did not do more to challenge the practices of my own fraternity. In the 1960s, however, Greek organizations throughout the nation, including the South, did face the challenges of civil and human rights on campuses. As universities and colleges moved toward integration, membership policies in fraternities and sororities changed. At CC, the color and religious barriers came down earlier than on some campuses, and Greek organizations on this campus deserve credit for their courage in effecting the changes that were demanded. But criticisms persisted along the lines that the Greeks were anachronisms; that they perpetuated adolescent behavior, were anti-intellectual, and increasingly fostered patterns of dangerous behavior, as seen in their penchant for hazing new members. Greeks countered by pointing to impressive academic accomplishments among their members, examples of outstanding campus and community citizenship, and support of the College by loyal alumni throughout the nation. I jumped into the middle of this debate when I became Dean of Students in 1974. I continued it as Vice President from 1982–1991.

Greek organizations point to the ideals of fostering campus citizenship, leadership development, support of academic excellence, commitment to socially responsible behavior, and establishing lifetime friendship bonds as their *raison d'être* on college campuses. In many instances, our fraternities and sororities have lived up to these ideals. For example, I have great admiration for the leadership given by our fraternities and sororities in the area of community service. Long before CC established the Center for Community Service in the 1990s as an integral part of its liberal arts mission, Greek organizations had been engaged in numerous community service projects ranging from support of various youth organizations to hospital volunteer activities. One can list many other positive contributions of fraternities and sororities to Colorado College.

Unfortunately, since the late 1960s until the present some Greek organizations at CC have tended to lose sight of their ideals and even their identity with national organizations. For a time, one suspected that for some of the chapters the only significance of the fraternity name was that it provided the means for controlling socially desirable space on campus. There was always disagreement between Greeks and the administration over what constituted good, even if nonsensical, fun and what was aberrant and embarrassing to the College. Every February, I dealt with the St. Valentine's Massacre tradition featuring the teepeeing of the sorority quad by the fraternities, and I put up with the spring "star wars" battles between Figis, Kappa Sigmas and Phil Delts. I also negotiated with the Kappa Sigma's concerning what were acceptable shenanigans at their annual pledge performance ritual at the final CC vs. DU ice hockey game. My administration tolerated the pledge striptease act high in the west end seats at the Broadmoor World Arena at the beginning of the third period, although for many it confirmed the adolescent image of fraternities. On the other hand, the occasional offensive signs or body markings spelling out obscenities led to disciplinary action.

Similarly, annual parties and activities stressing drug use and alcohol binging led to sanctions by the administration. I remember a Beta pledge party where two initiates were encouraged to see who could down the most shots of Tequila. One student passed out at 18 shots and threw up, none the worst for wear. The other consumed a lethal dose of over 20 shots of alcohol and ended up on life support in intensive care at Penrose Hospital. (Happily, he recovered with no permanent damage thanks in part to the amphetamines in his system that counteracted the alcohol poisoning.) Most of our Greek alumni remember scores of pranks that they considered harmless, such as Scott Vann's amazing feat of climbing the Tiger flag pole at Homecoming to attach a stuffed Orangutan dressed in the football opponent's uniform. Such memories, though often santitized, certainly contribute to the development of loyal alumni. And, yet, there is a fine line of distinction between acceptable behavior and behavior that crossed the lines of public decency and legality. Older Greek alumni have difficulty accepting some of the more unsavory changes that emerged in our fraternities and sororities. They want to believe that life in fraternities and sororities remains essentially the way it was when they were at CC.

Many Beta Theta Pi alumni remember fondly, and selectively, Demolition Derby. They also remember me as the dastardly dean that brought down the curtain on Demo Derby in 1975. Demo Derby was an annual event when it first began. Members of the fraternity purchased old wrecks, got them in running order, staged a campus parade and ended up at Demo Flats on the mesa west of the campus. After a series of sprint races, the Betas conducted a genuine demolition derby for the entertainment of all. Let's say that Demo Derby carried the Betas away. Some Betas wanted two derbies a year—one each semester. Preparations and partying lasted several days and did not blend well with the academic intensity of the new block plan. The injury of a student participant, allegedly as a result of not wearing adequate safety equipment, spelled the sad end of Demo Derby at Colorado College. Conversely, the curtain had risen on the age of administrative concern with liability issues in the area of student activities.

At one time in the heyday of Greek organizations at CC, there were five sororities and five fraternities. The nonresidential sorority lodges were impressive, as were the five residential fraternity houses. In 1998, there are three sororities and three fraternities. A combination of lost interest and disciplinary problems has eroded the basis of student participation and administrative support Still, preparation is underway for new lodges in a special area set aside in the long-range campus plan. Greeks, beware! And good luck!

PLATO AND PUCKS

When Gresham Riley restructured the administration after assuming the presidency in 1981, my new vice-presidential responsibilities included supervision of athletics. Professor of Chemistry, Dick Taber, succeeded Jerry Carle as Director of Athletics in 1982. I worked closely with Dick for the next eight years. When Taber decided to return to the Chemistry Department, Gresham Riley persuaded me to assume the director's job beginning in 1990. I regretted leaving the Vice President for Student Life position, but the President needed someone with experience to provide leadership in tackling two major problems that were looming on the horizon: the future of Division I athletics and the development of a gender equity plan in athletics. My agenda as AD also included facility improvements, including a new basketball floor and, to the President's dismay, a new eight lane all-weather track and field facility.

As an undergraduate at Vanderbilt, I had completed a minor in philosophy. In preparation for coming to Colorado College in 1969, I had de-

cided it would be a good idea to reread Plato's *The Republic*. I also became
reacquainted with *The Republic* while team teaching Perspectives on the
Western Tradition with Doug Freed, Robert McJimsey, and others. When
I assumed responsibilities for athletics at CC, I remembered some of the
things Plato said about the relationship between mind and body and between the physical and the philosophical in education. I kept two quotations from Plato on my desk while serving as Director of Athletics:

> What I should say therefore is that these two branches of education
> seem to have been given by some god to men to train these two parts
> of us—the one to train our philosophic part, the other our energy and
> initiative. They are not intended the one to train body, the other mind,
> except incidentally, but to ensure a proper harmony between energy
> and initiative on the one hand and reason on the other, by tuning each
> to the right pitch.
>
> And so we may venture to assert that anyone who can produce the
> perfect blend of the physical and intellectual sides of education and
> apply them to the training of character, is producing music and har-
> mony of far more importance than any mere musician tuning strings.
> [Book Three, Part Three, lines 411e and 412.]

And

> On the other hand, there is the man who takes a lot of strenuous physical
> exercise and lives well, but has little acquaintance with literature or phi-
> losophy. The physical health that results from such a course first fills him
> with confidence and energy, and increases his courage ... But what hap-
> pens if he devotes himself exclusively to it, and has no intelligent interests?
> Any latent love he may have for learning is weakened by being starved of
> instruction or inquiry and by never taking part in any discussion or edu-
> cated activity, and becomes deaf and blind because its perceptions are
> never cleared and it is never roused or fed ... And so he becomes an un-
> intelligent philistine, with no use for reasoned discussion, and animal ad-
> diction to settle everything by brute force. His life is one of clumsy igno-
> rance, unrelieved by grace or beauty. [Book Three, Part Three, line 411.]

In one sense, the history of athletics at Colorado College has been the struggle to find and maintain the balance that Plato talks about in *The Republic*. For example, in my early years at the College I greatly admired Jerry Carle, Director of Athletics and head football coach. On more than one occasion, Jerry was willing to not take a player on an away trip if that player was having academic problems or had another important commitment. Laura Golden, whom Jerry hired to help with the expansion of our women's intercollegiate program in the mid-seventies, had the same capacity to put a player's academic life first. She encouraged all of her players in volleyball and basketball to take advantage of study abroad and off-campus programs, even if it meant missing all or part of a season. Frank Flood Leon "Red" Eastlack, Jerry Lear, Horst Richardson and Tony Frasca reflected the same values.

But in the opinion of some faculty and students, CC's efforts at achieving a proper balance between athletics and academics have failed, primarily because of the long tradition of Division I sports at the College. The College began playing ice hockey in 1939, became a charter member of the early version of the Western Collegiate Hockey Association, and with the help of the Broadmoor Hotel pioneered the development of NCAA ice hockey championships. In 1984 to comply with Title IX, a very successful Division III women's soccer program was elevated to Division I status with athletic scholarships awarded. Women's Soccer quickly became one of the elite programs in the nation and remained so into the 1990s. But opponents insist that Division I athletics have no legitimate place in a liberal arts college of academic distinction.

The debate over Division I has waxed and waned for the last thirty years or so. Critics argue that these sports cost too much, compromise admission standards, and create a subculture of students not fully committed to the College's academic mission. And they insist that, even at a place like CC, these sports are both corruptible and corrupting as witnessed to by our own NCAA ice hockey violation case in 1991. Supporters, on the other hand, argue that national publicity counters high costs, that concern over admissions is answered by a virtual 100% graduation rate, and that the College maintains institutional control over these sports. I'll confess that there has always been a side of me that sides with the critics of

Division I. In fact, during one particularly dark period of time in our struggle to rectify some of the imbalances in our Division I programs, I said at an Athletics Board Meeting that Division I poisoned the well of CC's intercollegiate program. Bill Hochman, a staunch opponent of Division I sports, never let me forget that statement. Yet, I was always too much of an administrative insider and a pragmatist to join those who wanted to eliminate this tradition. I was well aware of the strong support for Division I on the Board of Trustees and among many alumni. I also continue to think that these sports provide an important link to the Colorado Springs larger community. And the debate always made me uncomfortable by its tendency to put denigrating labels on an easily identifiable group of students. For example, critics frequently said that hockey players got special treatment in the admissions process. In one sense this is true. I would not deny that the cost of having a Division I hockey program includes flexible admission standards. Still CC does not have a rigid cut off point for SAT or ACT scores, nor do we say that applicants must rank in a certain percentile of their graduating class. We've used our flexibility to increase representation of students from all walks of life—international, ethnic minority, small town, rural and so forth. Division I students at CC are as academically and culturally representative as any other group on campus. Over the years, I've met some terrific young men and women who've made CC a more interesting place and who wouldn't have been here except for Division I athletics.

The cost of Division I made me most uncomfortable. Between women's soccer and ice hockey we budgeted yearly in excess of one and one-half million dollars during my tenure as Director of Athletics. In fact, the overall cost of intercollegiate sports continues to dwarf what we spend on recreational and intramural sports and calls into question our values as an institution of higher learning. I firmly believe that our priorities should include a greater commitment to recreational and outdoor activities with a high carry-over value for the average student at the College. Such things as biking, hiking, rock climbing, and camping deserve a place alongside of traditional sports at a place like CC. In theory and somewhat in practice, our intramural and outdoor recreational programs provide this kind of focus; in reality, traditional sports gobble up the lion's share of our financial resources. As Director of Athletics, I made very little progress in addressing the imbalance, but perhaps one day intramurals and outdoor activities will become a more integral part of a well ordered and expanded, broadly defined sports program at CC. In the meanwhile, a new Colorado Springs World Arena now provides an opportunity to offset the high cost of playing intercollegiate sports at the highest level. One can only hope that the edge can be taken of the objection to Division I, at least on the basis of cost.

Gender equity concerns continue to impact the future of intercollegiate sports at CC. Twenty-eight years ago, when the El Pomar Sports Center opened on campus, gender equity didn't cross the minds of those who designed the facility. El Pomar was seen as a facility for male sports—without apologies I might add. In those days, the administration assumed that women would be content to inherit the old locker rooms and facilities of Cossitt Hall. After, all, women participated only in tennis and skiing at the intercollegiate level, and intramural numbers were modest at best. Congratulations to those prescient women students who protested their exclusion from El Pomar Sports Center in 1971. The passage of Title IX loomed on the horizon, and women on college and university campuses already pressed for the right to participate fully in sports. Colorado College, to its credit, moved swiftly in the mid–1970s to begin complying with the new Title IX legislation and to do what was ethically right in the area of sports for women. Almost before the doors of El Pomar were opened, renovations began to provide locker facilities and space for women. In fact, a pattern of renovation and restructuring began which has continued to this day as CC moves toward full compliance with gender equity goals. The first steps were taken in the mid–1970s when, in addition to tennis and skiing, the College added intercollegiate sports for women in basketball and volleyball, followed shortly by swimming, cross-country, soccer and track/field. An intercollegiate field hockey program also flourished for a short time before lack of competition spelled its demise. As the decade of the 1990s approached, CC had eight intercollegiate sports for women and twelve for men. This imbalance was exacerbated by the change in the male to female ratios in the student body. For years, CC had deliberately followed an admission's policy that kept the ratio at approximately 60% male to 40% females. President Worner ended that policy in 1978 with the result that gradually the ratio changed in favor of females. (This trend continues.) Before he left office in 1993, Gresham Riley made full compliance with Title IX a goal. To this end he appointed special commissions to review intercollegiate sports at the College and to develop a gender equity compliance plan. I chaired the Committee on Gender Equity that completed its report during President Kathryn Mohrman's second year in office. President Mohrman adopted the recommendations of the committee and made their implementation a priority. Those recommendations included the addition of women's softball and lacrosse, the dropping of men's baseball and golf, the addition of more full-time coaches for women's sports, a review of budgetary commitments, and a further plan to make locker room space equal for men and women. The decision to drop sports for men resulted in scathing denunciations of the administration, especially since it came on the heels of a decision to drop intercollegiate skiing after the Broadmoor ski area closed its doors. Strong emotions flared on both sides of the issue of dropping men's sports. Some could not understand how the Director of Athletics and the administration could allow it to happen. One colleague stood up in the faculty meeting and declared that dropping baseball was basically un-American. The decision stood; patriotism suffered a blow!

Reconstructing Dirty Harry

Battered and bruised by my stint as Director of Athletics, in 1995 I began making plans for a hasty retreat to the faculty and the classroom. I always appreciated the fact that the presidents and deans with whom I worked encouraged me to take the time to teach, in spite of my demanding administrative role. Throughout most of my career at CC, I managed to teach one or two blocks each year. Usually I taught Religion in America and occasionally a section of Freedom and Authority or Perspectives on the Western Tradition. During my nine years as Vice President, Psychology Professor Gilbert Johns and I team-taught General Studies 425—Liberal Learning and the Human Imagination. This was a course for seniors in their last block at CC. We met in the magnificent parlor of Stewart House, my home during my vice-presidential years. The course was designed as the complementary bookend of a freshman course, The Idea of a Liberal Education. In Liberal Learning and the Human Imagination, we reviewed with our seniors their understanding of liberal learning after four years at CC. We also focused a great deal on the question of how one continues liberal learning after college is over. In fact, students soon dubbed the course, "Is There Life After CC?" Teaching General Studies 425 with Gilbert remains one of my fondest memories— the lively discussions with talented students, "Jumpers" staged in class with Chaplain Kenneth Burton as George Moore, the Denver opera, the outside visitors, and provocative readings. Since scholarly teaching is the central mission of the College, I was extremely grateful to Dean Tim Fuller and President Kathryn Mohrman who made it possible for me to leave the administration after twenty-seven years to conclude and reconstruct my career as an adjunct member of the Religion Department.

When I left the administration at the end of the 1995–96 academic year, someone asked me what I considered to be my most important contribution to the College during my years as a dean, vice president and director. At the time, I didn't really know how to answer that question, and I still don't. I do know that I tried to personify a philosophy of administration that I developed early in my career at CC. As a dean, I found myself applying and interpreting a dizzying array of college rules, policies and regulations that sometimes bewildered students and faculty, not to mention those of us who lived with them day in and day out. My wonderful executive secretary, Karla Roth who made my life bearable when I was Vice President for Student Life, once referred to me as the *Dirty Harry* of the administration. She was referring to the fact that so often directors, deans and vice presidents have negative and unpleasant duties to perform. She was right of course. I coped with that fact by resurrecting a lesson or two I had absorbed years earlier in seminary as a result of reading the works of Reinhold Niebuhr. Something he said in *Moral Man and Immoral Society* struck me as particularly relevant to my work as an administrator at Colorado College:

> In every human group there is less reason to guide and to check impulse, less capacity for self-transcendence, less ability to comprehend the needs

of others and therefore more unrestrained egoism than the individuals
who compose the group, reveal in their personal relationships.

In applying Niebuhr's thesis to my work, I concluded that even an institution as well intended as CC must be on its guard against a natural
propensity to give in to a kind of collective egoism expressed as institutional bureaucracy. Somewhere along the way I decided that I would use
whatever power and authority I had as an administrator to struggle
against institutional tendencies to lose sight of individuals and their needs
in applying policies and rules. Those tendencies in their worst form de-
humanize the very individuals a college is supposed to serve. My style as
an administrator emerged gradually and came to mean a willingness to
err on the side of the student or faculty member over against institutional
policy and regulations. I followed this slippery slope maxim so long as it
did not compromise the integrity of the College or jeopardize the institution legally. For me one of those rare moments of affirmation came at the
opening fall convocation in 1997. In receiving his honorary doctorate
from the College, Richard Skorman, CC graduate and local businessman,
pointed out that my flexible interpretation of the College's leave policy
during the Vietnam War provided him the time and space he needed to
become who he is today. I hope there are others who will remember my
administrative work similarly.

I was fortunate to have worked with a remarkable series of Deans of
the College who had similar philosophies—George Drake, Richard
Bradley, Glenn Brooks, David Finley, and Tim Fuller. Laurel McLeod
who became my Associate Vice President and later succeeded me as Vice
President for Student Life possesses the same ability not to lose sight of individuals under the pressure. In fact, what I always appreciated about
CC's administration was its fundamental commitment to fairness and
flexibility in general when it came to student, faculty and staff interests.
In many ways, we all learned from the example of Registrar Al Johnson
and his remarkable associates, Harriet Todd and Margaret Van Horn.
There is no question that the Block Plan succeeded in its early years because of the untiring and dedicated work of the Registrar and his staff.
Johnson pushed the College early toward a commitment to applying

emerging computer technology to a course registration process so vital to the Block Plan's future, and most importantly his staff set a style of service to students and faculty that continues to this day.

An End that Begins

As I finally complete my thirty-two year journey through the liberal arts world of Colorado College in 2001, I will be able to look back with appreciation for what this glorious institution has meant to me. I am immensely proud that both of my sons and my stepdaughter earned degrees from CC. I sometimes think how lucky I have been to have never really left college. Along the way, I have heard hundreds of lectures by some of the world's greatest scholars and leaders. I have attended great performances by artists from all walks of life. I have experienced wonderful theater and dance. I have had great outdoor adventures. I have enjoyed the role of being a spectator at Colorado College athletic events by the score, and I have played in my share of intramural contests. I have taught and been taught both inside and outside the classroom as a member of a remarkable faculty. I have broadened my understanding of the human condition. Simply put, I have been a part of an uncommon academic community that makes Colorado College the distinctive place that it is. And the students! I have been stung at times by their criticism, but always buoyed by their enthusiasm for learning and their zest for living. It is gratifying to know that the mission of Colorado College ups the percentages that the world can become a more decent place.

Let me close with a reminder of that early faculty critic's questioning in 1969 whether I as a boy dean could possibly know anything about liberal education. When it all ends in 2001, I will answer: "I know a little more about liberal education than when I arrived in 1969, and I am excited over the prospects of continuing to learn for yet a little while." I still think sometimes that I am just beginning.

Barbara Yalich
Vice President Emerita of Development and
Former Director of Alumni Relations

CHAPTER 20

FRIENDSHIPS AND ENDOWMENTS: MY LIFE AND TIMES AT COLORADO COLLEGE

Barbara Yalich
Vice President Emerita of Development and
Former Director of Alumni Relations

The 25-year period I write about spans, almost to the day, the era of my close involvement with Colorado College as a Trustee and staff member. As a recently elected Alumni Trustee, I had the exquisite pleasure of being present at the trustee meeting in January of 1972 when Russell T. Tutt, then Chair of the Board, and Lloyd E. Worner, President of the College, made the surprise announcement of a $7.5 million dollar gift from David and Lucille Packard. It was, as they say, an electrifying moment. It was the largest gift in the history of the College, and even now, would be momentous for almost any college or university. The Trustees immediately voted to embark on a Centennial Challenge, a campaign to raise a like amount in celebration of the College's centennial observance.

On that day I had no way of comprehending exactly how important the news really was, or that my own life would be so changed when a few months later President Worner persuaded me to resign my Trustee position and become Director of Alumni Support at Colorado College. I confess that it was not a difficult decision for me, even though at the time I was happily serving as Executive Director of the Health Association of the Pikes Peak Region. I already had a lifelong affection for the College, having grown up only a few blocks from campus, knowing its spaces and

309

places from walking there almost daily, then becoming a member of the freshman class in the fall of 1949.

As an administrator I spent the next 25 years working on programs that resulted from the Packard gift and other generous support that followed, as well as a commitment by the College to significantly expand and strengthen our relationships with alumni and other friends. The conclusion of my professional work with Colorado College came at the time of another landmark in our history, the arrival of Kathryn Mohrman, the College's first woman president. At that point, the College needed to begin planning another major capital campaign. Being in the thick of two such efforts is sufficient for any individual, so I made the decision to retire.

The reminiscences I make here would be greatly enriched if we had the benefit of more conversations and recollections of at least two individuals with whom I worked most closely and knew so well, Lew Worner and W.R. (Bob) Brossman, for many years chief development officer at Colorado College and later Vice President and General Secretary. By working with faculty leaders and Trustees, they created the vision and inspiration for the College in those years; working together they shaped and influenced the work we did in the era after the Packard gift and prepared the way for the Gresham Riley presidency. To our sadness, we lost both of these leaders in the past two years—Lew in 1996 and Bross in 1997. I make considerable effort to reflect what I think were their views.

My own view of the College always came from several perspectives that were often in conflict with each other. On a daily basis I corresponded and talked with alumni, parents and other friends of the College far from campus and in the local community. They freely shared their questions and viewpoints with me. I had to be a good listener, even though it was sometimes painful. I tried to bring good information and the College's view to these conversations. Meanwhile back on campus, I was a close observer of College Trustees, the administration, faculty, staff and students and tried to make them aware of outside views and questions.

It was important to evaluate these differing views in the context of what was happening in higher education in Colorado and elsewhere in the country. My involvement in national professional organizations, particularly those relating to alumni programs, fundraising and public relations, helped me keep a balanced view for the most part. Sometimes there were no easy resolutions for outside constituents on such issues as changing from a nine-block to an eight-block academic calendar, defending academic freedom or a tenure decision, problems within the Greek system, explaining a losing era for a sports team, moving the Earle Flagpole a few feet to the west to accommodate the new Worner Center or changing the style and content of the Colorado College *Bulletin*.

As time passed, with more information, dialogue and greater understanding, we simply moved forward with tasks at hand. I believe that Colorado College realized greater change in relationships with alumni and other outside constituents and in fund-raising momentum in these last 25 years than throughout the first 100 years of our history.

There were many reasons for this: the College's need for an important and generous circle of friends; attaining a large enough constituency to achieve successful results; inexpensive communications technology that easily keeps people in touch with each other and the College itself; transportation that made it feasible to be back on campus more often for reunions and meetings; and a national awareness, developed over the years between alumni and others, that they have a continuing responsibility and role with their *alma mater*, particularly private liberal arts colleges. And of great importance, during the Gresham Riley presidency, the College Trustees and administration made a major financial commitment for staff and budget as well as improved publications to expand efforts with our outside constituents.

LOOKING BACK

We had a good history to build upon. Near the turn of the last century, staying connected to the small number of College friends might have seemed easier. The very early College presidents simply walked down Tejon Street or Cascade Avenue to talk with local businessmen who were very much aware of the struggling educational academy trying to survive and expand on the tract of land provided by General Palmer in his original plan for the town. They obviously had their own struggles to survive, so the presidents also made occasional trips to the east, with meager results. Only a few years later, President William F. Slocum greatly expanded that circle of friends and increased gifts to the College with his more frequent trips to the East Coast, particularly to the Boston area, to meet with Congregationalists who continued to have keen interest in the fledgling Colorado institution they had established in 1874.

Mary Slocum, wife of the President, and other women in the community had been very supportive of Cutler Academy (as the preparatory program was called) and Colorado College from the beginning. At first this was simply to help with fund raising for small projects. Then in 1889 they established the Women's Educational Society which continues to exist today and actively supports the college with gifts, scholarships and other needed projects.

Alumni numbers were very small for many years because graduating classes were small; it was not until 1897 that the first group came together as an Alumni Association and sought recognition with a representative on the Board of Trustees. It seems likely that asking these former students for gifts would not have yielded much success in those first decades. Many of these students had attended on scholarships and there were numerous instances of their having to leave before graduation and even drop out for several years to help their families. Later on, it was my privilege to know many of these early alumni and appreciate their generosity to the College. Names like Thomas M. McKee '10, Harriet Stoneham Dietzel '24, Agnes Bartlett Pugh '16, Lyman Linger '30 and Donald E. Autrey '40, and Harold E. and Martha Francis Berg '36 and '37 are only a few examples of the many remarkable donors grateful for the difference a college experience made in their lives.

In addition to the general struggle for economic stability, the growth of the College's alumni body was to be interrupted by World War I, the 1918 flu epidemic, the Great Depression, and then by World War II and the Korean War. These world events were reflected in student and graduation numbers, and consequently, in alumni numbers.

The arrival of President Louis T. Benezet in 1955 signaled a vital period of growth for alumni involvement. He was fresh from Allegheny College—the East!—and had a strong sense of the need to develop relationships with constituencies. He also knew how this should be done, having observed other East Coast institutions that had been in the alumni business for decades. His ties with emerging foundations all across the country were invaluable for Colorado College, so far removed from major cities where most of these offices were located. He brought know-how, courage, energy, vision and high purpose.

Benezet was responsible for bringing W.R. (Bob) Brossman from Cornell University to Colorado College as Vice President for Development. Brossman's contacts with colleagues at the foundations, as well as his extraordinary planning, writing and public relations skills, were ideal for supporting the efforts of President Benezet and later Lew Worner. Brossman's tenacity and professional leadership, from 1959–1981, were sometimes not well understood or recognized by those less closely involved. From my close view, he provided the continuity and energy so essential in the development of strong constituency programs.

I emphasize this point because there are few endeavors which require more long-term thoughtful and careful nurturing than that of building the close relationships with alumni and other friends of an institution that result in strong financial support, especially large gifts from individuals and sustained support from foundations. Benezet, Brossman and Worner had extraordinary success in obtaining large grants from major national and Colorado foundations for new campus buildings as well as academic programs and endowment. J. Juan Reid documented these in his centennial publication, *Colorado College: The First Hundred Years*.

Lou Benezet was always well remembered for his meetings with alumni clubs as he made his way around the country calling on foundation officers and potential donors. The Alumni Annual Giving campaign, begun in the late 30s and carried forward almost exclusively by hardworking volunteers, was reinvigorated by these two presidents and the staff work of Bross. Leo Hill '48, who served as president of the Alumni Association and as a member of the Board of Trustees in these years, deserves much recognition for his role in energizing alumni giving and bringing in new volunteers.

Even though there had been a philosophical commitment to expand significantly the College's fund-raising and "friend-raising" (as it was called then) efforts, budgets were extremely lean by today's standards and the highest priority, of course, remained for faculty support and academic programs.

No new staff positions were added for these efforts, and staff members were expected to handle two, three or even four areas of responsibility. Whatever support was provided for the volunteers came from loyal staff members like Lorena Berger, longtime alumni secretary, and Irene Peterson, Lorena's popular and effective office secretary. These two wonderful women were rather like old fashioned "housemothers" for generations of alumni, and I was amazed to find that their continuing correspondence with these individuals and families generated dozens of Christmas cards, wedding and birth announcements. This sense of "family" among alumni proved to be a wonderful base for future relationships.

Richard E. Wood arrived on campus as Director of Development to help with annual giving, but soon moved onto his lifelong career of student recruitment. J. Juan Reid completed an outstanding 43-year career at Colorado College, the last seven of these as Director of Alumni Affairs. In the 1970s and 1980s, we came to fully appreciate the meticulous addresses and student records these individuals and all of their predecessors had kept for each and every student, alumnus or alumna. These names and addresses, kept on three by five cards and Addressograph plates, were the basis for the constituency data base that exists today. These were used for the 1980s conversion to a computerized data base, even though this was too late for the era of Smedley, the College's first computer.

THE ERA OF GREATEST CHANGE—
1975 AND BEYOND

I have vivid memories of my first years at the College, perhaps because the contrasts were so great. On the one hand, we were in a state of euphoria about the Packard gift for a long while. On the other hand, the country had just passed through a period of great student unrest and unprecedented change on college and university campuses. For those on the outside, giving students a greater say in student life issues like housing, alcohol on campus, fraternities and sororities, dorm hours, dress codes and in other matters usually reserved for trustees sounded as though all structure and tradition had broken down.

The College's position as the only higher educational institution in Colorado Springs until that time had always engendered a strong town and gown relationship that meant large fits and close involvement. Other institutions now had a presence in Colorado Springs: the Air Force Academy, a new community college (which later became Pikes Peak Community College) and a branch of the University of Colorado (UCCS) which held some of its initial classes on our own campus. All of these developments caused a shifting of the higher education dynamics among our local supporters.

Student and faculty protests during the Vietnam War, a controversial symposium on violence and the unusual attire of students in those days (headbands, long hair, ragged blue jeans, and sandals) caused a severe breach in relationships with our constituents, just as it did for colleges and universities everywhere. Most well-loved traditions like Homecoming, Winter Carnival, formal dances, the publication of a traditional year-book, and Commencement activities had fallen by the wayside. For example, in the early 70s only around 50% of the graduates chose to march at commencement.

Add to this uneasy atmosphere the complicated change to a system called the Block Plan, a truly courageous redesign of the academic calendar initiated by the faculty and approved by both faculty and Trustees in 1969. The new calendar was perhaps the most difficult concept to explain and defend, aside from all the other issues. Sometimes it seemed that we spent at least ten to twelve years criss-crossing the country with our charts and graphs, speaking with alumni and parent groups, large and small, rebuilding their confidence and creating a new understanding of the College. It was tremendously important that Glenn Brooks, founder of the Block Plan and later Dean of the College, spent so much of his time with this effort. Later Deans Richard Bradley and David Finley continued these conversations with outside constituents during their own terms as chief academic officers.

In view of this unusual climate "out there," the prestige of the Packard gift and the sense of urgency about the Centennial Challenge, this campaign was not conducted in the same manner as those we are more familiar with now. There was no feasibility study, no large volunteer structure, no "silent period" in which a start-up nucleus fund was solicited and no outside consultants. It focused on a relatively small number of key foundations and individuals. Over the short life span of the campaign, all alumni were invited to make gifts, but only a modest effort was made to call personally on large numbers of potential donors. These calls were made by campaign chair William I. Spencer '39, other trustees, and a few key volunteers. The Centennial Campaign was successfully concluded two years after the Centennial celebration. As I write about this achievement, I am struck by the simplicity of an effort that was so important and timely in the life of Colorado College.

We used this period and the remaining years in that decade to begin rebuilding the Alumni Annual Fund, the class agent system and encouraging the return to familiar campus traditions. We were thrilled to have a senior/parent dinner dance for 600 guests in the spring of 1976; this number grew to 1,000 the following year. Successful Homecoming/ Parent weekends became part of each year and class reunions began to attract small crowds. The Fifty Year Club, suggested and planned by Juan Reid, came into being under the capable leadership of A. Earl Bryson '16, father of current Trustee Nancy Bryson Schlosser '49, along with his good friends Ed Taylor '16, Kenneth Sewell '25, Lester Hanes '19, Grace Berkley Brannon '27 and so many others.

GRESHAM RILEY ERA AND BEYOND

When Lew Worner retired at the close of the 1981 academic year, it was clear that important progress had been made toward more active and involved alumni organization and a much broader fund-raising base. A bit more than five years earlier, the goal for the Annual Fund was $366,000. By 1981–82, Annual Fund contributions had reached $906,000 from 5,530 donors. The President's Council, established by the College Trustees in 1968 as a recognition group for major donors, was thriving and the annual President's Council dinner was a major social event for the community. The College was well positioned for the capital campaign that was to come, an idea very much supported by Lew himself.

The Trustee Development Committee was a very active standing committee of the Board, showing their ongoing sense of the importance of the College's financial stability and the number of key fund-raising volunteers had grown. We had begun to talk more openly to larger groups about the College's ongoing need for resources, especially the importance of alumni participation in the Annual Fund. In earlier times, we had been less inclined to raise the topic of "giving money," afraid that alumni might be offended or—worse yet—not come back to events or reunions. This reflected the general "good manners" and "what's appropriate" style carried over from earlier times, when talking about one's money or giving habits was considered bad manners. We slowly moved into a different way of thinking and talking.

We were working hard to build the volunteer base at other levels as well. The National Alumni Council, the leadership group for the Alumni Association, had been transformed from a very small executive committee to a large and more representative group from all across the country and representative of the age range among alumni. This sounds like a simple process but, as with major change in any organization, it took several years and the dedicated leadership of many individuals throughout that period. Among the leaders in these transition years were Patti Jean Harrington '52, Barbara Anson Freyschlag '52, Tom and Billie Jean Fitzgerald '57, William J. Campbell '67, William J. Hybl '64, William R. Ward '64, Peter Susemihl '66 and Susan Arnold Mitchell '57. David B. Shaw '57, Gary Knight '67 and Malcolm Person '76 later helped bring these changes to life in a new era.

We had reestablished committees in metro areas. We experimented with new formats for alumni meetings in these cities. We began to have a few meetings in smaller suburbs to accommodate alumni who had long commutes to more centrally located gatherings. These programs often featured faculty members or popular administrators as star attractions. A favorite guest speaker who drew big crowds at these Colorado College meetings was Trustee Gerald H. Phipps who at that time was owner of the Denver Broncos.

No star attraction, however, out drew the presence of President Lloyd E. Worner who agreed to make a farewell sweep of the country just prior to his retirement. Crowds of 150 or more people were the norm in larger cities and more than 350 people attended his party in Denver. It's difficult to explain the personal magnetism of the man. He was not a brilliant or spellbinding speaker, and he knew nothing of "working the crowd" as we know it in today's terms. He would frequently get bogged down in a corner with an old friend, talking politics, sports or the Civil War, while other guests patiently waited for their turn to visit with him. These close relationships knew no age or interest distinctions, and ranged from our most senior alumni to current students, athletes and artists, politicians or philosophers, men or women. He obviously enjoyed himself in these settings, and this was a perfect way to complete his work at Colorado College.

Planning and support for all of these events flowed from Cutler Hall. The entire staff for alumni, development and college relations (public information, publications and sports coverage) was cozily housed on the first floor of that building. This included Bob Brossman and three fund-raising staff members in the north-end of the first floor, my own office of Alumni Affairs (four people) in the central area, and the four college relations staff members at the south-end of the hall. It had always been a joy to walk into this wonderful historic building each morning, but we were beginning to feel the need for more room. We struggled with space and budget problems on a daily basis because of the growth of programs and expectations. But we had more fun than I can remember at almost any other period of my work at the College. The camaraderie, energy and sense of shared purpose were extraordinary.

Even so, things were about to change. When Gresham Riley was being interviewed for the presidency, I remember gathering all my courage as the Director of Alumni Affairs to push for his answer to my question about his commitment to a bigger and more well funded alumni program. We were aware that the new president would be charged with the task of leading the College through our first ever constituency-wide capital campaign. I certainly can't recall his exact response to my question, but I was left with the strong impression that he understood what would be needed and would be a strong advocate in improving our situation.

This proved to be true. Bob Brossman had made the decision to retire shortly after Lew Worner. Gresham appointed Richard D. Chamberlain as Vice President for Development and College Relations. Dick came from a very strong development program at UCLA and, like Bross, proved to be a wise choice for a new president with a large task ahead of him. Dick chose the center office in Cutler Hall and, with some remodeling and the move of the Education Department to new quarters on San Rafael Street, our division expanded to the second floor and basement (garden level!) areas of the building.

Three important aspects of the alumni program changed dramatically during the first years of the Riley/Chamberlain era. The first was the conversion to a computerized data base, a long and complicated process. This particular system, with excellent support from the college's in-house computer staff, had a long and productive life-span extending until 1995. Ruth Phillips Wilson '51 and Jean Robertson Lemmon '77, who were responsible for the Records Office staff at that time, made a remarkable contribution to the College with their dedication and careful work on this project as well as other alumni programs.

The second change was the establishment of the Alumni Leadership Forum, designed to be an annual working session for 75–80 alumni leaders from all across the country. We had learned, by trial and error, that it was virtually impossible to sustain a nationwide network of programs without benefit of meetings and training sessions on campus. By this time, alumni had expanded their efforts to work with student recruitment and career advising for recent graduates. This was in addition to fund raising and work in metro areas. Other committees needed to meet, particularly those involved with the selection of recipients for the alumni honorary degrees awarded annually at the fall Convocation, and for the Lloyd E. Worner and Louis T. Benezet Distinguished Service awards established during these years.

Costs for the Alumni Leadership Forum were covered by the College making it possible for young alumni and those from varied personal circumstances to attend. This was, perhaps, one of the most beneficial investments made by the College, providing a steady number of well-informed and highly committed volunteers for years to come. It is also a program that has been adopted by a number of other institutions.

The third major development was the conversion of the former Charles Leaming Tutt, Jr. family residence at 1205 North Cascade Avenue into a permanent home for the Colorado College alumni program. This was to be my last and most exciting project as Director of

Alumni Affairs. The property had been gifted to the College twenty-five years earlier but, because of zoning issues and its location in the North End Historic District, had never reached its full potential to say the least. It had been a rental property for a number of years and was in embarrassing physical condition. Gresham had a grand plan in mind for it and provided his full support to bringing this about. My task was to work with City planners and the College legal counsel to assess what needed to be done to meet City zoning restrictions, to begin working with the Physical Plant staff to plan for renovation of the property and to rally neighborhood support to insure that the zone change or conditional-use variance would be approved by the City Council.

The prospect of having this beautiful turn-of-the century building as our alumni house kept me firmly on track; this was a dream come true for any alumni director. It was not an easy process, and I learned a great deal about confronting neighborhood objections and trying to change viewpoints. With the help of a very fine professional advisor, we scheduled many neighborhood meetings and made sure that alumni living in the north end were supportive of our plan. Eventually we were able to persuade all but a few people that the College would indeed be a good neighbor and that we would be mindful of the "small number of staff offices" called for in the agreement, as well as the requirement to limit the size of events and meetings. Eventually we placed the item on the City Council agenda and were elated when it passed with much enthusiasm. We continue to owe alumni living in the area north of the College a great deal of appreciation for rallying to support the effort and smoothing our pathway.

In the fall of 1985, the renovation was very nearly completed and we were ready for the big move! As the moving van filled with all our files and worldly possessions, and alumni staff left Cutler Hall headed north to Tutt alumni House, I went back into Cutler and moved to a new desk. As things turned out, I had just accepted a promotion to become Director of Development, and Diane Brown Benninghoff '68 had been appointed Director of Alumni Relations. Needless to say, I had mixed emotions, but felt confident about Diane's abilities and her passion for working on behalf of the alumni program.

In my new position, I was responsible for the day-to-day direction and management of the development program during the course of the 1984–89 Colorado College Campaign which had a theme of Securing the Tradition. This was a campaign in a much more contemporary format including: a new campus master plan (the Dober Report); a priority-setting process involving faculty, staff, trustees and other key people; a feasibility study to ascertain what we could expect to raise; new campaign publications and a video to use in off-campus meetings; kickoff events in eleven major cities; an expanded annual fund effort and personal solicitations of literally hundreds of prospective donors. Trustee John L. Knight '58 chaired the Campaign Executive Committee and did a superb job with the help of other trustees and key volunteers. The fund-raising staff expanded to work with more formal constituencies including planned giving, major gifts, corporations, and a foundations and grants office.

The $43.5 million campaign goal was reached six months before the date set for completion. This was announced at the President's Council dinner on November 11, 1988, at which Gresham Riley, new Board Chair William I. Spencer '39 and John Knight cheered all of us onto even greater heights. In the next six months, the total amount raised increased to $50.1 million in private gifts and agency grants. The new facilities and added endowment funds resulting from this campaign are all around us as we close out this century: the Lloyd E. Worner Student Center, including a major renovation to include the former Rastall Student Center; the Barnes Science Center named for Otis A. and Margaret Tyson Barnes, two major philanthropists, in gratitude for their generosity in providing full scholarships to generations of science students; and renovations to Olin Hall of Science and Palmer Hall. The academic program was enriched by endowments for the McHugh Distinguished Chair in American Institutions and Leadership; the Maytag Professorship in Comparative Literature; the Harold E. Berg '36 Fund for Art, a gift of the J. Paul Getty Trust; The Gaylord Endowment for Pacific Areas Studies; the Schlessman Executives-in-Residence program; the National Endowment for Humanities Distinguished Teaching Professorship in the Humanities, the NEH Endowment for Southwest Studies supported by the William H. Keck Endowment for the Director of Southwest Studies. Other major gifts came in Hewlett-Mellon Funds for Faculty Development and more than $14 million in endowment for financial aid. El Pomar also made it possible for the College to begin purchasing the property just east of the College, the area being developed as the new East Campus these ten years later.

To say that we all celebrated a good bit after such a sustained effort and peak experience would be an understatement!

The period following the campaign continued to be strong fund-raising years even though we soon moved back to fewer staff positions and a regular development budget. We missed the luxury of those extra campaign budget dollars and, in retrospect, I think we may have made that change too quickly. Prior to the campaign our general guideline for fund raising was to raise $3–5 million each year. Following the campaign we established a $6–8 million goal and were successful in remaining at that base and surpassing it several years.

In fact, in 1993, we experienced the third best fund-raising year in the College's history with an $11.1 million total, as a result of the generous bequest of Robert C. Cosgrove '49, which eventually reached more than $6 million. Although he was well remembered by some of his classmates and was frequently in touch with Planned Giving Director Kathleen Peterson and me, the size of his estate was a complete surprise to all of us. His is one of those extraordinary stories of a grand philanthropist.

There were many other things to keep us busy as well. Richard Chamberlain resigned, feeling that the assignment he had taken on was completed. He left us with an Alumni Participation Challenge, a commitment to spend the next three years bringing the College's percentage of donors to the Annual Fund to rank among the top liberal arts institutions in the country. We were successful, eventually reaching almost 65% alumni participation. I think all of us would agree that this is not a sustainable number for most colleges even though it was an interesting experiment for us. It certainly served the purpose of mobilizing volunteers and staff at a period when energies were flagging after so many yeas of intense activity.

Several months after Dick Chamberlain's departure, I was appointed to the position of Vice President for Alumni, Development and College Relations, which I held until retirement in 1994. The Development and College Relations offices were relocated to the former Plaza Building acquired by the College. It was renamed, much to our pleasure, the William I. Spencer Center in recognition of Bill's long and distinguished service to Colorado College.

Transitions continued as Gresham Riley announced his plans to leave Colorado College after 11 years, and we embarked on a year of farewell and thank you events in his honor. Professor Michael Grace '63 was designated to serve as acting president while a presidential search committee selected the individual to become the 11th president of Colorado College. These were busy times for us in that such major departures and arrivals at a college or university need to be celebrated and observed in important ways, especially to remind all of us of academic protocol and tradition, and College constituents need to be kept fully informed and involved in the process of changes in top leadership. In addition, ongoing events as well as projects with more immediacy need to move forward. One such project was the strategic planning process begun by the Board of Trustees while Gresham Riley was in office. We made strong efforts to continue with the preliminary data gathering and early drafts, leaving the new president to bring the major recommendations and finishing touches to the final version. I was privileged to be involved closely with all of these matters while serving as Vice President.

I mentioned at the beginning of these reminiscences my belief that these past 25 years represented more growth and change in programs relating to outside constituents and College fund raising than in all the years before. The number of alumni grew in those years from about 11,000 to more than 21,000 at this writing. The total dollars raised each year and in campaigns speaks for itself. Alumni participation in annual giving has more than doubled and remains at high levels. College publications are impressively better, more readable and informative. The staff numbers grew from 14 in the division when I arrived to 57 at the time I retired— this included KRCC, now the College NPR radio station which beams our messages, news, commentary and music all the way to the San Luis Valley. The quantity and quality of volunteer involvement with the College are immeasurably better.

What was the meaning of all this for me personally? No question—it was a career filled with close and enduring friendships, productive and challenging work along with some stress and anxiety from time to time. I always felt a great sense of being at the right place at the right time at Colorado College working with faculty and other staff members I respected and appreciated to the fullest.

Being an alumni director is without doubt the best job in town. I'm sure Juan Reid and Diane Benninghoff would agree. Strangely enough, being a vice president was the least enjoyable for me. There were too many meetings and seeming unsolvable problems. I always preferred being in the thick of things and seeing more immediate and tangible results.

Of course, no one deliberately sets out to be a fund raiser, and I certainly never expected to be one. I've come to feel, however, that my efforts in development were the most fulfilling and important for me of the many opportunities I had. It's difficult to articulate, but the feelings of deep trust, responsibility and satisfaction that come from working over a long period of time (sometimes three, five, or even ten years) with a friend who has the capacity to make a generous commitment, exploring with them their interests and dreams; then knowing well the needs of the College and helping that donor actually make the gift is a wonderful experience. I have been privileged to know a great many such philanthropists. Their acts of kindness, generosity and their special spirit will always be a cherished part of my memories of Colorado College.

And then there are the truly magnificent gifts that have been made at a crucial juncture or consistently over a period of time. This extraordinary generosity has without question transformed Colorado College, creating a future as a nationally recognized liberal arts college, rather than simply a very good regional institution. I have previously mentioned several of these donors from this recent era: David and Lucille Packard, Otis A. and Margaret T. Barnes '27, and Robert J. Cosgrove '49. I now refer to the faithful generosity of the El Pomar Foundation, The Boettcher Foundation, The Adolph Coors Foundation, The Helen K. and Arthur E. Johnson Foundation and of two families in particular: E.K. Gaylord 1897 and his daughter, Edith Gaylord Harper '36, both of whom were trustees of the College and close friends of Lew Worner; and Trustee Gerald L. and Florence Fabling Schlessman '17 and '21 and their son and daughter, Lee E. Schlessman '50 and Susan Schlessman Duncan '52, who also served as a trustee. To have known those responsible for gifts of such magnitude and to have had even a small role in the effort to bring these gifts to Colorado College was a high calling indeed.

Things came full circle for me when the College was preparing to announce a $4 million gift from David Packard as I prepared to retire. It seems to me a curious irony that these years began and ended with gifts from the great gentleman. I'm very happy to have been part of such an era at Colorado College.

COLORADO COLLEGE: Memories and Reflections

Designed by Sally Hegarty
Composed by Rachel Hegarty in BaskervilleMT with QuarkXPress
on Apple Macintosh systems
Printed by Fittje Brothers Printing Company, Colorado Springs
on 70lb Luna Matte Finish
Bound by Mountain States Bindery, Salt Lake City
in Lexotone, Emerald Green in an edition numbering 2,500 copies
One hundred of this title and companion book, *COLORADO COLLEGE:
A Place of Learning 1874–1999* by Robert D. Loevy, were bound in
boxed sets by Karen Pardue, White River Studio, Colorado Springs
in Campanetta Acid-free Cloth